Black Company

Black Company
The Story of Subchaser 1264

Eric Purdon

BLUEJACKET BOOKS

NAVAL INSTITUTE PRESS
Annapolis, Maryland

To the memory of Christopher Smith Sargent, 1911–1946

"He was always on the side of the person or group who was in danger of being misjudged. He was always the advocate for the defense of the people, always the advocate for the prosecution of justice."
—Capt. Mildred McAfee, USNR, first director of the Women's Reserve

Naval Institute Press
291 Wood Road
Annapolis, MD 21402

© 1972 by Eric Purdon
Foreword © 2000 by the U.S. Naval Institute, Annapolis, Maryland

First Bluejacket Books printing, 2000

Library of Congress Cataloging-in-Publication Data
Purdon, Eric.
    Black company : the story of Subchaser 1264 / Eric Purdon.
       p.   cm. — (Bluejacket books)
    Originally published: Washington : R. B. Luce, 1972.
    ISBN 1-55750-658-2 (alk. paper)
    1. World War, 1939–1945—Participation, Afro-American. 2. United States. Navy—Afro-American troops. 3. PC1264 (Ship) 4. World War, 1939–1945—Naval operations, American. I. Title. II. Series.
D810.N4 P87 2000
940.54'516—dc21   00-30573

Printed in the United States of America on acid-free paper ♾
07 06 05 04 03 02 01 00   8 7 6 5 4 3 2 1

All photographs are from official U.S. Navy sources.

Foreword

Black Company is the true story of a naval experiment conducted during World War II. This experiment did not test equipment or weapons of war. Rather, it was designed to test the ability of a group of African Americans to live, fight, and survive under wartime conditions on a small U.S. Navy subchaser. It gave these men the opportunity to disprove the opinions of high-ranking naval officers, opinions shared at that time by most Americans: that African Americans could not become able seamen, that African Americans could not take orders from each other, and that whites would not take orders from African Americans in positions of authority.

When the Japanese attacked Pearl Harbor on December 7, 1941, the navy allowed African Americans to enlist only as messmen. Like most of American society, the service was completely segregated. However, it sorely needed manpower. So a plan was devised to accept and train African American men in the various shipboard ratings—but not as officers. And African Americans still would not be permitted to serve on combatants except as messmen.

By late 1943 there were approximately one hundred thousand African American enlisted men of varying rates and ratings assigned to large naval bases ashore. Plans were made to commission a handful of officers and to man two ships with predominantly African American crews. On March 13, 1944, twelve African American ensigns and one warrant officer emerged from the Great Lakes Naval Training Center, and on March 20, 1944, the first of two ships—the USS *Mason,* a destroyer escort—was commissioned.

Black Company is the story of the second ship, the USS *PC 1264,* as told by its first commanding officer, Lt. Eric S. Purdon. At 173 feet long, the ship was home to a crew of sixty-three for about twenty-two months. There were five white officers, eight white leading petty officers, and fifty African American enlisted men of the different rates and ratings necessary to fully man a subchaser of its class. It was homeported at Staten Island and assigned as an operating unit of the Eastern Sea Frontier command. This book reviews the entire life of *PC 1264,* from its beginnings and its shakedown cruise to its arduous duties as an antisubmarine escort with several convoys up and down the East Coast.

Seven months after the ship was commissioned, the first phase of the experiment was completed. Lieutenant Purdon transferred the eight white leading petty officers, replacing them with eight African Americans. There was no noted loss of efficiency.

On May 2, 1945, I reported aboard *PC 1264* for duty as communications officer. For me it was a dream come true, the answer to years of prayers. After about ten minutes, I was surprised to discover that I was the duty officer. So I spent my first couple of hours aboard inspecting, learning the ship, checking our lines, and making sure we were secure. I met several former shipmates from my enlisted days and learned that there were several more aboard. Respect was mutual. Most were proud that I was there—and so was I.

The next morning I met the captain, Lieutenant Purdon, and the other officers. Lieutenant Purdon was a knowledgeable man and an excellent teacher. He was firm and almost stern, but not overbearing. As someone who led by example, he was admired by his officers and men alike. He was a perfectionist, and he expected the same from his men. Most important, in the face of injustice he quickly came to the defense of his men. I will always be indebted to him for his conduct the time I was arrested for impersonating an officer. COMNAVBASE Miami insisted that I be tried by general court-martial. When Lieutenant Purdon refused to do that, *PC 1264* was ordered out of Miami.

Life aboard ship was just what I had been trained to expect. It was a constant learning experience, and I thoroughly enjoyed the shipboard atmosphere. But I soon learned that the navy ashore, the other fleet units, and the civilian community were not prepared for the arrival of a ship like *PC 1264*.

We were scheduled for ten days of training in Miami and three in Key West before proceeding to the Pacific via the Canal Zone. The ship was at Key West when the war in the Pacific ended. Ultimately, USS *PC 1264* was ordered to return to New York via Norfolk. It served as the lead ship in the 1945 Navy Day Presidential Review and was later used as a submarine target ship operating out of New London. Finally, on February 8, 1946, its mission completed, the USS *PC 1264* was decommissioned.

Black Company is an enjoyable book to read. It is the history of a small group of men with a grave responsibility. On their shoulders rested the hopes and desires of generations of people, born and unborn. Every man aboard knew the mission of *PC 1264*. Shortly after its commissioning, the ship's motto was chosen: "We will never fail."
—Vice Adm. Samuel Gravely Jr., USN (Ret.)

Acknowledgment

During the five years it took to research and write this book, a number of friendly people were of great assistance. Nearly a quarter of a century had passed since the commission pennant was lowered from USS *PC 1264*'s mast, what few official records had been preserved were filed in government archives, and the officers and crew dispersed.

To tell the story of USS *PC 1264* required a national search; to find as many of the crew as possible and record their memories. For the story of a ship is the story of the men who served in her; from the captain, insulated by his position from the men, even on such a small intimate ship as a subchaser, down to the seamen and firemen whose adventures on liberty and in their human reactions to life aboard and ashore are diligently kept from him. This endeavor was a most pleasant, interesting and educational undertaking.

From the beginning, the Navy Department gave unstinting co-operation, without any requirement for review whatsoever. Rear Admiral Ernest M. Eller, USN (Ret.), Director of Naval History, when approached in May, 1966, said, "I want to help you all I can . . ." and he and his staff, particularly Dr. Dean Allard and Mr. Bernard Cavalcante, fulfilled this wish. The help Miss Anna C. Urband in the Office of Navy Information's Magazine and Book Branch gave was invaluable in providing the answers to a variety of questions, and Journalist third class J. R. Kimmins similarly merits my sincerest gratitude for his interest in this book. Mr. Harry Schwartz simplified my searches through the National Archives, with the same energy shown by the librarians at the U.S. Naval Academy, especially Mrs. Lucille Porter.

Mr. Lee Nichols, author of *Breakthrough on the Color Front* (Random House, 1954) and Mr. Maurice J. Mac-

Gregor of the Army's Office of Military History, gave me early advice on the methods of historical research and steered me to likely sources. Lieutenant Commander Dennis D. Nelson, USN (Ret.), whose book, *The Integration of the Negro in The United States Navy* (Farrar, Straus & Young, 1951), was one of the first to study the subject, gave me access to his records. Dr. Willard Hurst, Judge D. W. Gilmore, Mr. Charles Dillon and Mr. Donald O. Van Ness, former members of the Special Programs Unit, were generous in their help. Dr. Hurst's monograph written for *The Administrative History of The Bureau of Naval Personnel* was particularly helpful for an understanding of this Unit's role in the Bureau's organization.

There were many, many others: Mr. Lester Granger of the Urban League and Mr. James Evans, former Special Assistant to the Secretary of Defense, whose efforts greatly advanced the cause of racial justice in the armed forces. There were the postmasters, telephone operators and newspaper editors in towns throughout the country who helped me develop leads to former crew members; an example was Mr. H. Milt Phillips, editor and publisher of the well-named Seminole (Oklahoma) *Producer*. Printing my letter of inquiry in his paper resulted in a telephone call from Benjamin Shanker in Oklahoma City, four days later.

My deepest gratitude goes to all my shipmates named in the following pages for their stories and the memory of their experiences; to Dr. Jack W. Sutherland, the last commanding officer, and Will F. Otto—today, both California educators—whose diaries were invaluable. And to Samuel L. Gravely, Jr., whose career from ensign in charge of the subchaser's communications department to rear admiral in charge of all the Navy's communications, has proved beyond all doubt that which USS *PC 1264* set out to demonstrate.

And for my wife, who lived this time with me, her devotion my anchor against self-doubt and the fear my inexperience might harm the ship, I thank God she's with me still.

"Arden," Harwood, Maryland   August 20, 1971

Contents

Prologue

This is the story of some young Americans from a variety of backgrounds and of different heritage. They were as diverse a group, geographically, as could be gathered to live together in close quarters. They were together because America was at war. Yet these particular men were together for another reason and an added purpose, whose results would have a far greater impact upon their country and the cause of freedom than their contribution to the defeat of the Axis alliance.

Their home for nearly two years was a ship; a very small ship. For twenty-two months, an average number of sixty-two enlisted sailors and five officers lived together within an area of less than 25,000 cubic feet. Privacy was practically nonexistent; even the captain shared his cabin. Of these sixty-seven men, some were college graduates, the majority had attended high school, and some had never finished their elementary school education.

None was a professional sailor during the sixteen months of her service, nor wanted to be one, although some did become such. One is still on active duty and, in the twenty-six years since he reported aboard this ship from midshipman's school and the Submarine Chaser Training Center, has had a distinguished naval career, including command of ships far larger and mightier than this one in which he began; a career marked by a number of distinctive "firsts."

He was the first black man to be commissioned from a college Naval Reserve Officers Training course. On Thursday, May 3, 1945, he integrated, for the first time, the wardroom of a Navy combattant ship by being a member of it; he was served a meal instead of serving it. And, in the same month of 1971, he was selected to be the first Negro admiral in the United States Navy.

Neither he nor the other officers who ate that historic breakfast together, twenty-six years ago, can remember the occasion. Indeed, none thought that what he was doing was particularly historic. Everyone aboard that small subchaser was there simply because his country was at war; otherwise he wouldn't have been in a ship alongside a dock in the United States Naval Frontier Base, Tompkinsville, Staten Island, New York. If the captain, he would have been four miles away on Manhattan, working on an author's manuscript in a New York publishing house; if the storekeeper, teaching and coaching the basketball team in a school in North Carolina; if the chief engineer, servicing vending machines in Washington, D.C.; if one of the radiomen, a farmhand in Oklahoma. Others would have been finishing high school or college, or living where they had always lived, with never the expectation of leaving the bayou or sharehold where they were born, for cities like New York, Guantanamo, Miami and others they would see by crossing the waters of the Atlantic on a ship they had made reach there.

This is not to say that each one of them didn't have some idea of the purpose of this ship, and therefore of his individual part in it. They had only to look at one another to see that this ship's company was not as others were.

Yet, what was important was the way they were similar to other ship's companies: They wore the same uniforms with the same embroidered insignia on them—crossed guns, quills, flags, a spoked wheel—some of the eighteen specialties, out of approximately two hundred of the seagoing Navy, that were needed to run this ship.

Two years before, none of these seamen would have been allowed to wear these badges; they could not have enlisted to receive the training necessary for qualification in these ratings. For, between the two World Wars, the only branch open to them, and to others of the "colored" races—Filipinos and Samoans—was the messman branch. Indeed, even this rating was, in practice, closed to them for half of this period. Only Filipinos were recruited for this branch from 1919 to 1932, when active recruiting of Negroes was resumed.

Frank Knox, the Rough Rider friend of Teddy Roosevelt, who was Secretary of the Navy between 1940 and 1944, explained one of the reasons for the Navy's policy in a letter to Charles Poletti, Lieutenant Governor of the State of New York, on July 24, 1940.

"Experience of many years in the Navy has shown clearly," he wrote, "that men of the colored race in any other branch than the Messman Branch, and, promoted to the position of petty officer, cannot maintain discipline among men of the white race over whom they may be placed by reason of their rating. As a result, teamwork, harmony and ship efficiency are seriously handicapped. . . ."

This opinion was only one of several sterotypes or uncritical judgments held unquestionly by a majority of Americans in the decades since the Emancipation Proclamation. It was axiomatic that there were only certain things that certain people could do.

For instance, it was well known at the time of Frank Knox's letter to the New York lieutenant governor that orientals, especially Japanese, had a congenital trait of myopia, making it impossible for them to fly airplanes with any precision. Moreover, their industry was incapable of competing economically in the modern world, except by the marketing of shoddy copies of western products.

Less than a year and a half later, the Japanese themselves challenged these stereotypes and, by so doing, started a chain of events that were to undermine a number of American conceptions; slowly and painfully, to be sure—and by no means completed to this day—but with a definiteness that couldn't be ignored.

Within the time that it took the news of the attack on Pearl Harbor—that bright, crisp, early Sunday morning—to reach everyone on the mainland, the simile of America being a melting pot was a fact. Everyone's thoughts were instantly fused to a single determination. America was united, with a common anger and passionate indignation.

On Monday morning, at every recruiting station, lines formed and lengthened of young men who, the day before yesterday, had been hoping fervently that their luck would hold and their draft numbers not be called. Unions dropped plans for another tilt at management. Shipyard workers volunteered en masse to ship out to Honolulu to repair the damaged fleet. Young men already in service found that their uniforms had a new and added mystique for women. And industry that had been gearing up to supply our now *de jure* allies in Europe, hustled to gear up even more to fill the total war needs of the United States as well.

Americans now had a common purpose. Anglo-Americans, Mexican-Americans, American-Americans of every Indian tribe, Italo-Americans, Scandinavian-Americans; Americans of every hue and ethnic tie. German-Americans, who were becoming increasingly the target of suspicion and nascent hostility, found uncomfortable relief in a redirection of animosity toward Japanese-Americans that erupted in a better forgotten spell of concentration camps and economic genocide.

Not the least among all these immigrant American groups in its anxiety to do something actively, was one that had been resident in the United States for thirteen generations; not by choice originally, but for three generations now its people had been citizens, and their stake was in this country—and in the outcome of a war publicized to be for freedom.

The country's ponderous preparations for possible involvement in this war that had been underway in Europe since Hitler invaded Poland in the summer of 1939, had included provisions for the young men of all these American groups.

For about a year, young men had been receiving form letters from the President with the salutation "Greetings . . ." and a ukase to report for induction into the armed services, under the provisions of the Selective Service and Training Act of 1940; an act that specifically provided that ". . . any person, regardless of race or color, between the ages of eighteen and forty-five, shall be afforded an opportunity to volunteer for induction into the land and naval forces of the United States for the training and service prescribed in subsection (b). . . ." Subsection (b) of the preamble read: "The Congress further declares that in a free society the obligations and privileges of military training and service should be shared generally in accordance with a fair and just system of selective compulsory military training and service."

The Navy had long prided itself on being an all-volunteer outfit and, together with its accessory, the Marine Corps, viewed with horror the thought of having to accept forced labor in the form of draftees. It was understandably concerned that its efficiency, its esprit de corps would suffer, and a sort of Gresham's Law take effect: the lower standards of reluctant enlistees would infect the whole establishment. By recruiting only volunteers, the Navy could be more choosy and select only those whose education and background skills could be more easily incorporated in the Navy's system.

No one should fault the Navy for this. It is good management practice in a free enterprise system. But the military is a creature of Congress, and therefore not free.

At first, the Selective Service Act helped the Navy and, particularly, its sister service, the Coast Guard. A potential draftee could be realistic as well as patriotic. There was more glamor to life aboard a ship than hiking through mud, and the reported quality of Navy chow was infinitely superior to C-rations. And who would have thought, in 1940 and 1941, that future invasion craft, heading for the beaches of islands with the unknown names of Iwo Jima, Saipan, or Eniwetok—half a world away—would be manned by U.S. Coast Guardsmen?

Because of the reported higher standards of Navy training, there was an added incentive for an ambitious young man to enlist voluntarily—before the day he would be drafted anyway—and so be able to choose the specialty he could be trained in; a specialty he could use in civilian life after the war was over. Under the circumstances, it was as good a deal as could be expected.

For all, except one group in American society—the "colored." For them, as Frank Knox explained to Charles Poletti, the only Navy specialty they could choose was the messman branch. A college degree was the passport for everyone else to a direct commission as an officer. A bachelor's degree in English led to the command of USS *PC 1264*, but not until June, 1942, could a graduate of Howard University with a master's degree in electrical engineering be able to serve his country in the Navy other than as a wardroom attendant or as a cook. And it was not until 1944 that he could become a commissioned officer.

The passage of the Selective Service and Training Act of 1940 gave hope to Blacks that there would be a change in the Navy's policies. After all, a pretty definite obligation had been placed by the Congress on the military services in a provision of this act: ". . . in the selection and training of men under this Act, and in the interpretation and execution of the provisions of this Act, there shall be no discrimination against any person on account of race or color." Spearheaded by Negro organizations, pressure was put on the Navy Department, but it wasn't until the Pearl Harbor attack gave impetus to their efforts that the Navy began seriously to give consideration how "to best utilize the services of these men."

On Tuesday, December 9, 1941 the National Association for the Advancement of Colored People (NAACP) sent a telegram to Secretary Knox, asking whether the Navy would now—because of the increased need for recruits— accept Negroes for other than the messman branch.

The personnel chief, Admiral Jacobs, was given the job of replying, and his answer followed the current policy: no change was contemplated. This was hardly a satisfactory answer, so on December 17, the NAACP wrote the President an indignant letter, which was bucked "for reply" to Mark Ethridge, the chairman of the Fair Employment Practices Committee.

On New Year's Eve, Mr. Ethridge told the President in a letter that he had discussed the matter with the Navy's General Board—the group charged with the formulation of Navy policy—but that his committee, under the Executive Order forming it, had no jurisdiction over racial questions in the armed forces, so he couldn't very well answer the NAACP, except to express his committee's personal opinions. These included that, even in continuing a policy of segregation, the Navy ought to be able to use Negroes in the Caribbean or on harbor craft. He added that perhaps the President might want to consider the matter further.

"I think," wrote the President in a note sending this letter on to the Navy secretary, "that with all the Navy activities, BUNAV [the Bureau of Navigation, precursor of the Bureau of Naval Personnel] might invent something that colored enlistees could do in addition to the rating of messman."

So the problem was bucked back to the General Board on January 16. It reported back to the Secretary on February 3, and a month later got it again. The trouble this time was the Board's recommendation: either, or. Either Negroes be enlisted in the messman branch, or, "if this proved not feasible," for general service.

The idea was still segregated units. The Board felt strongly that integration just wouldn't work. Discrimination, it said, in the written report, "is but part and parcel of similar discrimination throughout the United States, not only against the Negro, but in the Pacific States and in Hawaii against citizens of Asiatic descent." The reasons, "are rather generally that: (a) the white man will not accept the negro in a position of authority over him; (b) the white man considers that he is of a superior race and will not admit the negro as an equal; and (c) the white man refuses to admit the negro to intimate family relationships leading to marriage. These concepts may not be truly democratic, but it is doubtful if the most ardent lovers of democracy will dispute them, particularly in regard to inter-marriage."

Ergo: Integration couldn't work, and how can you properly segregate aboard ship?

In his letter forwarding the board's current recommendation, Secretary Knox added: "The only special service that I can think of where segregation could be possible would be in the Marine Corps."

President Roosevelt agreed that ". . . to go the whole way at one fell swoop would seriously impair the general average efficiency of the Navy . . ." but still felt that Negroes could do some other things besides being messmen, so back to the Board it went—"for further study and report."

The General Board was in a bind. Composed of the highest ranking flag officers in the Navy, they were men who had spent their lives in the service of their country and the Navy, guided by higher precepts of honor and integrity than any comparable group in civilian society. As human beings, they had their own personal and differing views, but they were professionally dedicated to the defense of the United States and, especially now, with the nation at war, this was of paramount importance; of more concern than personal goals and interests. And nothing should, nor must, take precedence over fighting this war in the most efficient manner possible.

While war developed technological experiments in weaponry and tactics, those charged with the conduct of this war generally felt that to experiment with anything else—especially fixed customs and folkways—would only create new problems, disrupt the efficiency they needed, and hamper their efforts to win the war.

Its report, submitted to the Secretary of the Navy and forwarded to the President on March 27, 1942, restated its view that segregation was an essential principle of naval administration, writing, "The General Board fully recognizes, and appreciates the social and economic problems involved, and has striven to reconcile these requirements with what it feels must be paramount in any consideration, namely the maintenance at the highest level of the fighting efficiency of the Navy . . ." adding that "if so ordered" Negro units could be used "with least disadvantage" in naval shore establishments, small local defense vessels of Naval districts, construction and composite Marine battalions, and some selected Coast Guard cutters.

The decision was the President's, and he made it. On April 7, 1942, the Navy announced that, beginning June 1, Negroes could enlist for general service as well as in the messman branch.

Although no one even contemplated it at the time, there could now be a crew for USS *PC 1264*. Unnamed, unbuilt, her future ship's company in all parts of the country, two years would pass before this ship became a reality. And, in the meantime, the Navy struggled to set up some sort of administration for this new program.

Following the announcement that Negroes would be accepted for general service, the coordination of everything dealing with their enlistment and training, together with the voluminous correspondence that naturally resulted, was given to one individual—a Reserve lieutenant commander in the Bureau of Navigation. To this was added the job of bureau public relations officer, no sinecure in itself.

However, there was hope on the horizon. Government agencies have a long-established habit of periodically re-organizing and, during the summer of 1942, the Bureau of Navigation went through this exercise.

The Navy had obtained the services of a professional management consultant firm, and among the many recommendations it made was one for the establishment of a Planning and Control Division, whose function would be the dissipation of the inertia that any large organization has in meeting any new and strange problems. In their wisdom, the consultants suggested that this division should have a Special Programs Unit, to take the initiative in planning and coordinating new programs.

It took a year to get the Special Unit functioning. Inertia, inadequate staffing, due largely to the hesitancy of some to become involved in such a controversial program and, to be fair, the greater number of seemingly larger problems throughout the Navy that the Planning and Control Division had to undertake, were some of the reasons for the delay.

What was needed was a push. And that push came from a most unlikely quarter in such an established, seniority-conscious organization as the Navy.

It was a young lieutenant (junior grade), with less than a year's service, who got the Special Unit on the track. He was the one individual who, by his intellect, personality, background, and a natural political sense, was responsible, more than any other person, for the eventual integration of the Negro into the United States Navy.

Christopher Smith Sargent's eyes were weak; he had to wear glasses. The Navy has always been very sticky about a volunteer's eyesight—20/20 or nothing doing—even if his expertise is in finance, supply or being able to get along well with congressmen. He could have a hernia (that can be fixed) or ulcers (unrecognized as an ailment), but near-sightedness or color blindness! . . . Heaven forbid, how could he see and recognize the port running light from the starboard? . . . Never mind that he would never go to sea; he would wear the uniform, wouldn't he?

Many a young man applied to the Navy and was turned down because of some weakness in his eyes, and went on to distinguish himself in the Army, which has different standards. Chris Sargent applied to the Army and turned down because of his eyes. To the Navy's everlasting credit, it granted Christopher Smith Sargent a waiver, and commissioned him a lieutenant, junior grade, in October 1942, and assigned him to the Planning and Control Division of the newly named Bureau of Naval Personnel. In the thirty-eight months that he served the Navy, he left his mark upon it; for, despite his age and junior rank, he was the catalyst, the one above all others, who led the Navy and the administration through the tortuous ways toward the solution of the so-called "Negro Problem." This was not the only problem he helped solve. When the WAVES were getting started, they were, in the words of Mildred McAfee Horton, the first Director of the Women's Reserve, "constantly getting . . . embroiled in difficulties with the regulars who could not believe that anybody, even women, could be so ignorant as to make so many mistakes innocently. I began to hear of a 'friend of ours,' who seemed remarkably gifted in pulling chestnuts out of the fire. When we wanted to accomplish something very special, WAVE officers began to say, 'Let's get Chris to help us.'"

For Chris Sargent had a way with people. He was flexible, a diplomat and, in the best sense of the profession, a consummate politician. He was also an able administrator; the first and most important thing he did was to organize the Special Programs Unit, and staff it with able people.

In a memorandum, dated June 29, 1943, signed by Captain H. G. Hopwood, USN, the Director of Planning and Control, he recommended that "A captain, carefully selected for his sympathetic understanding of the Negro problem as much as his naval experience, should be detailed as Special

Assistant to the Chief of Naval Personnel" to administer the Negro program.

While this would have given organizational strength to the running of such a complex program, it would have made it an independent office, similar to that for the Women's Reserve. It was felt that properly it should be placed under Planning and Control as a self-contained unit. And there it was placed.

As a start, in July, Chris Sargent enlisted Lieutenant Charles M. Dillon, USNR, and brought him to Washington from his job as executive officer of the Naval Training School, Hampton Institute, Virginia, and, in October, he brought Lieutenant Donald O. Van Ness, USNR, who was the Officer-in-Charge of Negro Recruit Training at the Great Lakes Naval Training Center.

The Special Programs Unit was in business. Later, it did obtain its captain with "sympathetic understanding of the Negro problem as much as his naval experience," in Captain Thomas F. Darden, USN, who, as Officer-in-Charge of the Plans and Operations Section of Planning and Control, became the immediate supervisor of the Negro program.

It was a Brobdingnagian task to mesh and meld the various administrative, organizational and operational features of such a complex program and still exercise imagination and innovation. There was so much to do—that had to be done—yet with an appreciation and understanding of so many factors; not the least being the emotional one the sociologists now call "interpersonal relationships," meaning racial prejudice.

Chris Sargent was a crusader. To him, a lawyer and former law clerk to Supreme Court Justice Benjamin N. Cardozo it was a matter of simple elemental justice that all Americans should have equal opportunities. He may have been a crusader, but he was also a practical one. His powers of persuasion were great but not infallible. His were the ideas of commissioning Negroes and of giving chief cooks and chief stewards the right to wear chief petty officers' uniforms, and he politicked successfully to help the Special Programs Unit get these through. But he lost his biggest battle, to allow stewards to transfer to general service ratings when they were obviously qualified.

Sargent was tenacious, but not to the point of no return. When he found himself against the metaphorical stone wall, he could gracefully retire most amiably, leaving the way open for future assaults.

Captain Darden and Lieutenant Dillon seem to have been, by contrast, necessary devil's advocates. Both of them believed that segregation should be ended in the Navy as soon as practicable, but Sargent's approach for the immediate ending of it, they felt was too precipitous. They felt that their opinions should be backed up "by a few experiments and a prior conditioning process."

No records can be found in the Navy Department showing how or when the decision was made to commission two ships with, eventually, an entirely Negro enlisted crew. It is likely that the idea was a natural culmination of a number of events; starting with the suggestion of the General Board in 1942, that "if so ordered" and general service rates were authorized, that Negro seamen could be used on small vessels. This, followed by the continuing political pressure of Negro organizations and the press, arguments within the Navy Department about the capability of black sailors, and the discussions between Captain Darden, Christopher Sargent and the Special Unit on the best experimental method, probably combined to point the way.

At any rate, an experiment was decided upon. There would be two ships commissioned. One a destroyer-escort, the other a 173-foot submarine chaser, a PC. In this autumn of 1943, the shipbuilding program for escort vessels was well underway. Whatever ships were chosen as the guinea pigs, by type they would probably operate on escort of convoy from American ports, and return to American ports. Thus, they would be within easy access for inspection by the Special Programs Unit, or for conferences in Washington with the Special Unit by the commanding officers, between voyages.

The experiment called for the detailing of black enlisted men trained in the various rates needed aboard such ships. At first, white petty officers with seagoing experience would be assigned, for the blacks' experience, obviously, would be mainly theoretical. As soon as the blacks reached a level of competence at sea, the white petty officers were to be transferred, and blacks rated into their positions. Then close scrutiny of their abilities could be assessed and a determination made of the validity of the sterotypes.

USS *Mason* (*DE-529*), building at the Bethlehem Shipyard in Quincy, Massachusetts, was designated as the destroyer-escort, and USS *PC 1264*, being built at the Consolidated Shipbuilding Company yard in Morris Heights, New York, was named the subchaser. These ships would demonstrate the practical parts of the experiment and, with the definiteness of actual experience, prove or disprove the opinions many Americans held about the capabilities of a people.

The destroyer-escort was the first to be commissioned. On March 20, 1944, at four o'clock in the afternoon in the Boston Naval Shipyard, to the notes of the national anthem, the commission pennant was hoisted to the top of her mast.

One month and five days later, at Pier 42 on the North River, Manhattan, a similar ceremony made USS *PC 1264* an active fighting ship of the United States Navy.

This is the story of the second ship, for it was upon her that the experiment ultimately rested, as the destroyer-escort was unable to complete the first stage of the experiment—to transfer the white petty officers and replace them with qualified blacks.

Seven months after commissioning, USS *PC 1264* put this first phase into operation. The eight white petty officers, considered by the ship's officers and men as instructors, had done their jobs well. Eight black petty officers replaced them without fanfare or difficulty.

USS *PC 1264* was now admittedly a segregated ship, but, to evaluate the efficiency and capability of such an enlisted crew, it had to be, if the new-found policy of general ratings for blacks was to continue, and ensure that individual jobs could be filled solely on the basis of rating and ability. Otherwise, it could be charged that any success was due to the white personnel and any failure to the black. For the enlisted crew, it was "fish, or cut bait." In their hands was the proof.

From this could come—if it worked—true integration. If it didn't work? . . . Back to the galley for the Black? . . . It was possible, but not probable. The winds of war, with the announced Allied aims of freedom from tyranny, were stirring the long-lying leaves of social order and established ideas and beliefs.

In Washington, the Special Programs Unit of the Office of Planning and Control, Bureau of Naval Personnel, watched and went on about new business. The two officers of the unit divided the responsibility: Charley Dillon would watchdog the *Mason;* Don Van Ness, the *PC 1264.*

And Christopher Smith Sargent, now a Commander and Assistant to the Director of Planning and Control, would keep one eye cocked on the ships' progress . . . when he had time.

The PC 1264

One

Morris Heights

The Harlem River in early 1944 was, even then, heavily polluted. Debris of every sort sat on the thick, oily scum that prevented even a ripple to show that somewhere, below this unnatural surface, was water. Discarded lumber, wood shavings, cans, cotton waste, and three jaundiced, sordidly wrinkled condoms floated stolidly off the stringpiece of the Consolidated Shipbuilding Company's pier, forming a cordon of filth around the hull of an unfinished ship moored there.

It was February and snowing. The small, white flakes fell thinly from the overcast, losing themselves in the black river or into the mottled slush of the land. On the dock, a man in naval uniform stood looking at the ship, his hands pushed deeply into the pockets of an overcoat. On his shoulders were the two gold stripes of a lieutenant.

He was a young man, just past thirty, and heavy-set. His face, half-hidden by the coat's lapels upright to shield his ears and cheeks against the cold, showed annoyance, disappointment—not at the ship herself, for this was the moment of the start of their personal relationship—but at the "they." Those faceless, anonymous powers that played with names and file numbers in the newly constructed Naval Annex in Washington, and directed men's lives by the authority of Randall Jacobs, Chief of Naval Personnel, whose signature was rubber-stamped on everything "they" ordered.

His annoyance was the usual reaction of one affected

by a bureaucratic goof. The morning before, he had been
having breakfast in his apartment on Miami Beach, before
leaving for his job at the Submarine Chaser Training Center,
when the telephone rang. His wife answered and called him
to it. It was the Communications Watch Officer, tipping him
off that his awaited orders had arrived during the night's
TWX traffic. He was tipping him off, in advance of letting
the personnel officer tell him, because the orders called for
him to "proceed immediately" by commercial air to Morris
Heights, New York, for the commissioning and fitting out
of the United States Ship *PC 1264* and, upon commissioning
of the ship, to take command.

The precipitousness called for by these orders surprised
and shocked him. To "proceed immediately" meant that he
would have to report within twenty-four hours at his new
duty station, instead of being allowed the usual four days
plus travel time.

He needed the usual "proceed" time. It would have allowed him to drive his family north. For his wife, pregnant
with their second child, it could be a rough trip for her, her
mother, and their year-old son, driving through the snows
that were blanketing the northern states. When he tried to
have the orders amended, the personnel officer merely
shrugged *c'est la guerre* and explained that the orders were
such because the *PC 1264* was about to be commissioned,
and he'd better get up there pronto to be in time for the
ceremony.

He had flown from Miami last night on an Eastern Air-
lines plane, checked in at the Commodore Hotel and, the
first thing this morning had taken the subway and a taxi to
the shipyard.

Now, on this cold, gray, snowy morning of the third of
February, nineteen hundred and forty-four, he could see
that quite a few weeks would pass before the commission
pennant could be raised to the top of her mast. She lay there
in the turgid water, her sides and unfinished superstructure

dappled with yellow zinc chromate, power cables festooned across her deck, disappearing into her bowels. From within her came the sounds of work: strange thumps, the grinding of some sort of machinery. There was no motion topside; no outside work could be done in this weather, anyway.

He felt a duty to go aboard, but he couldn't. Somehow, it didn't seem quite right. Like calling upon a future mistress before she was ready to receive; before the circumstances were such that the memory of their first meeting would not taint the close affection that every prospective captain has for the vessel he will command, be she tub or ocean greyhound. I'll wait until I have my working clothes, he rationalized. The day's too lousy anyway. I'll find my office and get the paperwork started, beginning with my letters reporting to the Commandant of the Third Naval District and the Atlantic Fleet Representative here in New York. . . . And find out if any of the crew have shown up.

But he didn't leave immediately. He looked again over her long, thin, slim body, and tried to visualize her as completed; finished with the workmen and their hammers and torches, bright and clean, smart and strangely beautiful, despite the dullness of her camouflage gray paint, gliding through undefiled waters, her ensign at the truck stretched tightly by her speed. And he, on the flying bridge, in control at the conn, his men at their stations. . . .

She would be, he promised himself, as no other subchaser in the so-called "Donald Duck Navy"—the fleet of the smallest oceangoing warships, manned by reservists, "wartime sailors." Nor, for that matter, would she be as any other ship in the United States Navy . . . now or later.

The thought was suddenly sobering. Of course she wouldn't be, she was meant to be different. She was being put into service for a reason. The difference he meant was her operational performance—how she would do her job as an antisubmarine warship, as an escort to the convoys she would serve.

By God, he swore, we'll show them. The "Sixty-Four" may be small, one of hundreds of mass-produced subchasers, similar in design, armament and equipment, she may be disdained by the regulars, but we'll run this ship better than a goddam battleship and do more with her, too.

Despite the weather, the foul-up in his travel, and the snow that was managing to creep down his collar, he was elated. He grinned. This is an occupational reaction of all prospective commanding officers, he thought; this is the same as I felt last July at John Trumpy's Shipyard in Gloucester City, New Jersey, when I went to pick up the *SC 1073*. But this time there is a difference. We've got something more. Some icing on the cake. An additional purpose to the overall one of winning this war. "They" in Washington, and here in New York at the Third Naval District and the headquarters of the Eastern Sea Frontier, and the Atlantic Fleet in Norfolk, and one-tenth of the population of the United States and God knows who else, will be watching to see how we perform.

He turned and started trudging back to the shipyard building to find the space he would use as an office for the next two months.

Selecting the Crew

The selection of the enlisted crew for USS *PC 1264* had started seriously only two months before the future captain of that ship stood in Morris Heights and peered through the snow at one of two ships designated for an experiment. The Navy Department had sent out a letter to all Naval Districts asking that Negroes with general rates on duty within the districts be nominated for sea duty aboard two ships—USS *Mason* (*DE 529*) and USS *PC 1264*.

The idea, at first, was to select a cross-section of the Navy's Negroes, but this was changed to ask for the men best qualified in their ratings, their selection to be a reward for their past work. Men for *Mason* were to be sent to Norfolk for training, while those for *PC 1264* were to go to the Submarine Chaser Training Center in Miami, Florida.

Five days before Christmas, 1943, two third-class petty officers were shoveling snow on a dock in Portland, Maine. It was cold, as Maine winters are, and, as both men were from below the Mason-Dixon line, they felt it, however hard they worked at this seaman's job.

The taller of the two was a signalman. His home was in Birmingham, Alabama. His name was Jarvis Guice. He was twenty-one years old.

Willie L. Gray was about the same age, and his home was in Baltimore, Maryland. He was a motor machinist's mate.

Jarvis Guice was in his sophomore year at Tuskeegee Institute when the Navy announced that Negroes could enlist in other rates besides the stewards' branch. He promptly enlisted. His country was at war, and he wanted to be among the first of his race to be a seaman in the United States Navy. He did his recruit training at Great Lakes, Illinois, and qualified for Signalman's School at Camp Robert Smalls—also at Great Lakes.

He felt he was lucky to be on duty in Portland. Many of his classmates at Great Lakes had completed their training in a specialty such as his, and then were assigned to labor battalions. He had his share of chores here, but he did have the chance to practice his art. He was often detailed to the small local defense vessels that patrolled in Casco Bay, so he was able to keep up his speed at sending and receiving messages by blinker and signal flags, and in reading and understanding the meaning of flags and pennants flying from hoists to the ships' yardarms.

But it was lonely, too, in Portland. There was no Negro community to speak of, and nothing for a young, healthy male to do on liberty except go to the movies with his buddies. From time to time, the recreation department would have a dance and USO busses would bring young women from Boston, but the girls would have to go back as soon as the dance was over.

Guice pushed a shovel-load of snow to the edge of the dock and shoved it into the water. "Man," he said, "I think I'll take off for Florida."

"Me too," agreed Gray.

Guice, to this day, is convinced that extra-sensory perception works. Within five minutes of his wishing for a warmer climate, he was called to the base personnel office. Five minutes after that, Gray received a similar call. There, the two of them were told they had been selected for transfer to USS *PC 1264*. But first they would have to go to Miami, Florida, to train for duty aboard a subchaser. "Would you like that?" they were asked.

"When do we leave?" Guice answered.

Two days later they were on their way. At 3:30 A.M., on December 23, the day before Christmas Eve, tired from the long train ride and the changes they had to make—at Boston, at New York, and into a special car when they crossed into the South—they reported to the Duty Officer of the Submarine Chaser Training Center on Pier 2, Miami.

The duty petty officer looked at them in surprise. "But we're not ready for you, yet," he said.

Guice and Gray looked at each other quizzically. So we're the vanguard of a pretty important group. Special arrangements have to be made . . . which haven't, as yet. Well, no matter. They could put up temporarily with practically anything.

They should have known better. The Chief picked up the phone and dialed a number. He waited.

"This is Pier Two duty desk," he said. "Crew of *PC 1264* starting to come in. Where do I bunk 'em? . . . Can't put 'em there, they're *nigras*. . . . No, can't put 'em there in the Everglades Hotel, that's for steward's mates. These, here, are *general* rates. . . . Okay, okay. I'll put 'em there for tonight."

There was discrimination within discrimination. The signalman and the motor machinist joined their sleeping lesser soul brothers on a floor of the Everglades, one of the many Miami hotels comandeered as billets by the military for the duration.

Within a week, they were joined by about sixty others from all parts of the country. For three months they went to classes on the pier and aboard the school ships, concentrating on the equipment they would find aboard a 173-foot subchaser.

At the end of March, fifty were selected to be the black crew for USS *PC 1264*. Their training completed, they were transferred to the Receiving Station, Brooklyn Navy Yard, New York, to await the commissioning of the ship in which they would serve.

Most took advantage of the time to take leave. All looked forward to the day and the chance they had to prove themselves, to contribute equally with other thousands of young Americans in bringing victory to their country. Each believed, with impeccable logic, that victory over an enemy preaching a master-race ideology would bring, with peace, the end of racial discrimination in America. The Office of War Information covered the world with its propaganda of the Allied aims of the "Four Freedoms." It was designed to bring hope to the peoples of the enemy-occupied countries.

It was also heard in America.

Selecting the Commanding Officer

The choice of officers for the subchaser was left to Captain Eugene Field McDaniel, USN, the commanding officer of the Submarine Chaser Training Center. He reserved to himself the assignment of all officers to the subchaser fleet.

With wisdom, the Navy agreed to this. It was carried out, of course, by the training center's personnel office, which notified the Bureau of Naval Personnel in Washington what orders it wanted issued. These wishes were invariably fulfilled.

Captain McDaniel was the Submarine Chaser Training Center, and vice versa. His strong, hard, dedicated character was imprinted upon it and upon every officer that went through the course. There were a few spectacular military commanders during the Second World War whose colorful personalities made good newspaper copy; fortunately they had ability too, and their names are secure in history. But there were others whose job was not glamorous, nor dramatic in the popular sense, yet whose effect upon the successful outcome of the war was probably greater, though unrecognized. "Captain Mac" was one of those.

Captain McDaniel ran a "Ninety-Day Wonder" school on the shore of Biscayne Bay in Florida. Every week, reservists arrived to spend three months of intensive training, learning how to be seagoing, how to operate ships. He took the young officers from ROTC and Midshipman's schools and, often, directly from civilian life. Within those three months, he had to motivate them, to give them knowledge about seamanship, communications, navigation, engineering, gunnery, administration . . . and that war meant the necessity to kill the enemy.

"Blood and Guts," he was called. And the speech he gave to each incoming class, at the orientation lecture, became a classic remembrance for every officer who attended SCTC.

The Naval Academy's yearbook, "Lucky Bag," of the class of 1927, says of him: "Mac heard a minister say that if something were not so, it ought to be, and that has been his password ever since. . . ." The defeat of the Axis powers depended upon the safe arrival of war goods across the oceans. American productive ingenuity could build the escort vessels in ever-increasing numbers, to shepherd the tankers, merchantmen and freighters in convoy; the great need was to man them with adequately trained officers and crews.

This Captain Mac did. But he didn't stop there, with the three months' training. He sent them off to new construction, and when they had outfitted these ships, he made them sail their subchasers back to Miami for shakedown. For two or three weeks, or however long it might take, he tested them. By night and by day his shakedown staff examined them, probing for weaknesses, correcting deficiencies and strengthening each ship's individual fighting efficiency, until Captain Mac was satisfied that this small unit of the fleet could do its job.

There was little relief, seven days and nights a week. A ship could be tied up after a strenuous day's operations. At two, or three or four A.M., a shakedown officer could suddenly appear and announce, "Dive bombers attacking from astern," and test the quickness and skill of the crew in coming to their battle stations, and beating off the attack.

The arrangement between SCTC and BuPers on the assignment of graduates of the school was practical and therefore sensible. During a student officer's instruction, the staff could assess his abilities in the classrooms and afloat on the school ships and, together with the aptitude test he was given, the personnel assignment officer usually put the round pegs in the round holes.

No method dealing with human beings by human beings is absolutely foolproof, and tales are told of great and sometimes hilarious mistakes, but SCTC's record was extraordinarily good. There were, of course, the usual charges of favoritism. As the subchaser navy was composed almost wholly of reservists, the reserve officers most experienced to serve on the staff as instructors and administrators, were graduates of ROTC colleges in the first few months of the training center. Miami being on the east coast, most of them came from Harvard and Yale. When there were more Harvard men on the staff, the "Yalies" grumbled that the choice assignments were being given to the Charles River sailors, and vice versa. The graduates of other colleges grumbled all the time. However, the situation changed frequently, for Captain McDaniel had a hard and fast rule: the tour of duty for the staff was six months—no more; then back to sea, from whence they had come, half a year before.

The prospective commanding officer of USS *PC 1264* first came under the influence of Captain McDaniel in the class that started on November 3, 1942.

He reported aboard at eight o'clock in the morning, after flying down from New York during the night. He had been granted "proceed time" in his change of duty from the Local Defense School in Boston, and he had spent it anxiously and hopefully waiting with his wife for the birth of their first child, who was then three weeks overdue.

The child could take his time in arriving, but his father couldn't in reporting. But when he presented himself at the desk of the duty officer on Pier 2, a telegram was there for him. His son had been born at 5:18 A.M.

This was cause for celebration, but even here the fates were against him. It was election day, and the bars and package stores were closed until after the voting was finished that evening.

For three months he studied subchasers. He learned Morse code, signaling by flags, communications, navigation, piloting, seamanship, administration, the logistics of supply, military justice, gunnery, protocol and naval customs, and tried to understand the workings of diesel and gasoline engines. (His aptitude test showed negative comprehension of engineering.)

The Yalies may have controled the personnel detail office the second month of 1943 when he graduated. He was ordered to a *PC* building in Houston, Texas, as engineering officer. The skipper was from Harvard.

From February to June he served aboard USS *PC 1252,* helping to put her into commission and fitting her out in New Orleans, and then going through shakedown in Miami and riding her to New York. There, he received orders making him the prospective commanding officer of an SC—a wooden-hulled, 110-foot subchaser—building in a yard across the Delaware River from the Philadelphia Navy Yard.

Although he had been attached to USS *PC 1252* for four months, he had spent precisely seven days underway at sea.

As commanding officer of the USS *SC 1073,* he served a few hours less than three days at sea.

Two of these last three days were spent en route from Philadelphia to Miami for shakedown. "They," however, had decided to transfer this *SC* to the Union of Soviet Socialist Republics, under a new Allied venture called Lend Lease. So he was, upon the substitution of the Stars and Stripes by the Hammer and Sickle, and a few days of pleasant and bibulous liaison work with the Russians, assigned to the staff of the Submarine Chaser Training Center as Officer-in-Charge of the Tactical Library. His record showed that as a civilian, he had been an editor in a book publishing house.

Neither memory nor naval records reveal what faction was in control of the personnel office of SCTC in late January, 1944. It is inconsequential, for he was a Trinity man. A New England college, to be sure, but without any ties to military training at all.

Why he was chosen to command a ship with such social, political and, indeed, such historical ramifications is unclear. It probably was because he was available. His six months on the staff was coming to an end. His record showed he had served on both a *PC* and an *SC*—as commanding officer of the latter. And among his colleagues he was known as a staunch defender of the *PC* class of ship over the new and more popularly desired destroyer escort.

Perhaps the last factor was the governing reason. For when the telephone rang in his office telling him to come over to the personnel office to talk about his next assignment, he was asked, "Do you still think *PC*s will win the war?"

When he learned of the assignment, he was both happy and hesitant. Elated at the possibility of commanding his favorite-type vessel; unsure about his experience under these particular circumstances.

This ship, he was told, would be a guinea pig: to prove or disprove a number of beliefs about the Negro race. Many Americans were convinced that blacks had serious physiological differences beyond the mere coloration of their skin, than whites. His brain was smaller, therefore he could never be the intellectual equal of the white. Animalistic, personal cleanliness was unimportant, and so bunking them together in the confined quarters of a ship woud make it into a pesthouse—why, during the days of the slave trade, a slave ship could be smelled from beyond the horizon! And, although there were some isolated examples of a black man defending his master, generally they were cowardly and couldn't be depended upon in battle. There were a number of such theories axiomatic to those who claimed special knowledge and experience of blacks.

On the other hand, he was told, ships were now being built faster than men could be found to sail them. If it could be demonstrated that Negroes could successfully fill seagoing billets, they would be an invaluable source of manpower. But maybe they'll prove to be as lousy sailors as they are reported to be as soldiers. At any rate, the personnel officer said, the duty will be a headache, you'll have BuPers breathing down your neck, watching you continually; your disciplinary problems may drive you nuts. I don't know why I'm telling you all this, because I've got to get a nomination into BuPers right away, and you don't have to take the job if you don't want it. This is one military assignment you can't be ordered to—you have to volunteer.

"What about the other officers? Do they volunteer, too?"

"Natch. If I can find any. All of this graduating class want destroyer escorts."

"How about letting me find them?"

"Okay. But do it quick. I've got to get this subchaser buttoned up. . . . So you volunteer, eh? . . . Good. Congratulations, maybe. Here, sign this paper; proof of agreement."

If he could choose his officers, most of his worries would be gone, for there were friends of his, serving in the fleet, with months of seagoing experience who, he was sure, would be challenged by such an assignment. The rest of the afternoon he spent writing them.

But it was wasted. The following morning, the assignment officer called him and asked how many junior officers he had found. My God, he was told, I've only just written to some likely candidates. My God yourself, was the reply, you don't write them, you haul them out of class. You can't get any pals who are already serving at sea. You've got to get them from this graduating class. Come on over here, and go through their service records. And hurry, BuPers is on the line, eating me out, every hour on the half hour!

He had gone to the personnel office, deep in discouragement. The chances of finding any officers with seagoing experience here, he felt, was slim. They will probably have even less hours at sea than I have. It will be the *SC 1073* all over again, where I was the most experienced man aboard —as I should have been, being the captain—with a week at sea behind me; the other two officers and the twenty-six men had had zero.

And even if there are some experienced officers, will they volunteer?

He went into the personnel office and to the conference table, where the brown, Manila-covered service records had been thoughtfully stacked for him.

Selecting the Officers

The first, and most important, officer to select was the prospective executive officer. Second in command, his primary duty would be the administration of the ship's personnel and their training.

It seemed to the captain that this ship, more than any other, needed an executive officer with uncommon competency. He would have to have, not only strong managerial ability, with the specialized knowledge of naval shipboard procedures, but also—as the captain Chris Sargent wanted to head up the Negro program in the Bureau of Naval Personnel—"with sympathetic understanding of the Negro problem as much as his naval experience." A wide naval experience, particularly, was what the prospective skipper of USS *PC 1264* wanted him to have.

He leafed through the brown records. There were some good possibilities for the three other officer billets; he put those aside for later consideration.

He had to find his exec first. The personnel responsibilities of an executive officer include the junior officers as well as the enlisted men, so he should help decide who the rest would be. There's a Navy saying, that the wardroom—meaning the members of it, the officers—sets the tone of a ship. On a small ship such as this, with such constricted quarters, all the officers would have to be compatible; they would have to get along, each with the other. He burrowed deeply into the records of the graduating class.

As it turned out, the executive officer found the captain.

The detailing officer was getting impatient. The captain had found an excellent prospect and interviewed him. He filled the bill perfectly; he was interested in serving aboard a *PC*, especially this one; he was challenged by it. He had had sea experience in the South Pacific, and was now completing refresher training at the top of his SCTC class. His name was promptly proposed to Personnel.

"Sorry, no soap," the captain-to-be was told. "We've already tagged him for a new *DE*. His name's with the Bureau, now."

"Can't you send a correction, or something? Dammit, I need him."

He was told: No. There'd be too much red tape; besides it would give this assignment office the reputation, with the Bureau, of not knowing its own mind. The prospective commanding officer didn't buy this, but there was nothing he could do, except try to get another before he, too, was sewn up by the detailer.

That evening, his wife was putting their son to bed and he was morosely sipping a martini in his apartment on Miami Beach, when the doorbell rang. He answered it. A stocky, junior grade lieutenant made his apologies for calling unexpectedly.

"I understand," he said, "you are going to have a *PC* with a colored crew. I'd like to see if I could serve on her."

He had heard about the *PC 1264*, only shortly before, at the Officers' Club in the Tatum Hotel. Finding that the prospective skipper lived within walking distance, he decided to look into it right away.

"Frankly," he confessed, "I'm interested because I hear you are going to operate out of either Boston or New York. I've had a year in the Solomons, and I'd like to be closer to home for a while."

It was understandable, and honest. No cant with pseudoheroics. They talked for three quarters of an hour. He accepted a drink, but not dinner.

He was a jazz aficionado. Through this interest, he had met and was friendly with a number of musicians, most of whom were Negro; he had no hang-ups on color, whatsoever. An avid yachtsman in his native Massachusetts, this experience had made him the skipper of USS *SC 760*, thirteen months before, while still an ensign. He had sailed his ship across the Pacific, engaged in several operations around the Solomon Islands, and was now at the Submarine Chaser Training Center for routine refresher training. He liked small ships, and much preferred *PCs* to *DEs*. He would be 28 years old next month.

The following morning, as soon as the personnel office was opened for business, the two of them were there, and agreement reached with the detail officer to mark Lieutenant (jg) George Russell Poor, D-V(S), USNR, for assignment as executive officer of USS *PC1264*. Then they went to work to round out their officer complement.

Lieutenant (jg) Ernest V. Hardman, D-V(E), USNR, came from Wenatchee, Washington, where he was born 25 years before. He had a degree in chemical engineering from George Pepperdine College in Los Angeles, but had joined the Navy as soon as he graduated in 1942. He had been trained and commissioned a Reserve ensign at the Navy's trade school in Annapolis, and then sent to study diesel engineering at Pennsylvania State. When he finished this latter course, he was ordered back to the west coast and ordered aboard a "Yippie"—a Yard Patrol vessel—which spent most of its time patrolling the coast, south of Monterey, California. He was a natural for engineering officer.

Wilbur F. Otto, also a Lieutenant (jg) and a west coast native, was a graduate of the University of California. Before going to SCTC, he had been trained at the Armed Guard Gunnery School at Treasure Island, near San Francisco, and had been in charge of a merchantman's armed guard. The same age as Ernie Hardman, he was a young man with an insatiable appetite for adventure, new experiences; the possibility of serving aboard such a distinctive ship whetted his already instinctive enthusiasms. "Boy, oh boy!" he kept repeating, during his interview in a deserted classroom on Pier 2, his face breaking into a series of ingenuous grins. "Sounds great!" He was nominated to be Gunnery Officer.

Frank W. Gardner, Ensign, D-V(S), USNR, a serious and earnest young New Yorker, readily agreed to volunteer for duty aboard USS *PC 1264* as Communications Officer. Newly married, he doubtless didn't find the possibility of operating out of New York as unattractive duty, but he was deeply interested in sociology. Because of the nature of this ship, he would probably have agreed to serve aboard her, wherever she might be based. At 22, he was the youngest.

The officer complement was now complete. It was formed, not a minute too soon, for the next day the prospective skipper received his orders to "proceed immediately" to Morris Heights, and look upon the *PC 1264*—a ship he had never heard of, two weeks before.

Precommissioning

The captain may have felt some chagrin at the precipitousness of his orders, but when he began to delve into all that he and his precommissioning detail was supposed to do, before this ship was ready for sea, the two months and three weeks were hardly enough time.

Mail had already piled up in the small office allotted to him; he'd have to start the filing system, if only to get them out of the way. There were reports to be made on the progress of building, on deficiencies, of Navy-contracted supplies not arriving. The spectre of paperwork was no wraith.

The first letter he wrote read: "It is requested that Paul G. Davis, Yeoman 2/c, 647 61 52, be assigned to duty to the Consolidated Shipbuilding Company, Morris Heights, New York, in connection with the fitting out of USS *PC 1264*, and be placed on subsistence." While he was at it, he wrote similar letters to bring Chief Street, Boatswain Donald Briggs, Radioman Donald Frazier, Electrician Harold Hunt, and Quartermaster Charles Phelps. He knew that Lieutenants Hardman and Otto would be arriving in a few days.

The remainder of the crew continued their training in Miami until the middle of March, then were transferred to the Receiving Station at the Brooklyn Navy Yard to await the commissioning. George Poor and Frank Gardner came up at the same time and reported to the shipyard.

But, before they left Miami, both George and Frank experienced what the crew had known all their lives.

Captain McDaniel's school had a curriculum designed to be practical. With only three months to turn landlubbers into seagoing sailors, it cut through the theory and provided the tools for results. For instance, in navigation, it taught the officers how to work a sextant, then supplied a form to fill out. All the embryo navigator needed to know in mathematics was arithmetic—to add and subtract. Starting with a, hopefully, accurate measurement from the sextant and of the moment in time when he'd taken it, he could plot the line of position of that star sight on the chart. With two or three more, he could fix his position.

Similarly, short cuts were taught in every other course. The latest information on new stratagems by U-boats, and successful methods developed to combat them, were passed on to the students. The courses were constantly being pruned or enlarged, to keep up with the rapid changes in this technological war. Captain Mac wanted the men of his navy to be prepared, for anything.

It was found, early in the war, that an unnessarily large number of men were dying, after their ship had been torpedoed, simply because they didn't know how to abandon ship properly, or how to swim through seas that might be filmed by burning oil.

So, every ship's company that went through the Submarine Chaser Training Center was scheduled, at least once, to go to the municipal public beach on the island of Miami Beach for instruction.

At the end of a pier, a tower had been constructed, with a platform approximately the height of a ship's top deck. Each man was first shown how to jump from this platform, then he did it himself. In the water, he would learn how to save a drowning shipmate. On the beach, he was taught first-aid and artificial respiration. Then, his instructional period over, two hours would be left for fun—recreational swimming, it was called.

It was a popular class, ships' crews looked forward to it; the two hours recreation during working hours, lying on the warm sand under a Florida sun, or running, cavorting, on the beach and in the water, outweighing the trauma of jumping from a high platform.

The crew of the *PC 1264* was routinely scheduled for such a day toward the end of February.

Then with no explanation it was canceled. The executive officer demanded a reason. He was given it. The city government of Miami Beach refused the use of its public beach for the training of Negroes. Period.

Considering the philosophy of the staff of the Submarine Chaser Training Center regarding the preparation of its students—commissioned and enlisted—for war service at sea, it is difficult today, to understand how it would accept, so supinely, such a decision.

But this was 1944. Military bases, within the United States, conformed to local customs—often, even, within its own boundaries. The commanding officer of any installation, who might want to change local attitudes towards his men, had no legal recourse against civilians, nor against their municipal governments.

In fact, few wanted to. USS *PC 1264* would experience such indifference again.

Lt. Eric Purdon, USNR, reading the official orders directing him to assume command of the USS PC 1264, at the commissioning ceremony, April 25, 1944

Two

Ship Acceptance

On Monday, April 24, 1944, the *PC 1264* left her builder's yard forever.

Through the rain, with the shipyard pilot at the helm, she made her way through the debris-covered waterways of the Harlem River and Spuyten Duyvil Creek and under the Henry Hudson Parkway bridge into the North River, and headed south to the Navy's Pier 42 on the lower west side of Manhattan.

Spanking new, her one hundred and seventy-three feet of freshly painted length glistening in the wetness, her bluish-gray hull relieved only by the bright white painted letters and numerals of her name on either side of her bow, she glided through the muck, responding easily to the turns of her wheel to avoid the floating rubble in her way.

The precommissioning crew was aboard, as were the shipyard superintendent and a representative of the Navy's Supervisor of Shipbuilding. This would be the ship's last voyage as a civilian. Upon arrival at Pier 42, the SupShips man would sign an acceptance form, give it to the shipyard superintendent, and the *PC 1264* would become the Navy's property. Tomorrow, shortly before noon, she would be enrolled as an active unit of the fleet.

The commissioning was something to look forward to, as indeed they had for some weeks, but after their arrival at the pier, there was still much they could expect to do in preparation. Supplies—food and equipment—would have to be loaded, the rest of the crew move aboard and stow their personal belongings in their living quarters, the cooks and stewards get the galleys going for chow, and have everything tidy for the next morning.

The captain and the exec were fairly sure that everything had been thought of, and prepared for, to have this twenty-four-hour interim run smoothly and efficiently. The outfitting office in the Brooklyn Navy Yard had been alerted. It assured them that everything was in hand; supplies and the balance of the crew that had been waiting at the Brooklyn Receiving Station would be on the dock when the ship arrived.

Just before leaving Morris Heights, George Poor had made a final telephone call, saying the ship was getting underway. No sweat, was the complacent answer.

A bad wedding rehearsal is said to mean a successful marriage. When the ship turned into the slip at noon and, maneuvering past two amphibious landing craft, tied up at the pier, the crates of equipment and the balance of the crew were waiting there, but no food supplies. Moreover, the Receiving Station had agreed to feed the men before sending them over, but had not. These supplies did not arrive until evening but, nevertheless, Clarence C. Young, the ship's cook, managed to feed all hands their supper that night.

Another mistake the captain blamed himself for not noticing before the ship left Morris Heights, was the condition of the compartments. Clean and sparkling on the outside, inside the ship was a mess. The months of building had accumulated more grit and grime that it seemed possible to dispose of before the next morning's ceremony. The living compartments were so dirty that the captain didn't see how the men could possibly sleep there that night, and was tempted to have them all taken back to the Receiving Station for the night. But the crew would have none of that.

They wanted to get aboard. "We'll have her shipshape," said the petty officers grimly.

Soon after the ship tied up at the pier, the crew was called to quarters on the afterdeck. It wasn't a pep rally or for pronouncements from the throne; merely a chance for everyone, for the first time, to look at everyone else with whom he'd be living and working. The captain explained the schedule for the ceremony the next morning, after introducing himself, the officers and leading petty officers— Chief Motor Machinist's Mate John Z. Street, Boatswain's Mate First Class Donald Briggs, Gunner's Mate First Class Leland A. Young, Quartermaster First Class Charles E. Phelps, Radioman First Class Donald C. Frazier, Electrician's Mate First Class Harold E. Hunt, Radar Technician Second Class Aaron Maerowitz, and Pharmacist's Mate Second Class Edward Weber—the white instructors, whose job it was to train their replacements as soon as possible.

He then turned the meeting over to the executive officer. George Poor announced another snafu ("situation normal, all fouled up"). Word had just arrived that the day after tomorrow, the Navy Yard would conduct some inclination tests, to see how the ship would act in a heavy sea, what its roll might be, what the chances were of her turning turtle; information that the crew would certainly like to know. It would be done at the dock by some obscure scientific method, but it meant that the equipment on the dock could not be put aboard until the tests were completed.

However, there was a bright side to this. Not having to load the equipment made cleaning the ship a great deal easier, and meant that there was a chance of hitting the sack before dawn.

The group of faces were expressionless, with the tautness of enlisted men being talked to by a commissioned officer; and, too, with the wariness, suspicion of a people listening to one of another kind, stifling any indication of their thoughts.

The captain hoped that he, too, did not show his own feelings. Now that the entire crew was all together, in one group—sixty-two, besides himself—he was awed by their number. He felt again the enormity, the seriousness of what he believed was the purpose of their being here: that they, the sixty-three of them, together with the one hundred and fifty-six aboard the now commissioned USS *Mason* in Boston, would be the makers or breakers of a new personnel policy for the Navy.

And his was the responsibility for one of these ships; for the operational effectiveness of a combattant ship in time of war. This was his overriding responsibility, to see that USS *PC 1264* more than carried her weight against the enemy. Yet with this obligation was a sociological one, which might—or might not—affect his primary mission. This, he was to find out.

The fact was, he was undertaking both with little experience in either. He was aware there was racial discrimination in the United States, just as there was discrimination against Jews, Catholics and now Germans and Japanese, but it had never consciously touched him. He was a WASP—a many-generation White Anglo-Saxon Protestant, who had been raised and educated mainly in the British Isles until he came to America to go to college. His status he accepted as an accident of birth without giving it any thought whatsoever. He had never met or known a Negro socially, but then he had never met an Indian. He did know and was close to some Filipinos, Mongols and Chinese, for, following college, he had worked in the Far East.

He knew that as the Navy would learn about the Negro through this ship, he would, too. And there was so much for him to learn. A month before, Lieutenant Charles Dillon of the Special Unit in BuPers had sent him an Army pamphlet, entitled "Command of Negro Troops." It was an advance copy, for it hadn't been officially approved. It had started him reading more; he was now ploughing through the recently published two-volume edition of Gunnar Myr-dal's "An American Dilemma."

Here now, clustered on the fantail of his ship, was his crew—black and white. Except for the few who had been with him at the builder's yard, and those from the Receiving Station who had attended the Defense Recreation Committee's party in Harlem a few nights ago, they were complete strangers. He knew nothing about them, nor did they know anything about him. But they were now together, by virtue of administrative detailing. Living as closely as they would from now on, knowledge would come. And understanding. Leaders would emerge to take the places of the white petty officers. Later, perhaps, there could be even Negro officers.

He felt a warm sense of assurance. We've got everything going for us, he thought. The white petty officers are fully qualified with a world of experience, and, thank God, George, Ernie, Will and Frank were at SCTC at the right time!

He dismissed the crew.

Commissioning

A commissioning ceremony is a tradition of the sea. Perhaps a little less important for the future of a ship than the launching. The smashing of a wine bottle against the hull placates the gods; it is a religious sacrifice to ensure against misfortune—that however hard the gales may blow, however high the seas may get, this ship, with the men within her, would sail in safety on fairer seas and with friendlier winds.

The launching placates the gods, the commissioning placates The Organization. In its way it is a sacrament, too; the outward and visible sign of Authority: the witnessing of the legal appointment of a ship to the active list of the fleet, and of the individual who is to command her.

PC 1264 was scheduled to join the U.S. Navy at 11:30 A.M., Tuesday, April 25, 1944. Two weeks before, printed invitations had been mailed to the crew's families, friends and naval officials. There was no bar to guests, although it was wartime and commissionings were ordinarily considered classified—to be conducted in secret with the ingenuous hope of keeping the enemy unaware that another weapon had been added for use against him.

For *PC 1264*, however, publicity was encouraged. The Navy's Public Relations Office at 90 Church Street had prepared a barrage of press releases and made arrangements for coverage by the press, radio and motion pictures. It was a natural for the press and, with the temporary lifting of wartime censorship, they took advantage of it. Well in advance of the scheduled time, reporters, camera crews and still photographers staked out their claims at vantage points on deck, on top of the stack and on the top story of Pier 42's warehouse.

The ceremony is simple. A commissioning officer, representing the senior naval commander responsible for the outfitting of the ship—in this case, the Commandant of the Naval Shipyard in Brooklyn—comes aboard with a chaplain. He is met at the head of the gangway by the prospective commanding officer and escorted to the place where the officers and crew have been lined up. The chaplain solicits the help of a nondenominational God, the commissioning officer directs the prospective commanding officer to place the ship in commission.

To the music of "The Star-Spangled Banner," the commission pennant is raised to the masthead, simultaneously with the national ensign at the stern and the Union Jack— a blue flag with stars—at the bow. The captain then reads his official orders appointing him the commanding officer, and directs the executive officer to set the watch. The most junior officer (usually), and the petty officer of the watch march off to the gangway, members of the engineering force disappear below to take care of their machines. The captain then introduces the commissioning officer who gives a short speech followed by one by the captain. The chaplain gives a benediction. There are congratulations and the ceremony is over.

The crew had worked the night before until after two in the morning, washing, scrubbing and swabbing every compartment down to the bilges. The cooks and stewards had stowed all the food supplies, served an evening meal, and then had prepared refreshments for the expected guests and spectators.

No one had much sleep, but all were able to get some. And in clean quarters. Six o'clock came almost immediately.

The morning was spent in rehearsals. The last had a grand finale with the distribution of Plankowner's certificates. These were momentoes, certifying that each one of them was a member of the first crew to serve aboard. They were distributed now, so those, who wanted to, could turn them over later in the morning to their families for safekeeping.

The rain of the day before had gone. It was a clear, springlike day with a slight chill. There had been a question whether the Navy Yard Band would show up, but it did. And with the arrival of the first guests about eleven o'clock, periodically performed a repertoire of popular music interspersed with John Philip Sousa. It was a great help in entertaining the waiting visitors, for Commander H. F. Sasse, USN (Retired), the commissioning officer, was twenty minutes late.

The band's bugler had been alerted to watch for his arrival. The chief bandmaster was keeping himself warm with a spirited conducting of "The Stars and Stripes Forever," when the commandant's representative and the chaplain were spotted walking briskly down the pier. The music stopped in mid-quaver, and the bugler sounded, "Attention!"

The rehearsals had done their work. There was no slip-up. The loudspeakers on the dock enabled the guests to hear what was going on. There was even a moment of drama, remarked on afterwards by a few, caught up in the pagentry.

At the moment of commissioning, with all hands facing aft toward the stern and beyond to the river, as the band broke into the strains of the national anthem, and the ensign, the union jack and the commission pennant were simultaneously being raised on their staffs and mast, the sun suddenly broke out from the overcast, its rays focussing upon them.

Then slowly, majestically, beyond the slip, down the North River passed a naval ship and a heavily laden merchantman. The swell from their wakes made USS *PC 1264* strain at her moorings. It seemed to be a sign of her anxiety to go at once and take her place in the fight for which she, more than any other ship, was symbolic.

Lieutenant (jg) George Poor, the executive officer, set the watch upon the captain's orders, and the shrill whistle notes of Donald Briggs' boatswain's pipe sent Ensign Frank Gardner, the first officer of the deck, and Louis T. Ellison, GM 2/c, first petty officer of the watch, to their station by the gangway.

His chore over, Commander Sasse was in a hurry to leave; so much so, it didn't look as though the four sailors, who were to act as ceremonial sideboys and give him side honors at the gangway, would get there in time. But the press effectively blocked him, insisting that he and the new skipper shake hands and smile while flash bulbs flashed. By the time the photographers were satisfied, the gangway was ready. Frank Gardner had the spyglass tucked properly under his arm, and Briggs was tuning up his pipe again.

The visitors were naturally anxious to get aboard and the crew was just as anxious to greet them. But the press wanted a reenactment.

The March of Time took closeups of the captain reading his speech, the men in ranks. Jarvis Guice, the signalman, had to raise and lower the commission pennant three times before the impatient families and friends could come aboard.

With over three hundred visitors, the real waterline of America's newest warship must have risen a foot. Cookies, sandwiches, potato salad, coffee and ice cream were ready for them in the mess hall and wardroom.

Mrs. A. D. Berning, who had christened the ship four months before by breaking a bottle of domestic champagne on her bow, came with her husband for this next most important event in her nautical godchild's life. Mrs. Willie Parris, the director of the Harlem Center of the New York Defense Recreation Committee, whose generous organization had already had one ship's party, and would have more before the war was over, was accompanied by Mr. Samuel Allen of the recreation committee. Lieutenant Commander Donald O. Van Ness of the Special Programs Unit had come up from Washington, as did Connie Davis, the year-old daughter of Isaac Davis, MoMM2/c (motor machinist's mate second class), with her three aunts. Connie had left home at three o'clock that morning, but was not at all fretful; she promptly fell asleep on the captain's bunk during the reception.

The father of the yeoman, Paul G. Davis, semi-paralyzed from an accident some years before, had insisted on seeing his son's ship commissioned. "Take good care of our boy," he told the captain, who replied candidly, "I'm relying on him to take care of me."

And there were two young ladies from Boston, Miss Ethel Ferguson and Miss Althea Saunders, who had met Jarvis Guice at the USO dances in Portland. The former would become Mrs. Guice, and the latter Mrs. Henry Perry, the wife of the brawny young Californian who later became the ship's boatswain's mate.

By two o'clock in the afternoon, the party was over. Early liberty had been granted, and men from the off-duty sections were leaving the ship, when a young man came, half-running, down the dock. He shouldered by the men on the gangway sidling past, with mumbled, breathless excuses, up to the deck. He announced that he was a reporter for the *Herald-Tribune,* but had got lost. Please, could someone tell him what had gone on at the commissioning?

He was brought into the wardroom. The way he acted, convinced the captain that this was probably the first assignment he had been given by his city editor; a cub reporter sent to get some experience. He was given some coffee and left-over sandwiches, and the events recounted in detail. Then he interviewed a number of the men.

The results were excellent all the way around. The *Tribune* ran the Associated Press story the next day; this young man's report was much more detailed and made an excellent follow-up the day after. So the ship had two day's worth of publicity in the same paper.

The wire services' account of the event was picked up by newspapers, coast-to-coast. There were items in all the leading Negro press: the Pittsburg *Courier, Amsterdam News, People's Voice,* and all the New York papers—*Times, Herald-Tribune, World-Telegram, Daily News, Mirror, PM, Journal-American* and *Post* carried photographs and articles.

That night, there was more celebration. At the Savoy Ballroom, a majority of the liberty section—the men who could go ashore—danced through the night, their plank-owner's certificates an instant passport to the arms of every young girl there.

Underway up the Hudson

For the next four days, USS *PC 1264* remained alongside the dock at Pier 42.

The day after the commissioning, a lighter with a crane arrived in the morning for the inclination tests. The crane hoisted heavy weights on the deck and measurements were taken. Then the weights were shifted and more readings made. Though necessary, it was a nuisance, because it delayed the proper stowing of all the gear that had to go on board, before the ship could be taken out on her own.

This was an adventure everyone looked forward to. But, before it could be undertaken, there was more than the loading of the stores to do. Although this took up most of their time, checking the crates that came almost continuously from the Navy Yard, putting them in their proper places below, and keeping out of the way, as much as they could, of the workmen who still streamed aboard to complete jobs the shipyard had not finished, each officer and man had to practice what would be expected of him under various circumstances arising at sea and in battle.

Every man's job, his station during general quarters and emergencies, his watch section and responsibilities, his bunk number and his liberty section, were all listed on the Watch, Quarter and Station Bill, posted in the mess hall. Individual cards were also made up for each man to carry and be able to refer to, until he was sure he knew what to do. The only way to respond easily and quickly and with certainty, came through practice. So, before USS *PC 1264* put to sea, there would have to be drills.

It was hard to fit them in during these four days, but they were.

Sunday, April 30, was set to be *the Day*.

The purpose of the first voyage of USS *PC 1264* was to make her into the weapon she was designed to be; to change her from a ship into a warship. To do this, she would first sail fifty miles up the Hudson River, to Iona Island, near Bear Mountain. There, she would take aboard and store in her magazines and ready boxes, the ammunition for her 3″50 caliber, 40 mm and 20 mm guns. Then she would return, continue on through New York Harbor to The Narrows and Fort Lafayette for her depth charges.

With her armament complete, she would cross New York Bay to Staten Island and report to the U.S. Naval Frontier Base, Tompkinsville, for about a week's pre-shakedown training, equipment testing and adjusting, before setting sail for Miami and a rigorous shakedown at the Submarine Chaser Training Center.

The operations officer of the Third Naval District, recognizing that it would take most of Sunday to get to Iona Island and load the shells for the guns, suggested that the ship either stay at Iona or anchor in Haverstraw Bay, below Peekskill, for the night, before returning. The captain said he would take it under advisement.

The captain was merely hedging. He appreciated the suggestion, but an idea was forming.

Iona Island is a small, wooded island nestling in the most beautiful part of the Hudson River that runs from Haverstraw Bay on the south to above West Point and the Military Academy on the north. The grandeur of the highlands, with their mountains—Storm King, Bear, Dunderberg, Sugar Loaf—dropping sharply into the river, make it one of the most spectacularly scenic places in the northeast part of the nation. It is also a place that was close to the heart of the captain of USS *PC 1264*.

Directly across the river from the Military Academy at West Point is a village called Garrison. Here, his wife was born; here, her family still lived; and here was where his wife and son would live while he was at sea. They had moved there after the commissioning on Tuesday.

At least, it would be interesting to see Garrison from the water.

After breakfast on Sunday morning, the daily quarters was held on the afterdeck. It was announced that a Roman Catholic Mass would be held in a room on the pier, and anyone interested in attending, could. However, if any would like a Protestant service, the captain would be happy to conduct one aboard.

A number of the men said they would like a service

aboard, so, shortly before the engines were tested, prepara-
tory to getting underway, one was held. Within at least one
man's heart was a plea for help and guidance, particularly
during the next hour.

The morning was bright and warm. As the captain
climbed up to the flying bridge when special sea detail was
set, he realized he was approaching his moment of truth.
Within a few minutes, he would give the orders that would
put this five hundred tons of steel into motion. He would
have to guide her away, sliding from between the pier and
a *PC* that now was moored alongside, out into the narrow
slip, backing past two amphibious ships lying astern, then,
still backing, out of the narrow entrance into the North River.
Thank God, there is no wind in here, he thought. I wonder
what the current's doing beyond the slip. This is one hell
of a spot to get out of, for the first time we run the ship.
How fast can the engine room respond? How long will the
dead time be, between the moment I give it the order and
when the screws take their first bite of the water?

George Poor clambered up the ladder to the flying
bridge. "All departments ready for getting underway, sir.
All lines are singled-up on the dock."

"Very well." He leaned over the bridge screen, the better to see the deck force on the fo'c'sle. He said to the talker
with his phone, next to him, "Cast off three, four, five
and six! . . . Hold two! Take one to the winch!"

Alongside, the *PC 1217*'s men were taking in the lines
holding her to the *1264*. On the main deck, Briggs and his
men were hauling in the released forward bow and after
quarter spring lines, the breast and stern lines. The bow
line they were wrapping around the capstan. Holding Number Two—the after bow spring line—and heaving in Number One—the bow line—would bring the stern out.

But there was no need for this. The current swirling
under the dock, carried the stern gently out and with it the
PC 1217.

"Cast off one and two! . . . Starboard engine back one-third!" He clicked his stop watch. Four seconds later, the starboard engine was turning the screw. They were underway at 9:52.

Gently, smoothly, USS *PC 1264* eased astern, around the two ships behind her, straightened and backed into the North River, giving one long blast of her whistle as she left the slip.

The captain couldn't believe it. He had brought the ship out with only one bell to the engines. And the dead time between his order and the response was only four seconds! It was incredible, miraculous, for a new ship, a green crew.

"Pass the word to Chief Street," he told the talker. "My congratulations for a job well done."

Out in the stream, USS *PC 1264* turned her nose northwards. The special sea detail was relieved and the regular cruising watch took over. The talker put away his phones; from now on, the officer of the deck would relay his orders to the bridge through the voice tube.

The captain kept the conn. He didn't want to give it up . . . yet. He was too exhilarated by the ship's performance. He was like a kid who finds he can stay upright on his bike for the first time: I can drive this thing; it isn't so hard after all. But the responsibility of this ship was his, and would be his alone as long as he was captain. And he knew he needed all the experience he could get in piloting his command. The Hudson River was a busy place, even on Sunday.

Cruising at about ten knots, the ship made her way up the main channel, past the anchored merchant ships and under the George Washington Bridge. With the bright sun and seventy-four degree temperature, it was the sort of day that made being in the Navy the best way of life imaginable. Spuyten Duyvil slipped by on the starboard side, Yonkers lay ahead and the rocky cliffs of the Palisades stood steeply on the port.

Euphoria is good for the soul, but it breeds laziness.

The captain turned the conn over to George. "I think we'll have some drills. Later on, we should come upon some fishing nets. Watch out for them."

By the time the ship reached Peekskill on the east bank of the river, all the standard emergency drills had been practiced: general quarters, with all hands rushing to their battle stations; simulated depth-charge attacks; Sing Sing, playing the part of a Nazi fortress, came under heavy, imaginary fire from the 3"50 gun forward and the 40 mm Oerlikon aft; battle casualties were taken to the wardroom, where Pharmacist's Mate Ed Weber's hospital had been set up to perform immediate cures; Ernie Hardman, as damage control officer, and Donald Briggs, the boatswain, led their team to the engineroom where they saved the ship by shoring up a shell hole at the waterline, then rushed to the paint locker forward on the bow to put out a sudden conflagration. Below Peekskill Bay, where there was room to maneuver, a man in the form of a life jacket fell overboard and eventually was rescued.

Over and over again, they practiced; the captain on the flying bridge timing their reaction. They were much too slow for the results that would be expected in Miami by Captain Mac's shakedowners, but each drill showed improvement. After all, this was the purpose—to iron out the bugs, to give each man practice in how to get where he had to go in the fastest, smoothest manner, without falling all over someone going in the opposite direction, and what to do when he got there.

The drowning life jacket was rescued and left to dry on the deck. The ship headed northeastward around Jones Point on Dunderberg Mountain. There was Bear Mountain before them, with Iona Island nestling at its foot.

"Secure from emergency drills!" the captain bellowed. "Set cruising condition three!"

"How about special sea detail, Captain?" George Poor suggested. "We're almost there."

"We're early. Iona doesn't expect us until fourteen hun-

dred. Another forty minutes. We'll go on up to West Point
and give the guys a chance to see some really beautiful
country."

Bear Mountain Bridge, a mile beyond Iona Island, con-
necting the west bank of the river to Anthonys Nose on the
east, towered a hundred and fifty feet above them. Four
miles beyond lay West Point, the Army's citadel, its gray
granite buildings impressively dominating the steep shore,
against a backdrop of thickly wooded hills and terraces.

At Arden Point, the captain slowed the ship to one-
third on the starboard engine, and ordered a series of blasts
on the whistle.

George Poor and Will Otto knew what he was up to,
but Guice, standing the signal watch, wondered. He wasn't
alone. The noise brought the off-duty sections to the rails.
Collison? They couldn't see anything wrong. They gazed up
at the flying bridge. What was the Old Man doing?

He was leaning on the bridge screen, binoculars
pointed at the eastern shoreline.

The chart showed plenty of water to within a few yards
of the shore. He headed the ship in, closer.

Then he saw what he was looking for. A blue Buick
convertible came streaking down the hill to the Garrison
ferry landing. A young woman jumped out, waving.

The captain lowered the glasses and moved over to the
starboard signal lamp. He switched it on and slowly flashed
H-E-L-L-O.

The girl darted back to the car, reached through the
door for something. She turned, and then came the weak
light of a flashlight. H-I, it spelled.

"Starboard engine stop!"

The captain clacked the shutter a little faster. W-I-L-L
C-A-L-L Y-O-U F-R-O-M I-O-N-A

A-R-E Y-O-U C-O-M-I-N-G H-O-M-E T-O-N-I-G-H-T
W-I-L-L T-R-Y

It was time to close this off. "All engines ahead one-third. Left standard rudder. Steady on—what course, George, back to Iona?"

"One eight five, to start, Captain."

"Thanks." He leaned to the voice tube. "Steady on one eight five."

From the shore came an "R" for "Roger." End of transmission.

Iona Island

It was exactly fourteen hundred hours, when USS *PC 1264* tied up to an ammunition barge at Iona Island. She had come in headed downstream, so the lines were over her starboard side. A warrant gunner came out of the shack. He walked over to below the bridge.

"Captain," he hollered, "would you turn your ship around? We've got your 40 millimeter ammo down there, and your 3-inch stuff here. We can load you better if you're heading the other way."

"Can do. . . . Cast off all lines! . . . Starboard engine ahead one third!"

Seaman First Class James E. Johnson, in the pilothouse, rang the engine telegraph for the starboard engine to go ahead one third.

In the engineroom, Motor Machinist's Mate Second Class Arnett E. Gibson was at the starboard throttle. "Hey, Chief!" he yelled. "Shall I give it?"

"There's the order," Chief Street answered. "Give it! Follow it!"

"But—" Gibson was desperate— "we're up against some ammunition!"

"Give it," said Street, inexorably.

Up on the flying bridge, the captain suffered as the seconds ticked by, his earlier elation at the speed of the engineroom to answer his orders, completely deflated. Then the starboard engine roared into action and the ship moved away from the barge.

In the engineroom, Gibson awaited the explosion. Street took some cotton waste and studiously wiped the engine telegraph.

"Gibson," he said. "We're blind down here. Those fellows up there can see. But they can't move without us. So when they say they want to move, we move 'em."

The ship eased away from the barge. When her propellor guards were well clear, the helm was put over to port, and the port engine put ahead one third. Out in the river, the helm was shifted, and she was guided in to another landing.

"Double up all lines, and secure!" the captain ordered. "We're spending the night here."

"Oh no, you aren't," bellowed the warrent officer. "This barge is leaving after you're finished."

"Okay. Then single up the lines. We'll find another roost. Secure the main engines. The smoking lamp is out. Hoist Baker. . . . Mr. Otto!"

Lieutenant (jg) Will Otto looked up from the fo'c'sle. "Sir?"

"Get your bullets on board, Will. Don't drop any."

"Aye, aye, sir! . . . Young, Ellison," he called to the two leading gunner's mates, "Let's go!"

The captain stepped down to the signal bridge, past Guice who was hoisting the large, red signal flag, "B" for "Baker" to the yardarm, signifying the loading of dangerous materials, and climbed down the ladder to the main deck.

Adolph Cork had the gangway watch. He had just buckled his belt, holding the .45 caliber pistol, when the captain crossed over to the barge. He smiled.

As a quartermaster, he knew Morse code. He knew where the captain was going. He was going to find a telephone. He noted the time of his departure in the log.

The captain made two telephone calls. The first was to

the duty office at the United States Military Academy. He explained who he was, and asked if a United States ship-of-war could tie up to the West Point dock for the night.

"A what?" he was asked.

"The United States Ship *PC 1264*. A submarine chaser. One hundred and seventy-three feet overall." Then he added, in clarification, "Navy . . . sister service to yours."

"Oh. Hang on. I don't see why not. But I'll have to find out."

He hung on—three, four, then five minutes. Then the voice was back again.

"I can't find who's supposed to be responsible for that dock. So why don't you come on, anyway?"

"Thanks. We're at Iona Island right now. We'll be up in an hour or two. Thanks again."

He hung up. The good old Army, willing to stick its neck out. Most outfits, if they didn't know, would say no, rather than take a chance. I'll write a bread-and-butter letter to the Superintendent, and add a commendation for the duty officer.

He took the receiver off the hook and dialed another number. Things were working out just fine. He'd have his wife meet him at the ferry dock.

West Point

The captain was a liberty party of one that night, but the officers and men were not neglected.

Shortly after the captain had left, turning down Ernie Hardman's suggestion that he should cross the river in the ship's boat, the wardroom had a visitor.

He was a major; punctilious, because he was unsure of himself in unfamiliar surroundings.

He was announced by the gangway watch, but he

marched in concurrently with the announcement. He stood stiffly by the door, and looked over each one of the officers silently and blankly, and around the room; at the coffeepot with cups in the serve-through opening to the pantry; at the green, baize-covered cleared table. The officers had risen in politeness. George Poor, executive officer and for the past half hour acting commanding officer, pushed his chair back to get up and welcome him.

"Sun's over the yardarm," the visitor said, his face absolutely without expression. His words, spoken with equal intonation, sounded more like a report of a unique meteorological event than a hackneyed, social phrase.

George had reached him. He put out his hand. "Welcome aboard. My name's Poor. . . . I guess you're right, but there's nothing we can do about—the yardarm, I mean. Not this Navy—"

The major took his hand, grasping but releasing it immediately. He turned and marched out.

"What the hell did I say?" asked George of no one.

"You told him you wouldn't give him a drink," Will Otto explained. "Kind of inhospitable of you."

"Damn Navy policy," growled George. "Not our fault, but his neighbor's—up the river at Hyde Park."

Frank Gardner asked, "Who?"

"F. D. R.," replied the Marblehead Republican. "That Man in the White House. When he was assistant secretary of the Navy, he took booze off the ships. Josephus Daniels got the blame, but it was Franklin. Take my word for it."

"This talk gives me an idea," said the practical Ernie. "There ought to be an Officers' Club somewhere here."

With the exception of George Poor, who had the duty, they were getting ready to go on a reconnaissance, when their visitor reappeared. No one saw him, except the gangway watch, and he disappeared almost as quickly as he arrived. He marched aboard, nodding to the petty officer, went into the deserted wardroom and left a paper bag on the table. Out again, he stopped by the gangway.

"If any of you fellows would like a tour of the Military Academy," he said, "there will be two busses down here in about fifteen minutes."

The major may not have known about Navy policy, but he could recognize a deficiency when he saw it. The paper bag contained a fifth of Old Crow.

Fort Lafayette

The next morning at 8:35, USS *PC 1264* left West Point. A number of the men had taken advantage of the academy's hospitality, and toured the post under the guidance of knowledgable sergeants. The officers gave up their quest for the officers' club. The ship's visit had caused quite a stir; no one remembered when a Navy ship had visited there before; a number of sightseers walked along the dock inspecting her.

Luther Wheeler, Seaman Second Class, who had the duty at the gangway, watched two young soldiers as they walked up and down the length of the ship, two or three times. He overheard one say: "That boat's kinda high in the water, ain't it?" The other studied the hull for a moment. "Naw," he answered with authority. "That's just because it's high tide." "Oh," said the first, satisfied.

By midday, the temperature had risen to 83°. On the long ride down the Hudson, as many as could be were topside, enjoying the warm sun and the scenery. The river, in this fourth decade of the twentieth century was still able to support a fishing industry, and the ship had to keep a sharp watch for nets stretching, almost invisibly, to the channel and beyond. She nearly ran into one, just below Peekskill, but its marker—a small red flag—was spotted just in time.

First stop was Fort Lafayette, a small island three hundred yards off the Long Island shore in the Narrows. Here, the depth charges, the three-hundred-pound cans of TNT, and the "Mousetraps," the anti-submarine rocket charges, were loaded. But not when the captain expected.

He was feeling pretty cocky, as he headed the bow of the ship toward the dock. These had been two very pleasant days, sailing up and then down the Hudson. He had been able to be with his family last night. His fears about his ability to pilot this ship had evaporated. His confidence in his crew was—well, almost absolute.

And there was nothing to this. His bow was headed just right. I'll coast to a stop right alongside. We'll hand the mooring lines to those shore sailors. A smart maneuver by any Navy's book.

"All engines stop!" He pressed the button on the stop watch. Let's see what the engineroom does it in, this time.

He never did find out. Instead of quietness from the exhausts, they roared even louder. The stern settled lower into an increased churning of wake. The captain found himself pushed back by the surge forward.

"Stop! Goddammit. All engines STOP!" The dock loomed ahead. "Left, five degrees rudder!"

Then the engines stopped; abruptly. But she sailed by the dock, her bow wave splashing against it, then her wake. Her nose headed for a flagpole on the parade ground of Fort Hamilton, a few hundred yards away.

"Right standard rudder! . . . Port engine, ahead one third! . . ."

Thus began a nightmare. The channel between Fort Lafayette and Fort Hamilton on the shore, was only five times as wide as the length of the ship. Manuevering with her engines; stopping, backing on one, going ahead on the other, stopping, starting again—the captain did it too often.

The ship was, at last, making her approach, gliding a little too fast, her engines stopped, when catastrophe almost occurred. Almost . . . for USS *PC 1264*, and the experimental program, survived.

Diesel engines are started by compressed air that is stored in tanks. Too many starts uses up this air; it takes an immoderate time to compress a fresh supply.

"Captain," the bridge talker announced, "the engine-room reports it's out of air."

The ship's heading was good, but she was coming in far too fast; she would have to be braked by an engine reverse. Could we hold her by the lines, if we can get them over? . . . Too risky, the momentum is probably too much. Even if the men on the dock could get them on the bollards, which I doubt, they'll snap, and we'll scrape the bejesus out of our side and the dock, too. And kill some seamen with the broken line in the process.

"Left, five degrees rudder! . . . Rudder smidships! . . . Steady as you go!" With luck, there may still be enough momentum to pass this little island and get out in the bay. "Fo'c'sle," he ordered. "Stand by to let go the anchor!"

As he said it, he saw that Briggs was already prepared for it. In these moments of agony, a warmth filled his chest. By God, he thought, we'll make it.

And they did, without anchoring. Her speed slowing constantly, the ship managed to slither around the end of the fort and into more open water. The captain was about to tell Briggs to let the anchor go, when he checked the engine-room. Through the talker, he asked, "How long before you'll have enough air to give me a start?"

"I might be able to start the starboard," was the reply.

"Starboard engine, ahead one third!"

The stop watch was forgotten. Time was important, but not the measurement of it. Gripping the bridge screen, he waited. Suddenly, a flume of heavy, black smoke broke from the starboard exhaust, instantly followed by a throaty roar. The ship shuddered.

The USS *PC 1264* was underway again.

Slowly, she headed from the shore. A short time later,

the port engine was able to start. It delayed lunch to the consternation of Clarence Young, ship's cook, but the captain decided on a short cruise to fill the air tanks before trying to dock again.

Lieutenant Knag, the officer assigned by the Third Naval District to administer Negro personnel, was on the Fort Lafayette dock when the ship tied up, five minutes before one o'clock. He was there, because the men assigned to load the ammunition were black, and he was naturally interested in their performance. He had never been underway aboard a *PC*, so he was invited to ride the ship to the Frontier Base at Tompkinsville, after all the depth charges had been carried aboard and put away. In the months ahead, he was to prove to be a strong and loyal friend of USS *PC 1264*.

The ship, now with its full allowance of ammunition for all its weapons, pulled away from the small island of Fort Lafayette, at twenty minutes to four, this May Day of 1944.

The short, twenty-minute voyage across to Staten Island, can be symbolized as a crossing from infancy to puberty for the ship. She now had all the physical powers of an adult but, before she could use them, she would have to be tested, educated, as an entity, disciplined with firmness but understanding, admonished when she went wrong, and taught her manners.

Her puberty would last a week. Called Indoctrination, it would be a pre-shakedown period; a check-up. The ship doctors would test her equipment, adjust it, make sure her green crew was seasoned enough to take her down the coast to the next stage of growing up, at Miami.

After those relentless weeks of development, she then should be ready to take her place in the adult world of a Navy at war.

During shakedown, in a simulated submarine attack, a depth charge
explodes astern

Three

Tompkinsville—Preshakedown

On the Staten Island side of the northern end of The Narrows, there was a parcel of waterfront real estate with an exotic name: United States Naval Frontier Base. It conjured up visions of a desolate, distant outpost, ringed with palm trees, isolated from civilization, built by Seabees, without a woman in sight. The name was rarely mentioned without adding its location, Tompkinsville, and this somewhat destroyed the image. But nothing could demolish it better than seeing it. So, the word "frontier" became a nothing, a noise in speech, a name . . . which, of course, it was.

What it meant was, a naval base for ships of the Eastern Sea Frontier; one of the four organizations set up to defend the North American coast against submarines, and other assorted depredations of the enemy. Each sea frontier stretched about two hundred miles out to sea, EastSeaFron covering the waters from Canada to Florida. Within their territories, the sea frontiers controlled convoys and were responsible for their protection.

New York was a main terminus for convoys; receiving them, reforming them, grouping single ships together, and sending them across the Atlantic or on coastal voyages south to Key West and Guantanamo, Cuba, or north to Halifax, Nova Scotia.

73

The frontier base at Tompkinsville cared for the ships that escorted these convoys; especially the smaller ones—the Coast Guard cutters, frigates and PCs. It was scheduled to be the home port of USS *PC 1264,* when she had finished her ordeal by shakedown.

It was well equipped to do so. It had five piers—numbered, north to south, from six through ten—and shops for all sorts of ship repair of less than major proportions. It had its own post office, sick bay, commissary, ship's store, and a training center for antisubmarine warfare, where appointments could be made for two-hour sessions practicing simulated submarine attacks on an ingenious machine called an Attack Teacher.

The character of the base, though, was reflected by the people charged with supporting the small ships. The so-called indoctrination of new ships was under a lieutenant commander, A. G. Meigs, who was well-known throughout the Donald Duck Navy, and often referred to as the New York father of *PCs.* He and his two assistants, a Lieutenant Hansen and a Lieutenant Rosenbloom, who helped the ships with questions of seamanship and gunnery, had the attitude —too rare, unfortunately, in shore establishments—that the operating effectiveness of the ships was more important than red tape and administrative procedures.

During this week, the structural strength of the hull was tested. At a firing range beyond Sandy Hook, all the guns were fired and depth charges dropped, set to explode at a shallow depth, their force spectacularly throwing volcanos of water behind, and shaking the ship with its energy.

On another day, the radio direction finder and the compasses were calibrated, and on still another day, the ship moved to the Navy Yard Annex at Bayonne for deperming—the installation of gear to nullify the ship's magnetism; a countermeasure against German magnetic mines and torpedoes.

Gismo

The weather was beautiful throughout the ship's stay in Tompkinsville, the days warming to the low eighties and the nights cooling to the fifties.

Each day's work was completed early enough to allow liberty for the off-duty sections at a reasonable hour. And as the base was only a five-minute walk to the ferry, it was easy to get quickly over to the bright lights and fleshpots of Manhattan.

It was easy to get to Manhattan and, at the Battery, catch a subway to 125th Street and Harlem. But, coming back wasn't as easy. The New York City transit system could be an incomprehensible maze, especially for a young man from the back country of the South. Forgetting to make the correct transfer could land him in the back country of Long Island, as desolate and less friendly than his native countryside.

The captain had realized this when, four days after commissioning at Pier 42, a seaman had been late from liberty, and had the distinction of being the first to stand a Captain's Mast. The captain had been understanding, giving him a warning and advice to study urban navigation.

The seaman either disregarded the advice, found the countryside more friendly, or a combination of both. The second night the ship was in Tompkinsville, he was in the off-duty section and eligible for liberty. He was gone for two days.

The ship was easing into the slip on the northside of Pier 6, after the day of structural firing, when a lone but recognizable figure was seen on the dock. Believing in speedy justice, ten minutes after docking, the captain convened his court of law on the top deck, appropriately next to the mast.

With the executive officer as prosecutor, and the yeoman, Paul Davis, as recorder, the accused was ordered to be brought forward. He had been waiting below on the main deck, in the custody of the boatswain, Donald Briggs, who was also master-at-arms. At the command, he began to climb laboriously up the ladder, his ascent impeded by a burden in his arms. On deck, he straightened up, came forward to the court of law and stopped directly in front of his commanding officer.

"Captain," he said. "A present for you." And he handed him a small, white puppy.

Thus was enlisted, for the duration, the mascot of USS *PC 1264*.

As the result of a competition, he was named Gismo.

A Lieutenant from the Past

Special sea detail had been set, and the ship was waiting for the arrival of the technicians from the frontier base.

Five minutes after the scheduled departure, the men from the base were seen walking slowly down the dock. As they drew nearer, it was apparent that their progress was slowed by one of the party, an elderly gentleman in the uniform of a lieutenant (jg). He walked haltingly with the aid of a cane and, reaching the gangway, hooked the cane on his arm, and pulled himself carefully aboard, grasping the handrails.

He was a picture of the past. His uniform cap was high-brimmed, a fashion abandoned two decades ago. On deck, he saluted the national ensign, then the quarterdeck, and shuffled into the wardroom.

With the party aboard, the ship got underway, the captain at the conn. His curiosity over his extra passenger grew the rest of the morning, for the lieutenant did not appear on deck. When the ship reached its operation area, he promptly turned the conn over to Ernie Hardman, whose OOD watch it was, and went below.

The lieutenant was sitting on the wardroom transom,

reading a copy of *Life*. He looked up and nodded.

The captain went over to the coffee urn and poured himself a cup. "Coffee?" he asked.

"Thank you, no," the lieutenant answered and leafed a page.

The captain carried his cup to the table and sat down. He sipped slowly, glancing momentarily—and every moment he felt he could—at the ship's guest. He certainly was a fine-looking old gentleman, he thought. But who the hell is he? He must be ninety if he's a day. But only a jay gee! What is this all about? . . . Suddenly, a thought came: Is this a plant? . . . Is it a test, or something? . . . A part of preshakedown? . . . They bring on a guy who couldn't possibly be in the Navy—is it a check of the ship's security? What else could it be?

He put down his cup. "Lieutenant," he said, voice conversational and, hopefully, not too obviously questioning, "are you assigned to the frontier base?"

The old man pushed the magazine aside, folded his hands on the tablecloth and looked benignly at his junior in age.

"Yes. Yes, indeed I am. Do you doubt it?"

That did it. He was challenging him. "Frankly, yes."

"Can't blame you. Weren't you told?"

"No. Should I have been?"

"It's easier, for me. Like today, when I get a chance to ride a ship. They'll only let me do it in good weather." He leaned back. After a moment, he went on, "Yes, I am assigned to the base. Here—to put your mind at rest. . . ." He reached into his pocket and brought out a wallet. He flipped it open, showing a card. It was the regulation Navy identification card, with his picture on it. It was a modern one, too.

"You wonder," he went on, "that I am still on active duty, is that it?"

The captain nodded.

"You well should." His smile was of amused accomplishment, of pride. "Young fella," he said. "Would you like to know why? Of course you would. And you've a right to know, for this is your ship, and I'm riding in her. . . ." He paused. "But I have something to ask you. You'll understand why, when I tell you my story. But I have to ask you not to tell anyone about what I'm about to tell you, until after the war. Agreed?"

"I promise."

The captain did understand why, after the lieutenant explained. He kept his part of the bargain, not even telling the other officers on his ship.

This lieutenant, j.g. was eighty-six years of age. He had been born two years before the War Between the States had broken out, and had enlisted in the Navy, two years before this country had celebrated the centennial of its independence. He had served in the Spanish-American War, had been with Admiral Dewey at the Battle of Manila Bay, and had retired after the first World War. He had reached the rank of warrant officer, but upon retirement had been promoted to lieutenant (j.g.).

When his wife died in the middle Twenties, he moved into the Home for Retired Sailors. With the outbreak of the Second World War, he had written the Commander of Eastern Sea Frontier, Admiral Adolphus Andrews, whom he'd known as a midshipman. He volunteered his services.

Admiral Andrews, whom he called "Dolly," had invited him to his headquarters at 90 Church Street. It was a pleasant visit, reminiscing, but "Dolly" had told him there was nothing he could do, that he had already served his country, that this was a war for younger men and, in fact, telling him to go back to his Snug Harbor.

This he had done; not willingly, but resigned to the obvious. He would be there, now, except for something extraordinary that had happened.

"About two months ago," he said, "I got a letter. From Washington. It was orders." He wagged his head. "Yes, orders. Addressed to me. And at the Home, too. They told

me to report to Eastern Sea Frontier for duty. I thought
Dolly had come through."

"Had he?"

"No, siree. Not Dolly at all. Well, I went to 90 Church
Street, and reported. Let me tell you, they were somewhat
surprised. But there wasn't anything they could do about it.
It was there, in black and white. 'Report for duty . . .' And
I reported. The trouble, then, was what to do with me. I
was all set for sea, but they'd not do that. So they sent me
over to Tompkinsville, and I've been there, ever since."

The captain chuckled. He didn't know whether to believe him or not. But there the old man was, and what other
explanation could there be? "Do you know how you got
those orders?" he asked.

The lieutenant looked crafty, pursing the ends of his
mouth downwards. "Well . . . I don't know for sure. And
this is the part that if I tell you, you promised not to
say . . ."

The captain nodded.

"Well, the orders were right enough. My name, and
the address, the rank and all. But there was one thing
wrong." He stopped, looked long and hard at the other for
effect. "The thing that was wrong, was the file number."

"The file number?"

"Yeah-up, the file number. There is some young jay gee,
sitting out in Iowa or Kansas or somewhere, with the same
name as me, sweating his heart out waiting for orders. . . .
But he ain't going to get 'em. Because I've got 'em."

At his age, he should have cackled, but he didn't. It
was a deep, satisfied laugh.

Voyage to the Ordeal

The last two days of indoctrination were over the weekend. The ship remained alongside the dock at Pier 6, re-
plenishing supplies and taking care of odds and ends, and

some administrative details. Clarence Young, SC 2/c (ship's cook, second class), who had worked so well and hard from the day before commissioning, had found that even the calm waters the ship had so far sailed upon, made him continually seasick. Despite this chronic ailment, he had done his job, but it was obvious that on the ocean, the situation would worsen dangerously. So, regretfully, but necessarily, he was transferred to the base. His successor, also a ship's cook second class, coincidently had the same last name. Occonnar Young would serve aboard until the end of the war.

On Monday morning, the captain made his farewell calls on Captain J. M. Gill, the commanding officer of the base, Lieutenant Commander Meigs, and Lieutenants Hansen and Rosenbloom. It was a pleasant formality, which he didn't prolong, for their job carried on. Another PC had arrived.

This was USS *PC 1209*, a sister ship, also built at Morris Heights. Identical to the *1264* in construction, even to the installation of a new type of engines, she was ready now, herself, to get ready for shakedown, and to follow USS *PC 1264*, first to Miami, then back to New York. Neither her captain, Lieutenant Russell L. Harris, nor the *1264*'s skipper could know how much their destinies would intertwine.

Before leaving, a visit had been made to the port director to file the route down to Miami, and Charles E. Phelps, QM 1/c, the leading quartermaster, had ensured the charts were corrected to date. So, all was in order, when USS *PC 1264* backed from the dock, slid to the entrance and through it to the bay, blasting with her whistle to warn the ubiquitous tugs that continually courted disaster by steaming up and down, as close as they could to the ends of the piers.

Headed down Ambrose Channel to the open sea, the crew watched the receding skyscrapers of New York, then, ahead of them came a sight, magnificently unforgettable; an augury of their own future. A convoy of over fifty ships was returning from Europe, their hulls empty of the supplies and war materiel they had successfully taken to the beleaguered allied countries. Now in safe haven, a baby flattop and destroyers, splotches of rust showing where the sea had stripped the paint away, were leaving their charges behind, to come quickly up the channel, toward their own deserved rest.

It took USS *PC 1264* three days to make the passage south. The weather was perfect, even the seas off Cape Hatteras were calm at noon on Tuesday. There were a few cases of sea sickness, but the men and officers were getting their sea legs.

The calmness of the sea was put to good purpose. Everyone realized the importance of the initial reputation USS *PC 1264* must make in the next few weeks. None doubted that his ship would be tested, studied and inspected with greater care and concentrated effort than any comparable new vessel.

Webster defines morale as the "moral or mental condition with respect to courage, discipline, confidence, enthusiasm, willingness to endure hardship, etc." There may have been some lack of confidence, for want of experience at sea, but the crew during the trip south showed great morale by any standard. Drills were actually welcomed and assiduously worked, seriously and hard. There was extraordinary enthusiasm. When not standing a watch, or in the lulls between drills, the departments made sure their records were in order, filed and maintained in the way SCTC expected them to be. Samuel Chadwick, SK 2/c, the storekeeper, vied with Paul Davis, Y 2/c, the yeoman, for the use of the office typewriter—an arrangement was finally worked out. The desk force peered at hidden corners for places needing a touch of paint. Anything polishable was polished.

The drills became more serious. Instead of merely simulating firing, the gun and depth charge crews went through their procedures, including the bang at the end.

The men fired rifles, to accustom themselves to the kick and noise. Then under the watchful eyes of the gunner's mates, Leland Young, GM 1/c, and Louis Ellison, GM 2/c, they stripped the weapons and cleaned them.

Landfall was made on Cape Canaveral at 8:30 on Wednesday night. The ship must have been riding the countercurrent of the Gulf Stream, for she was ahead of estimated time by three and a half hours.

Scheduled arrival at Pier 2 of the Submarine Chaser Training Center was 2:30 the following afternoon, so, during the night, the captain reduced speed. He wanted to put the finishing touches to the drills, and have a field day to be sure that USS *PC 1264* was in the best condition any subchaser could be, arriving for shakedown.

The seabuoy at the entrance of the Miami channel was reached at 1:40 P.M., Thursday. To make a grand arrival, regular gung-ho Navy, the captain had considered having all hands in whites. But there were small rain squalls about, so when the buoy was abeam, he passed the word that the uniform of the day would be clean dungarees for the men, and clean, pressed khakis with blouses, for the officers. He also directed that all men on the main deck would line the rail until they had to handle the mooring lines at the dock.

At slow speed, USS *PC 1264* sailed down the straight channel, toward the white, low buildings of the subchaser navy's headquarters. From atop the operations building, a light flashed.

Guice was ready. So ready that his signal lamp had been switched on, the light burning behind the shutters. Rhythmically, steadily he clattered the flashes announcing the arrival of USS *PC 1264*, and requesting berthing instructions.

The answer came: South side of Pier 2, outboard of *PC 452.*

"Hey," said Ernie Hardman, the engineer. "The four fifty-two!"

"So what?" the captain asked.

"That's the steam *PC*. The experimental one. They've been trying to get her to work for a couple of years."

Another experiment; seemed appropriate to put these two ships together.

"Don't let's tie up too closely to her," George Poor said morosely. "We might scrape some of her success off on us."

Shakedown

When the captain paid his official calls, after landing, he was assured the Arrival Inspection wouldn't take place until the next morning, and so the ship would remain alongside the dock the rest of the day. He took this to mean that they would be left alone, to rest up after their trip.

He gathered that the first impression of the ship was good. "You looked mighty sharp," Lieutenant Commander Morony, the head of the shakedown department said. "First time I've seen a shakedown ship arrive 'manning the rail.' The line handling was very good."

Back at the ship, the captain found that the Arrival Inspection was the first examination underway at sea, but shakedown had really begun in earnest. For the rest of the afternoon and evening, officers and petty officers swarmed over the ship, asking questions, inspecting logs and copies of reports. To add to the congestion, mere sightseers wandered aboard, interested, as one said, "to see the nigger navy." It was better the next day, being at sea.

The shakedown inspectors were thorough. For the first three days, there was a detectable, growing despondency among the entire crew. Nerves became strained; there seemed to be no way to anticipate what would be wanted next. So much went badly. The drills they had practiced so often and brought, they thought, to such precision, seemed amateurish and ineffective. Their latent suspicion, that the inspectors would pour it on, to show that they couldn't run the ship properly, appeared to be justified.

The effect could have been disasterous, apathy could have set in; the what-the-hell-they-won't-let-us-do-it-anyway attitude of centuries. Then, the evening of the third day, the mood changed.

They had been out all day, beyond the seabuoy. In the early evening they came back in, more discouraged than ever. The shakedown party was about to go ashore. The ship's officers were glumly seeing them off; a few of the crew were standing near by.

The senior shakedown officer, a lieutenant, paused by the gangway. "Well, another day . . ." he said tiredly. "But it went a lot smoother, today. Matter-of-fact, this ship is better now, farther along in less than a week than any ship I've worked with for ten days." He saluted and left.

It was just the spark of encouragement everyone needed. There was no let up of pressure, but there was belief now in its purpose, and in their ability to meet it.

A ship at the Submarine Chaser Training Center, during this period, received more than the constant evaluations of her crew's knowledge and ability. Other departments checked her equipment and made recommendations for modifications, sometimes discovering shoddy, if not downright dangerous, workmanship by the shipbuilders. Captain McDaniel had made arrangements with the local shipyards, and it was rarely that a ship did not have some shipyard availability, in order to repair badly installed equipment, or to add some new items he felt his ships should have.

The engineering department was particularly interested in USS *PC 1264*'s power. Being among the first to have a new type of diesel propulsion, the department was on the look-out for any bugs that could be expected with any new design.

The pressure on the crews was well recognized by the shakedown staff, and periodically the schedule would allow a day's escape. A day of "independent exercises" would be assigned. The ship could go out by herself with no inquiring inspector aboard, and work out her problems by herself. It was good psychology, and good practice, too.

Five days after her arrival in Miami, USS *PC 1264* had her first day of independent exercises. She did, however, have an outsider aboard.

The afternoon before, after their return from exercising in the Florida Straits, an officer whom the captain had known on the SCTC staff a few months earlier, came aboard. He was an intelligent young lieutenant, a New Yorker, but with as deep and fanatical a belief in racial stereotypes as any red-neck cracker. It was a side to him the captain had never realized; there had never been an occasion for discussion of it, until now.

"I think," the captain said, "you ought to see for yourself. We have a day of independent operations tomorrow. Why don't you take a day off, and ride with us? You ought to be able to arrange it."

The lieutenant mulled it over. "I'd like it," he said, at last. "Actually, just for a day at sea. But I can't. We're having a dinner party tomorrow night, and I promised Sue I'd be home early to fix the cocktails."

"No problem. The day is the ship's. We fix our own time. I'll have you back any time you say."

It was agreed. He'd be aboard at eight in the morning, and he was promised to be back on the dock by three in the afternoon.

The ship was underway at 8:25 A.M. She cruised down the channel, beside the palm-lined causeway, past the sea-buoy and on into the Gulf Stream. There was the usual activity off the harbor; charterboat fishermen were out in number with their vacationers; figures stood on the break-water casting. The broad, white beach stretching northward between the sea and the tall hotels was dotted with people. If there hadn't been the sight of the school ships—the *DE*, the *PC*s and *SC*s—steaming in the strait with their student crews, and this minor warship, it would have been hard to realize that there was a war on.

The hot Florida sun had already made the day a scorcher.

Will Otto was officer of the deck. "Request permission, Captain, to let the men take off their shirts."

"Negative."

There would be no relaxation of Navy spit-'n-polish during shakedown. Captain Mac probably had a high-powered telescope.

But, to get farther away, he set the course northeastward.

The guest stayed on the flying bridge, most of the time, for he could observe better there, and keep out of the way as the drills were carried out.

Down in the engineroom, Chief John Street was following his own course of instruction of the firemen and motor machinists. He had four non-rated men "striking"—working toward becoming motor macs—and he was giving them experience in operating the various machinery, assisted by the rated men.

He had all his engineroom gang with him, for the drills had started with all men at battle stations.

There had been few orders for engine changes. They had steamed at more or less constant speed, once they had entered open water; the usual drills being handled by the deck force. Chief Street expected more activity when the Old Man decided to have man overboard drill and when there was a simulated attack on a submarine.

At 10:35 A.M., however, there came an unexpected order.

The engine telegraph clanged: All engines back emergency!

The men at the trottles pulled them back. There was a grinding roar, and both engines quit—stopped—were dead.

Topside, the watch saw the ship glide to a stop. Not

almost immediately, as it should have with the fulfillment of the order, but under the normal manner of losing way with no power.

Ernie Hardman disappeared below to his engineroom. He came back, after a while, clambering up the ladder, Chief Street behind him. It was bad news they brought.

"Something bent within the engines, Captain. We'll be here a spell. I doubt, really, if we can repair them here. Looks like a yard job."

The captain spoke into the voice tube. "Quartermaster!"

"Aye, aye. Phelps here."

"Phelps, get a bearing for me and plot our position."

They were about five miles out, north of Miami Beach. Too far to raise the subchaser center by flashing light.

"Mr. Gardner!"

Frank scrambled up to the bridge.

"Frank, we'll have to break radio silence. Encode this message and send it to SCTC: 'Engine casualty. Request tug. My position twenty-six dash zero three north, seventy-nine dash five four west.' Make it operational priority."

When Gardner reappeared, it was to report the message had been transmitted and SCTC had receipted with a roger.

"Well," said the captain in resignation, "I guess we'll just have to sit and wait for a tug.' He cogitated for a while, then added, "We don't have to sit, though. Let's have a few jolly drills."

The ship sat, but she didn't remain where she was. She was well into the Gulf Stream when she lost power, so she floated with it, on an average of more than three nautical miles an hour northward. She wasn't totally devoid of power, fortunately. Her generators worked, so there was power for her interior lights, for ventilation below and, most importantly, for the galley.

"Don't worry," the captain told his guest. "The tug ought to be along shortly. I've got four hours to keep my promise."

But he wasn't able to. About three quarters of an hour

after SCTC had been notified of their predicament, it sent a message saying that a tug from Fort Pierce would rendezvous and tow them to Miami.

USS *PC 1264* waited and silently floated northward. As the shore was in sight, bearings could be taken continuously, and her position accurately plotted. Night was approaching, but still there was no tug. Just before dusk, a small coast guard cutter, with the numbers *83452* on her bow, came by and offered help.

"Can you take us in tow?" he was asked.

"Will try." And he proceeded to do so.

It was five minutes to seven, when the cutter took the strain on her line. For four hours the captain had avoided the eyes of his guest.

One hour later, the line was cast off. The cutter had barely enough power to move the subchaser, and certainly not enough to tow her faster than the four knots the Gulf Stream was now moving her north. With the disappointed thanks of the *PC* she roared off to her base.

"Mr. Gardner, let's send another message. 'Where the hell's the tug?' . . . No, belay that. Quartermaster, what's our position now?"

Frank Gardner went below to his coding machine to translate the message, giving the present position of the ship and enquiring about the tug, into the gibberish of the current communications word symbols.

The captain was in the combined chart and radio room, when Ensign Gardner brought in the encoded message. He gave it to James A. Mitchell, RM3c, the radioman on watch.

Mitchell took it and was about to turn on his transmitter, when he quickly dropped the message on his desk. "Something coming in," he said.

He swiveled to his typewriter and clacked out the letters coming to him through his headphones. Then he flipped on his transmitter, rogered, and pulled the message from the machine's rollers.

Frank asked, "Shall we see what this says, before sending our message?"

"Hell, no. Mitchell, go ahead and send it. Mr. Gardner, decode this one as soon as you can."

Mitchell glanced at the clock to see what the hour and minute was, for the date-time group to be put at the beginning of this outgoing message, for identification. He switched his transmitter on, and, with the seeming carelessness of complete control, his fingers harmonizing the Morse, he told SCTC what USS *PC 1264* wanted desperately the base to know.

When decoded, the incoming message said, simply: What is your position?

Frank questioned, "Shall we send them an answer?"

"We did," said the captain. "Pretty promptly, too. Maybe, now, they'll send us that goddam tug."

It was exactly midnight, when the *YT-338* took USS *PC 1264* under tow and headed south from the northern end of Palm Beach where she'd found her. It took ten hours and twenty-nine minutes to reach Pier 2.

Being pulled ignominiously up the Miami channel, the captain, his guest, and George Poor were on the flying bridge.

The captain again made his apologies. "I'm really damn sorry—and embarrassed—about all this," he said. "I hope your wife doesn't give you too much hell. She must have been pretty worried, too. I wish I could have gotten word to her—but I couldn't use our radio for that."

"Don't think a thing about it. I wouldn't have missed this trip for the world. You know something? . . . About nine o'clock last night, I forgot these fellows were black."

The captain stretched out his hand. "Check," he said.

A lookout called, "Message from the base!"

The light on the operations tower was flashing; slowly, deliberately. The letters read: Commanding Officer PC one two six four report on docking to Commanding Officer SCTC.

So Captain Mac is going to eat me out himself, the captain thought. Well, I deserve it for giving that goddam order to the engines. He turned to his executive officer. "George, what odds will you give me that in about an hour we'll be running through a change-of-command ceremony?"

"No bet. It won't happen."

But the captain would have laid odds that he would relieved. Old Blood and Guts had done it before. As soon as the ship tied up, he left and walked slowly up to the administration building and the second floor, where the holy of holies was.

"Go right in, Lieutenant," the yeoman guarding the outer office said. "You are expected."

I know damn well I am, he thought, as he opened the door.

It was a terrible, terrifying sight that greeted him.

Captain Eugene F. McDaniel was seated at his desk; behind him, ranged like cabinet officers at a presidential signing of a new piece of legislation, were all the department heads of the Submarine Chaser Training Center.

The skipper of USS *PC 1264* walked a few steps and stopped. He didn't think he could go farther.

Captain McDaniel arose from behind his desk. A tall, thin, scrawny man, he looked as tough and mean as his reputation. "Captain," he said, "I have all my department heads in here, to hear what I'm going to say to you, the commanding officer of a ship here for shakedown training."

Oh-oh, here it comes. Oh, God, please stop this trembling.

Captain Mac went on. "The purpose of this center is training. To do everything we can—*everything*—to prepare your ship to go out and kill the enemy—accurately and permanently. We don't allow many mistakes by the ships when they are here on shakedown; I don't expect any—*any* —from my staff."

He went on, "Last night, this center made a number of serious mistakes. You had an engine casualty, and you asked for help. It took this center thirteen hours to get that help to you. So we are here this morning, Captain, to apologise. All of us. We apologise. . . . That is all!"

The PC's skipper stood dumfounded. He didn't know what to do or say. Slowly, he started to turn away, then stopped. He returned and faced them. He nodded, still bewildered. "Thanks," he said ". . . Sir!" and started to leave.

"One thing more, Captain."

McDaniel was smiling, his crooked but remarkably affable smile. "One thing more. And it impressed me. Your ship has a good communications department, Captain. We sent you a message last night, asking what your position was. One minute after we sent that message, you had decoded it, encoded an answer and transmitted it. A remarkable performance. Good day."

Miami Life-Final Inspection

The damage to the engines extended the stay of USS PC 1264 in Miami by one month. The technical representative of the manufacturer arrived to oversee the repairs and to work out a modification, so that such a casualty couldn't occur on the other ships now being fitted with this particular type of propulsion. Before reversing an engine, it first had to be brought to a stop; then restarted in reverse. A failsafe system had to be worked out, to prevent any possibility of human error. At the same time, the damaged parts had to be replaced.

Most of this work was done at the Merrill-Stevens Drydock Company, on the Miami River.

While the ship was being towed up the narrow river, around the bends and through the drawbridges, the electrician, Harold H. Hunt, EM1/c, one of the white instructors, gave a lesson in seamanship to Lieutenant (jg) Will Otto and the pilothouse watch.

"I don't see," mused Will Otto, the officer of the deck, "how bigger ships—like *DEs*—are able to get up this river to the shipyard, when they have to have repairs done. Getting around these sharp turns, I mean."

"Nothing to it, Mr. Otto." Harold Hunt had the answer. "They have rubber beams and an accordian keel. There've been great advances in ship construction."

"Hey!" called out Henry James, S1/c, from the wing of the bridge. "Take a look at that!"

Apartments and homes bordered the river; set back to allow a lawn to drop to the water. Varying in size and luxuriousness, they nevertheless all had the common quality of design for pleasant living in a semitropical climate. The atmosphere was one of indolence, of rest, of sun worship— the search for the golden tan. Florida caters to the cult and, whether on the beach or in the garden alongside a house, the accoutrements for it are always there—mattresses, deck chairs, a plain blanket, or just the crabgrass. And, usually, there is a body on or in each.

James had found such cultists, spread along the banks of the Miami River. The ship listed to port and then to starboard and back again, as the ship's company who were topside, moved from side to side, the better to observe.

"This," said Hunt, with authority, "has all the requirements for long-glass liberty."

Will Otto, student, was eager to learn. "What's that?"

"An old Navy custom. Comes from the time when the spyglass was the only instrument for the enlargement of images. Hence its name." He called for the quartermaster. "Cork, break out the long glass. I'll show you what I mean."

No explanation was necessary. The more pragmatic Otto said, "You fellows use the long glass. I'll try the binoculars. Easier."

"Oh, no, Mr. Otto, sir." Hunt's voice was chiding, heavily disapproving. "That is not Navy custom, sir. Regular glasses are for Peeping Toms, which, of course, no sailor would stoop to. Long-glass liberty is recognized as an educational—!" He broke off. "Cork! Gimme the glass, there's one I can't miss!"

Harold Hunt's lecture on Naval customs and usages did not go unheeded. Adolph Cork, never a one to let an idea go unexploited, put the lesson to profitable personal use. After arrival at the shipyard, he found that the ship commanded an uncommonly good vista of the WAVE's barracks. As the junior quartermaster, one of his responsibilities was keeping all the navigational equipment clean and serviceable; including the binoculars. He managed to convince some of his shipmates that as custodian, only he could allow their use. For a while, he conducted a lucrative rental service.

While the ship was at the yard, shakedown was held in abeyance, but the time wasn't wasted. Officers and men, in groups, took instruction at the center—in fire fighting, gunnery, damage control, communications and on the Attack Teacher. The more fortunate were able to take leave.

An extra month in Miami wasn't favored at all by the crew. They had been here before, of course, and the discrimination against blacks made liberty an empty privilege. Miami Beach was completely shunned. There was nothing there for them, anyway, and a city ordinance made merely being on the street at sunset a misdemeanor for the "colored." Miami was not quite as bad, but nearly so; it had a midnight curfew.

There was a snack bar at the shipyard. This was strictly segregated. It had three sections: one for "white," one for "colored," or one for "enlisted." This was soon boycotted, for the woman attending the enlisted section refused to serve the *PC*'s men, ordering them to go to the one for their race. The yard, being a civilian establishment, there was nothing the ship could do, except object. This added to the resentment of the dockyard workers against the "uppity" ship. An example was the experience of the executive officer.

Returning to the ship, alone, late one night, he entered the gate and showed his identification card to the civilian guards.

"Are you from the nigger ship?" The two men stood in his way. They were big men, fat-bellied, their hands ostentatiously spread on the butts of their .38 revolvers, the holster flaps unsnapped.

"I am attached to USS *PC 1264*," Lieutenant Poor replied.

One of them brought his jowls close to George's face, in typical gangster-movie fashion, "let me tell you, you goddam Yankee nigger-lover. See that building over there? We'll string you and your goddamn niggers to the top of it, if they give any more shit to our white women. Y'all tell 'em to keep away from our women."

Such indignities were lessened only by numbers. When the liberty sections decided to get away from the ship for an evening in Miami's black ghetto, they went in threes or fours, as a minimum.

Such incidents, too, brought sharply into focus, for the white officers and petty officers, what some Americans inflict upon other Americans. Their own complexion was protective, so a real understanding of another's susceptibilities, what he had to live with every day of his life, was difficult to achieve completely. Gradually, they were learning.

The antagonism of the shipyard guards was particularly marked; suddenly, inexplicably, their truculence vanished. They certainly never showed any friendliness, but their treatment of the men, their checking of liberty passes as they came and went through the gate, became perfunctory. The reason for this small improvement in attitude was not learned for many months. Which one of the other subchasers in the yard for repairs at the same time as USS *PC 1264* was responsible for it, has never been identified.

About ten days before the ship's repairs were completed, some white sailors from that subchaser were drinking in a tavern near the shipyard entrance. They heard some men at the bar, whiskey brave, announce that a group of them were going down and shoot up that nigger ship. Quietly, the Navy men left, went back to their subchaser, roused their shipmates and, without letting their officers know, broke into the small-arms locker and outfitted themselves with .45s and rifles. As quietly, they left the ship and deployed around the main gate.

The startled gate security guards asked them what they were doing. They were told. No invasion occurred, but a great victory was achieved.

Miami's prejudice made it difficult for the men to feel comfortable anywhere, except aboard their own ship and the Negro section of town, which had to be reached through hostile territory. The normal recreational facilities ashore, principally the long, wide, sandy beaches—Miami's greatest attraction—were closed to them. So, the 1264's men went ashore less frequently than other ships' companies for the necessary change of scenery and non-male sociability.

However, they had to get away for some sort of different activity. The confinement of the ship, aggravated by the disruption of the repair work, was not only depressing but unhealthy for mind and muscle. Being young and healthy, they had to let off steam somehow. One way was through swimming parties—not to the segregated shores of Miami's vacationland, but where they could be by themselves, as free as possible from the suspicious natives. The most convenient waterway was the Miami River.

The ship's boat, a sixteen-foot wherry, would be hoisted from the deck behind the smokestack, and launched. Clad in swimming trunks, some would take the oars, while the rest—as many as could be in the boat without swamping it—would be self-appointed coxwains. Somewhat disorganized in rowing techniques, the craft would eventually reach a

secluded cove, the anchor dropped and a friendly Nature of
sand and water welcome them to isolated relaxation.

Ensign Frank Gardner went along on an early trip. As
they splashed their way up the flat-surfaced river, oars getting entangled then disentagled, a discussion started on the
fauna of the sea and its tributaries. Seaman Allen Conner, a
Philadelphian working to be an electrician's mate, expressed
some concern about sharks and barracuda joining them at
their swimming hole. It was a distasteful thought, enlarged
upon with relish by the two mid-Western authorities, Dick
Bennett and Adolph Cork.

"Bullshit," said Ensign Gardner when someone suggested timidly there might be too much danger, so why not
go back to the ship? "Sharks and barracuda have to have
deep water. They couldn't come up this far. Lay off, Cork.
You know damn well there's no possibility."

"Not even a little one?" suggested the irrepressible
Cork.

The boat was anchored, oars shipped. The hot sun, the
cool, clear water soon overcame any lingering fears.

Ensign Gardner, immersed to his chest, his arms
stretched along the gunwale, half-suspended, half-floated
beside the boat. Eyes closed, his thoughts were far from war,
his pale body enjoying the languid lassitude of the water's
comfort.

Suddenly, teeth closed on his left calf. In immediate,
unconscious reaction, he thrashed out, a foot grazing something disappearing under the boat.

"I've been bitten!" he yelled, as he scrambled up into
the wherry. "Everybody come back! . . . Quick! . . .
Hurry!"

On the other side, Cork surfaced and unconcernedly
floated as his shipmates churned the water, vying with each
other to reach safety.

On Wednesday, June 21, in the late afternoon, the tug,
F. W. Meade, tied up to the bow of USS *PC 1264* and, with

a smaller powerboat, *Lazy Bones,* aft, brought her to the fuel dock at the end of Pier 1. The following morning, at last under her own power, she returned to Pier 2, to complete her shakedown.

Ten days later, she had finished. On Sunday afternoon, July 2, 1944, the final inspection began at twenty minutes past one. Two hours and ten minutes later, it was completed.

The shakedown department was satisfied. There still remained three and a half days' exercises at the Fleet Sound School in Key West, but, as far as the Submarine Chaser Training Center was concerned, USS *PC 1264* was ready to join the fleet. In fact, her record for shakedown was rated, "excellent."

Before the captain went ashore that night with George, Ernie and Will to get drunk in celebration, he wrote a letter to the Special Programs Unit of the Division of Planning and Control, Bureau of Naval Personnel, reporting that fifteen men had been promoted: seven seamen to third-class petty officer, four to second class, and four to first class.

Key West

The early sun rose far too slowly out of the Bahamas across the Florida Straits, the day before Independence Day, 1944. At a quarter to seven o'clock, the ship had started on her one hundred and fifty mile trip to Key West. The first five miles was eastward through Government Cut—the dredged channel extending to the ocean—and throughout this length, the sun remained at eye level, directly ahead, its intensity torturing the scarlet eyeballs of a hung-over captain. The executive officer, in no better physical shape, was also on the flying bridge, but the responsibility for getting the ship safely out of harbor was the captain's, so he could lean against the wind screen, his back to the insufferable sun, facing without seeing the receding city of Miami.

Despite their agony, they had no regrets. The night before had been an appropriate celebration; shakedown was over; the ship had passed her trial by ordeal successfully; at last, they could leave Miami. Now, all that remained were three days at the Fleet Sound School in Key West to get some practical experience in submarine hunting. Then she would be ready to go to work.

Key West, Florida, is a coral island, four miles long and two miles wide, the southernmost city in the United States.

When USS *PC 1264* first entered the harbor through Old Nor'west Channel, and slowly made her way to the Naval Operating Base, the town shimmered in the late afternoon heat. It looked what it was—a tropical town. Beyond the commercialized waterfront, the green of guava trees, banyan, frangipani, the royal poinciana with their great umbrellas of orange-colored blossoms, marked the streets and surrounded the houses and their broad, sloping, rain-gathering roofs.

The crew found it was a quiet town by day and attempted to be a wicked one at night. They also found that it was really south of the Deep South. The town bell no longer rang at 9:30 each night to mark the time all blacks must be off the streets "under penalty of being whipped . . ." but there was curfew here, as in Miami, and by midnight the Negro population, mostly descendents of immigrants from the Bahamas and still preserving their cockney speech, were enclosed in their "restricted area."

For three days, USS *PC 1264* was a student at the Fleet Sound School. She practiced at sea, hearing for the first time the sounds of a real submarine through the electronic ears of her own sonar. She spent hours tracking the friendly target and, over and over again, simulated attacking it. But, when in earnest against an enemy she would have dropped her depth charges, she sent instead a signal underwater to the submarine, which then released a smoke bomb to show where she was at the time.

They were especially busy days for the men who stood their watches on the bridge and were the ship's attack teams —the officers, helmsmen, and the five soundmen: Jack Boggess, Henry James, Henry Perry, Luther Wheeler and William D. Williams; all of whom had been promoted to Sonarman Third Class during shakedown. The Sound School instructors concentrated on them. When not at sea, they were in the school's classrooms, training on the Attack Teachers, or listening to recordings of actual attacks, to the sounds of an approaching enemy torpedo, learning to differentiate between the peculiar sonar echoes returning from a whale, a school of fish, and from the steel pressure hull of a German U-Boat. They also listened to the taped sounds of a fatally wounded enemy submarine sinking to the ocean's floor, with at least one man still alive in a closed compartment, and heard a single pistol shot.

Key West was an even worse liberty town than Miami for this ship's crew. The prewar Latin coffee shops with their strong Cuban coffee and little cakes, the ice cream parlors selling custard of green coconut and ices flavored with ripe tamarind, sugar apple and sapodilla were among the very few places they could go. There were a constantly growing number of honky-tonks catering to the influx of soldiers and sailors assigned to the Army, Navy and Coast Guard stations within the town's eight square miles. But, as the majority of servicemen were white, even these were segregated. There was little enjoyment for a black.

The officers fared better. The Officers Club at the Naval Base served inexpensive but excellent food and drinks. On the night of the ship's arrival, Lieutenant Hardman established an extraordinary rapport with the slot machines in the lobby. His success was so constant, that in later months, whenever the ship returned to Key West, free dinners and booze on Hardman were not only planned for, but obtained. He was a generous host.

The three days, however, passed rapidly. On Friday,

July 7 their training was completed. The ship did not wait. At one o'clock in the afternoon, she cast off her lines and was on her way.

Thirty-six minutes later she rounded the seaward buoy and her bow was pointed along the route that would take her back to her birthplace—New York.

"Yabonah," the captain muttered as he increased the ship's speed to 600 rpms, and then relinquished the deck to Lieutenant Otto.

Nobody heard him. They couldn't have understood if they had. It is a Mongol expression, and means, "To home . . . at last."

The officers, crew and mascot of the PC 1264

Four

Inspection

USS *PC 1264* reported to Commander, Eastern Sea Frontier, for operational duty, on Monday, July 10, 1944. She was promptly assigned to Task Unit 02.9, the surface escort group based at the Naval Frontier Base, Staten Island.

The ship had completed shakedown and sound school training with a good record. The commander of the surface escort group wanted to find out for himself how efficient this new member of his task force was, so on Saturday, July 15, Captain H. F. Ely and officers of his staff appeared at the ship shortly before 9 A.M., to make a surprise inspection.

Actually, it wasn't unexpected. Every new vessel could anticipate being given a going over by the operational commander before assignment to the first job. Naturally, each hoped to give a good, initial impression; the degree of a task force commander's confidence could largely determine how she would be employed.

It seemed a fairly valid assumption that more than the usual interest would be shown in USS *PC 1264*. So, from the moment of arrival on the south side of Pier 7 in Tompkinsville, the ship readied herself for as searching an examination as any she had recently experienced at the Submarine Chaser Training Center.

The essence of a surprise inspection is, of course, to catch the ship's company off-guard. The actual condition of a ship can perhaps be better assessed by the sudden appearance of a team of investigators; the normal state of maintenance, morale, and discipline can, more easily and graphically, be seen and evaluated.

USS *PC 1264* had convinced herself that she was high in all the tangibles and intangibles that would be examined, yet, while recognizing such inspections were for her own good, as a child being led to the woodshed for the same avowed purpose would like to lessen the agony, preferred to be prepared. It was a matter of pride and the establishment of a reputation.

Success in any military operation depends largely upon knowing the intentions of the enemy; his timetable for an attack. So, an item of the highest priority in the ship's preparations for the expected inspection was discovering exactly the date and time of Captain Ely's visit.

Thus was born a private espionage network. Eventually it stretched from within the Base Headquarters on Pier 6, Staten Island, across the harbor to the headquarters of Eastern Sea Frontier itself at 90 Church Street on Manhattan; for how often might surprise inspections be made of this particular ship?

The ship had seventeen hours' warning. It was enough. By 8:30 that Saturday morning, the ship was gleaming from stem to stern. Even some bilges with water in them had been repainted, and Gismo given a bath. All hands were in clean, pressed uniforms. The compartments had been checked and rechecked for any loose gear.

The captain happened to be leaning on the rail when he saw Captain Ely and his party stride down the dock.

"Here they come," he said. "Let's go!"

Ensign Gardner, the Officer of the Deck, emerged from hiding in the wardroom, his badge of office, the spyglass, under his arm. The boatswain's mate, Donald Briggs, and the seamen assigned to give boarding honors as sideboys, clambered down from the pilothouse and lined up on the narrow deck by the gangway. Briggs played the shrill notes of welcome on his boatswain's pipe.

Captain Ely paused for a moment on the dock, and looked over the ship. Then ahead of his group, he started up the gangplank, stopped to salute the flag flying from the stern, then the quarterdeck, and came aboard.

The *PC's* skipper saluted. "Welcome aboard, Captain," he said. "This is certainly a pleasant surprise."

Captain Ely returned the salute. "I'm sure it is." He grinned. "For your information, Captain, this is an official Eastern Sea Frontier inspection. I would appreciate your men forming in ranks on the dock. We will start with a personnel inspection."

For two hours the Inspection Board looked around, in and over the ship. During most of this time, Captain Ely kept the captain in the wardroom, not only to learn something about him personally, but to keep him away from the inspection party so he couldn't, perhaps, influence the answers given the investigators by his officers and crew.

Toward the end, a lieutenant commander who had been looking into the communications department, came into the wardroom and slapped his cap down on the table. "Can't catch 'em at anything, Captain," he told his boss affably, with a trace of a chuckle. "Smart as hell. . . ."

He explained. He had climbed the ladder to the signal bridge. There, a tall, young signalman had come to attention smartly. "Signal bridge ready for inspection, sir." He identified himself, "Signalman Second-Class Guice."

The communications officer checked the flag bag—the flags and pennants were clean and stored in proper sequence; the log was being properly maintained; the equipment was in excellent shape.

"Guice," he said, at last, "I have a problem to put to you. . . . I know this ship hasn't operated yet in winter, but it will and this sort of a situation can arise. I want to know what you would do if it does." He paused and then went on, "You are escorting a convoy. It's cold and rough; water and spray has covered all the topsides here with ice.

You're on watch. Suddenly, you see the convoy commodore's flagship calling you up on flashing light. . . . What do you do?"

Guice moved to the 12-inch signal lamp at the side of the bridge. "I turn on the lamp," he said, pointing at the switchbox by the deck, "then I point it at the ship and—" he put his hand on the shutter handle—"acknowledge."

"Ah . . ." the officer said. "I don't think you understand. That lamp is covered with ice. It's frozen. You can't work it. So, what do you do?"

Guice didn't hesitate. "Sir," he said politely, "the *PC 1264* would never allow its equipment to get into that shape—not to work, I mean."

Before the inspection party left, a critique was held in the wardroom to give the subchaser's officers an informal report of the findings. A few recommendations for improvements were made, but they were minor and given—it seemed to the smug listeners—more to demonstrate the investigators' thoroughness and the belief that no ship could possibly be perfect.

Captain Ely punctiliously requested permission to leave the ship. "I think you are ready to earn your pay, now," he said. "You'll be hearing from us."

The ship's payroll would cost the taxpayer a little bit more. During this week, the executive officer, Lieutenant (jg) George Poor, was promoted to senior-grade lieutenant.

Convoys—Guantanamo

Now the ship was ready to go to work. In the months ahead, she would escort convoys from New York to Guantanamo, Cuba, to Key West, Florida, and back again; from Charleston, South Carolina to New York. She would accompany a French submarine from New London, Connecticut, to Key West, protecting her from Navy and Army Air Corps bombers, to whom any submarine was fair game. She would patrol, for a week or more at a time, various stations off the coast, when there was a suspicion that the Germans, in a last-ditch attempt, would bomb New York and Washington with rockets launched from U-Boats.

She also exercised one day in the waters of Block Island Sound with a submarine that had been fitted with a new invention, called a "snorkle," which enabled the U-Boats to breathe underwater and run on their diesels, instead of only by battery-consuming electricity. Naval officers and civilian scientists were aboard the subchaser to try and figure a way to detect submarines with this device.

She would operate in all kinds of weather. At the start of her career from commissioning and throughout shake-down, she had enjoyed relatively calm seas and fair winds. Her sponsor, Mrs. A. D. Berning, had christened her well at her launching. The relative tranquility allowed the men to become accustomed gradually to the pitch and roll that were a subchaser's greatest characteristics. There were still a few months before the winter storms would churn the Atlantic with fury, and encrust her decks and superstructure with ice from the driving spray.

Her first job was with a convoy from New York to Guantanamo—the Navy's leased base on Cuba's southeast shore—listed on COMEASTSEAFRON's operations board as Convoy NG-448. For a week at the end of July, USS PC 1264 patrolled the starboard beam of the rectangle of eleven freighters, eleven tankers, and two large landing craft on their way to the Pacific. Four other escorts protected other sectors: two Coast Guard ships, USCGC *Haste* (*PG-92*) and USCGC *Intensity* (*PG-93*), and two subchasers, USS *PC 1212* and USS *PC 1209*.

Constantly, the *piinngg . . . piinngg* of the sonar beams from her supersonic echo-ranging device probed in a search-ing arc for an underwater enemy; jarring the silence of the pilothouse like a discordant metronome; each high-pitched note fading before the next beat, lost in the ocean's distance.

This was now the real thing, the test of their months of training. The play acting was behind them; this was their war.

It was brought forcibly to them in the early afternoon of the first day at sea. USS *PC 1212* thought she had a contact and dropped a pattern of depth charges.

It was brought even more strongly to USS *PC 1264* the next morning. A few minutes after eight o'clock, a strong echo came back on her sonar. It might have been a school of fish or a whale. It could just as well have been a U-Boat about to fire its torpedoes. When in doubt, attack!

"Sound general quarters!"

The men scrambled to their battle stations. The sub-chaser raced to the point where her target seemed to be and dropped an urgent, shallow pattern of depth charges.

Everyone reacted at the alarm, and after the first attack, in his own personal, emotional way.

Back aft, Arnett Gibson, the big, burly, motor machinist's mate, was in charge of the K-guns which threw the three-hundred-pound ashcans of TNT into their high-arched flight from the sides. A veteran of the Army and, at forty-five, the oldest man on the ship, he found that his loading crew of three had become transfixed with the explosion of the first pattern and the upheaval of the sea astern.

"Get moving!" he howled. "Load these goddam guns! We've got to do it again!"

The ship was turning for another approach. Gibson grabbed two of the seamen nearest him, and with words best understood in the U.S. Cavalry, he told them he would throw them instead of the charge, if they didn't get hopping.

They awoke, understood, and in time for the second attack, had the guns loaded.

For three hours the *1264* hunted her quarry, attacking it twice again with the mousetraps. By then the convoy was over twenty miles away, and as there was no longer any indication that their target had been a submarine at all, but perhaps a properly disgruntled whale, the ship turned toward the distant convoy and increased speed to catch up with it.

On the bridge, the attack team was remarkably cool and responsive to each order. The sonarman operated his gear as precisely as if he were in the mocked-up attack teacher on shore, managing to regain contact quickly again after it had been lost in the depth-charge explosions and the churning water cavitation around the ship's propellers after passing over the target. Discipline was tight and controlled. But there was blood lust—what a coup, if USS *PC 1264* could get her sub the first time out!

But she didn't. This was the only excitement of the voyage.

At four o'clock in the afternoon of Thursday, July 27, the ship arrived in Guantanamo, and headed for the fuel dock to take on supplies of oil and water.

George Alexander, a seaman at special sea detail on the fo'c'sle, saw a Cuban standing on the wharf. He wanted him to take a mooring line and put it on a bollard. "Say," he yelled as the ship eased nearer to the dock. "Do you speak American?"

The man shook his head. "No," he replied, "but I do speak English."

The return trip with GN-148 was even less eventful than the voyage down. Yet, when the ship tied up again at their home base, alongside Pier 7 in Tompkinsville, on Tuesday, August 8, shortly after dawn, the officers and men of USS *PC 1264* felt somewhat they were bloodied and, therefore, veterans.

During the six days that the ship spent in her home port, supplies of ammunition, fuel and food were replenished. There were some personnel changes. Not only on the ship, but ashore. The captain's second son considerately arrived on the fourth evening, allowing his father to experience a hospital waiting room. On board, W. W. Hawk, a much-needed coxswain, came aboard to assist Donald Briggs with the deck force. A new seaman, F. A. Moore, also reported. The ship lost Ensign Frank Gardner. He became ill, the night before leaving for Guantanamo, and had to be rushed to the hospital.

No ship remains static in Personnel. There is natural attrition. Men leave, because they have been promoted and their experience and rate is needed more aboard another ship. Or they require medical attention ashore. Or they request and obtain a transfer to some other duty. Or they may be transferred for cause—in other words, they're fired. And, during the war, there was another reason. A man returning late from liberty or leave, and missing his ship, was automatically transferred off the ship to the base. He ran the risk of severe disciplinary action, because his ship had to sail short-handed.

When a replacement was needed, the procedure was to send a dispatch to Service Forces, Atlantic Fleet, in Norfolk, requesting such and such a rating. For USS *PC 1264,* this posed a particular problem; invariably, the request would be filled by the proper rating, but usually he was white.

Yet, there were a number of blacks who had been trained in the ratings needed, in the New York area, at the various ammunition depots—at Leonardo, New Jersey, and —as the ship had experienced—at Fort Lafayette. It seemed to the captain and executive officer, that some arrangement ought to be made to enable them to tap individuals from this supply.

When a man was needed, he was needed right away. If the captain could get authority to transfer a man he knew of to his ship, it would certainly help. The Special Programs Unit in BuPers was amenable, so an arrangement was made with Lieutenant Knag, who controlled Negro personnel in the Third Naval District.

It was a great arrangement. When a man was needed,

the captain could issue him orders, by name, based on "Verbal orders of the Commandant, Third Naval District." In his selection of replacements, the captain relied upon recommendations by the crew, who knew better than any the qualifications of certain individuals and their eagerness to serve aboard USS *PC 1264.*

But personnel officers at bases who would suddenly, and to them quite illegally, lose a man, became righteously indignant; especially if he was a lieutenant commander or above, and such a caper was being pulled by a lieutenant! But the system stuck, and for the first time since the war of 1812, a commanding officer was able to sign on his own crew. And conversely, he was able to get rid of any he didn't want.

USS *PC 1264,* short one officer, left to be an escort of the thirteen merchantmen of Convoy NG-453 before dawn on Monday, August 14. It would be her last voyage to Guantanamo. After this, she would be assigned to coastal convoys to and from Key West—a less happy assignment. Guantanamo was a naval base and therefore there was less discrimination.

Yet "Gitmo" had a discrimination of a sort, too.

Guantanamo was a main way station to feed cargo ships into the trunk line to New York. They came there from Galveston, Texas, from Aruba and Trinidad, Recife and Rio, and to and from the Panama Canal.

Escorts assigned to convoys running between Gitmo and the ports on the South American coast, relied on this naval base for their services; not the least being laundry. Ships' Services ran a very efficient establishment; if requested, it could return dry cleaning and wash within a few hours, at a very nominal fee. For all ships, that was, except those on the New York run. Its excuse was that the New York ships could use stateside facilities without burdening this outpost.

But the real reason was shown one evening, when the

captain sidled up to the bar at the Officers' Club, and stood next to an officer quaffing one of the club's celebrated ten-cent twenty-year-old rums. They started a friendly conversation, discovered where each had gone to college and what he had done before the war. Then the inevitable question came up.

"What run are you on?" the rum drinker asked.

"New York—Gitmo," the skipper replied.

The pleasantly relaxed face of the other suddenly hardened. His affable, gentlemanly, civilized expression changed instantly, showing almost apoplectic jealousy, hatred and self-pity. He dropped his glass on the bar, breaking its stem, and wasting the aged elixir on the mahogany top. He turned and left.

The unpopularity of the escort units assigned to stateside ports was due entirely to their believed access to unlimited quantities of women, American women. Guantanamo was a male society. There were two American women on the base. One, a Red Cross girl, the other, a nurse. They were the two most beautiful women in the world.

Sailors are not unduly chauvinistic. It should be remembered, though, that World War Two was a great educational experience and by its end had demolished a number of young Americans' insular ideas, not the least being the surpassing desirability of "the girl next door." But healthy young males, and those older too, are subject to temptation, and the only women available to the Guantanamo-based men were the women of Caimenera, across the bay. The overwhelmingly female population of "C-Town," or "Clap-town," contributed to a healthy Cuban balance of payments, and overworked the medics of the base's prophylactic stations.

One evening, before their ship left to return to New York, the officers were quaffing drinks on the lawn of the club, overlooking the anchorage. The well-kept grounds sloped to the edge of a cliff which dropped steeply into water deep enough to allow large vessels to moor close-by.

It was a beautiful night, warm with a gentle breeze bearing the fragrance of red jasmine blended with the scents of a dozen or more West Indian flowers. The towering royal palmtrees formed a backdrop, silhouetted against the darkening sky. Soft Musak wafted from hidden speakers. Attendants in scarlet jackets kept replenishments coming to the white-uniformed customers. It must have made a charming sight from seaward.

And a bitterly frustrating one, too, for the passengers of a troopship anchored only a few hundred feet away. They were WACs—members of the Women's Army Corps.

Soldiers are soldiers, of whichever sex. And these soldiers, after a week or so at sea, and knowing there would be many more of isolation for those going on to the farther parts of the Pacific, unmistakeably resented being kept aboard.

The Guantanamo Port Director was obviously no man of understanding in allotting this anchorage off the Officers' Club. It should have been somewhere in the middle of the bay, far from the maddening vision of a pleasanter way to spend an evening in the tropics. He probably thought that by anchoring this ship here, there was less chance of any hanky-panky and rescue operations by his woman-hungry enlisted men. The Army commander, wanting to preserve his charges, must have agreed. But officers are men too. And the sight of two hundred or more young *American* women festooned along the rails, hanging to stanchions, heads out of portholes, so near yet unattainable, was emotionally unnerving.

They lined the cliffside. Lochinvars pledging rescue; trying to heave miniature bottles of liquor across their separation. Bantering; some girls shouting their promises of unspeakable pleasures as reward.

The Port Director was right about his opportunity for supervision. The club's lights flickered for attention, then a voice came over the public-address system: "The club is now closed. Members will leave immediately."

The howls, screams, moans, whistles and shouts from the troopship must have been heard as far as Caimenera.

An Officer Reports

USS *PC 1264* was needed in New York to join a convoy leaving for Key West on September 9, so she was told to get up there, right away, by herself. In the late afternoon of Wednesday, August 30, she loosed her lines from the dock and left Guantanamo forever.

It took three and a half days of steady steaming to reach Tompkinsville; half the time needed for a convoy to make the voyage. Four hours after midnight, on the morning of September 3, Buoy "A", forty-five miles to seaward of the harbor was reached, and four hours later, the ship turned into the slip on the south side of Pier 7.

It was Sunday, but no day of rest. Stores had to be brought aboard, checked and stowed. Although she had just completed a voyage and wasn't scheduled to leave again for six days, the ship had to be ready for any possible emergency, to be able to leave whenever she got the word. The rule was: upon arrival, be prepared to go to sea.

The captain was in his stateroom shortly after nine, when Will Otto, in his capacity of Supply Officer, came to report that the stores were aboard, and that the fuel barge would be alongside within the hour to fill the tanks. He also brought with him a tall, thin, dark-haired ensign, whose long, narrow face was wet with perspiration; either from nervousness, or because he was wearing a winter-weight blue uniform in ninety-degree heat. More the latter, the captain decided.

"Ensign Stanley W. Rhodes," Will said. "Frank's relief. Straight from Miami and the trade school."

Technically, Frank Gardner was still on temporary duty for treatment at the hospital and had not yet been detached officially from the ship—his BuPers orders would not be received for two more days—but the captain knew that his convalescence would prevent his return. Every now and then, on the past trip to Guantanamo, he wondered what his new communications officer would be like. He would be the first officer that neither he, nor George Poor, had had a hand in selecting. Coming from SCTC, the character of USS *PC 1264* should be known to him. If he has any reservations about serving with a black crew, the captain thought, I don't have to accept him. This had been agreed with the Special Programs Unit. Now's the time to find out.

He thanked Will and dismissed him. He offered the only other chair in the small cabin to Ensign Rhodes.

If there had been no war, Stan Rhodes would have been in his junior year at the University of Washington at Seattle. He was a freshman and in ROTC when the Japanese bombed Pearl Harbor. At the end of his second year, in June 1943, his class of reserve midshipmen was put on active duty in the Navy's V-12 program and their naval courses accelerated. He was commissioned an ensign on the last day of February and, after two months' temporary duty in New Orleans and Corpus Christi, reported to the Submarine Chaser Training Center on June 28. When his course had ended, he heard that a volunteer billet aboard "a special ship" was open. He inquired, applied and was accepted.

He was born twenty years before, and raised in Spokane, which he described as "neutral ground, racially." In his high school of twenty-two hundred students there had been three or four blacks. He said they were popular, and took part in a number of school activities. To his knowledge there had never been any discrimination, but then he scarcely knew them; they could obviously be identified, and that was as much as he really knew about them, or any other minority group. He confessed he had mixed emotions about serving aboard USS *PC 1264* because of this inexperience. He had read about incidents of social injustice, but had never seen any—until he'd left Seattle and was on his way to Miami. He'd been shocked by the shades of subservience that were expected of, and by, Negroes. He felt the humiliation of segregated facilities; it disturbed him. He didn't know what he could do aboard this ship, but he felt he would learn something. He'd like to try.

Ensign Stanley W. Rhodes, D-V(G), USNR, was assigned the primary duty of Communications Officer, with collateral duties as Radar and Commissary Officer. He was advised to get himself outfitted with summer uniforms.

A Case of Bad Welding

Three days before the ship was to leave with a convoy to Key West, Arnett Gibson and Jacob Moore, both motor machinist's mates 2/c, were working in the engineroom. Chief Street had gone ashore, and Gibson was in charge.

Checking through the engineroom, Gibson discovered something that wasn't quite right. He called Moore over.

Jake Moore was a conscientious engineer; his great ambition was to convince Chief Street that he was capable of handling both engine throttles alone; indeed, he told his engineroom colleagues, he was a one-man engineroom force. A husky Alabaman, his most striking physical characteristic was a large, strong jaw, which gave him his below-deck nickname of Chinchilla.

"Don't look right to me," said Moore.

"Sure doesn't," agreed Gibson. "Chinchilla, go get Mr. Hardman."

When Lieutenant Hardman, the engineering officer, saw what had been discovered, he found the captain and took him below. Each of the main propulsion engines, weighing over eight tons apiece, were welded to heavy girders attached to the steel ribs of the hull above the bilge. These girders, called the engine bedplates, supported the engines the length of the engineroom, spreading their weight throughout their extent above the thin skin of the ship's hull, which was less than ½ an inch thick.

What didn't look right to Gibson, nor to Moore, nor to Lieutenant Hardman, nor to the captain, were a series of cracks running all the way along these welds between the engines and the bedplates. "Let's get the base engineering officer onto this," the captain said.

"Kee-rist!" exclaimed the base engineer. "A real lousy weld job. You get into any kind of a sea, these engines will shift and slide right off the bedplates, and drop right through the bottom of the ship. Big hole. No *PC* any more. I reckon we'd better get this fixed."

So the ship's voyage to Key West the following Saturday was cancelled, and another subchaser substituted in her place.

Three weeks later, the escort group USS *PC 1264* should have accompanied returned from the round trip to the tip of Florida. And a sorry sight it was.

It was the season of hurricanes, and the convoy's course had led it through one of the fiercest to strike the offshore waters and the eastern coast. Damage was extensive on all the ships, the small escorts being particularly battered. The torrents of water pouring over their superstructures tore away lifelines, stanchions, the ammunition ready boxes, rafts and even radio and radar antennae. Most tragically, the executive officer of USS *PC 1265* was swept from the bridge and lost. There is no doubt that, but for the watchful eyes of Arnett E. Gibson, USS *PC 1264* would have vanished within seconds, long before the height of the storm.

To repair USS *PC 1264's* engine foundations required that she be towed to the Navy Yard Annex, Bayonne, New Jersey, a couple of miles north on the Upper Bay. There, her afterdeck would have to be cut open and her engines raised. It would mean ten weeks of operational inactivity.

Operational inactivity, but not a stop to operational planning . . . nor to the crew's shore operations.

Six months before, in March, the first Negro officers in the history of the United States Navy—twelve ensigns and one warrant officer—had been commissioned at Great Lakes Naval Training Center, after a ten-weeks' indoctrination course.

The captain wanted one of them. The Special Programs Unit in the Bureau of Naval Personnel had been sympathetic but noncommittal, agreeing that the assignment of a Negro officer to USS *PC 1264* would be a desirable demonstration of the truth or falsity of another stereotype: that a Negro lacked leadership qualities, and that, anyway, Negro enlisted men wouldn't carry out the orders of one of their own race.

The falsity of this, of course, was demonstrated every day aboard USS *PC 1264*, the chain of command running smoothly down through the rating structure. For instance, in the engineroom underway at sea, each of the three cruising watches was run by a black motormachinist's mate 1/c; Chief Street stood no assigned watch except at general quarters and special sea detail, but was available at any time. The three first-class motormacs maintained discipline among their men.

Another, and more serious stereotype, was the belief that white sailors would not take orders from a Negro. What better opportunity was there to test this, than aboard USS *PC 1264?* Of course, the cards might be considered stacked somewhat, because the white petty officers had worked closely with the men of their departments, they had been able to judge them, to compare them with white crews with whom they'd served, they had had five months of racial education. That an ensign is inexperienced when he comes aboard a ship is a fact of life to Navy petty officers. The captain felt that these white petty officers would take a Negro officer in stride. They had taken their assignment to this ship that way, they had taken the inexperience of the commanding officer similarly. They were typical Navy leading petty officers, who did their duty.

The captain suspected this latter stereotype was generally accepted in the Bureau of Naval Personnel so there might be stronger objections to the idea of a Negro officer aboard his ship while the white petty officers were still there. Nevertheless, on September 27, 1944, he wrote a letter to the Chief of Naval Personnel, via (1) the Commander, Surface Escort Group, Eastern Sea Frontier, and (2) the Commander, Eastern Sea Frontier, requesting the assignment of a Negro officer.

The letter reached the Bureau of Naval Personnel with an endorsement from Admiral Herbert F. Leary, "recommending approval." But there, the captain's suspicions probably proved correct. On the letter, now stored in the Archives, there is a penciled notation, "strongly recommend against," by somebody with the initial "R." So, no action was taken.

However, the idea at the very outset had been to transfer the white petty officers when the men below them were trained to take their places. Very soon, now, the captain believed, he could recommend their transfer; there were a number of black petty officers who had shown their ability and qualifications to undertake greater responsibilities; indeed, there was strong competition within each department as to whom should be the leading petty officer when the time came.

The captain decided he should pay a visit to the Special Programs Unit. There were some other things on his mind, too.

Visit to the Special Unit

If Guantanamo was a desert, a wasteland, a void unoc-

cupied by women, Washington, the nation's capital, was a
paradise. Overpopulated with women, few of its houris were
nymphs of the Moslem variety, "created from musk and
spices and endowed with perpetually virgin youth and perfect beauty," but most seemed eager to offer their heavenly
art. The scents of musk and spices under assorted French
names were heavy in the expected masculine halls of the
military headquarters. And whenever a male walked down
a corridor, feminine heads turned unabashed, openly ap-
praising. In wartime Washington, the hunter was a huntress.

The secretary in one of the offices in the Navy Department building on Constitution Avenue was not unattractive, although her lips were too thin; a deficiency she recognized and worsened by the inartistic use of lipstick. She was
a bit heavy in the leg, too, the captain decided, and in the
hips as well. The latter would have been acceptable if coun-
terbalanced by a proportional bosom.

Alas, they were not; not the orbs of heavenly frame
praised by an Elizabethan poet, and, when found, so appreciated by the captain. But her personality was friendly and
straight-forward.

She took his name, writing it on a pad to take it to the
officer he wanted to see. "Where are you stationed, lieutenant?" she asked.

"Aboard a ship in New York," he answered. On the wall
was a poster showing a burning, torpedoed ship behind the
black-lettered words, "The Enemy is Listening!"

"How long have you been in Washington?"

"I just got here this morning."

The carmined mouth widened. "Have you found a place
to stay?" She went on, matter-of-factly, "Hotels are impossible these days. If you like, you can stay with me. I have an
apartment on 16th Street. Comfortable, quiet."

Startled, confused yet, by her generosity, momentarily
tempted, he stammered, "Gee . . . well . . . that's mighty
kind of you. But I guess I've got to get back to the ship tonight."

Her smile lessened, but her eyes were still friendly.
"Too bad," she said, picking up the paper and standing. "I'll
see if the commander can see you now."

The captain had been only half truthful. He and the
skipper of USS *PC 1209,* Lieutenant Russell Harris, had
caught an early morning train from Pennsylvania Station in
New York, but they hadn't decided when they would return.
They had agreed that this depended upon how much each
of them could accomplish with the individual offices and
bureaus they wanted to visit; the decision would be made
when they met that evening at five o'clock.

There were three things the captain of USS *PC 1264*
wanted to do. First, he had to talk over the state of the ship
with the Special Programs Unit of BuPers' Division of Planning and Control. Second, he wanted to push the idea of
assigning a Negro officer. And, third, he wanted to broach
the possibility of a change of operational assignment for his
ship.

Naïvely, he anticipated no problems at all in obtaining
a favorable response to his two suggestions. It seemed to
him they were natural steps towards fulfilling the purpose
of this naval experiment. Twelve black ensigns had been on
the Navy's rolls since last St. Patrick's Day. *PC*'s were covering landings of invasion forces throughout the central Pacific; others were in European waters supporting the assault
against the Nazi-dominated continent. He didn't disparage
the importance of his ship's convoy duty but there were
serious, historical allegations about the Negro's reactions
under enemy shellfire. The captain certainly didn't relish
the idea of being a target for enemy shells, bullets, mines or
torpedoes, but such an experience should be made available
for the record of this avowed experiment. It could well, he
feared, prove something about him.

The reception he received from the Special Programs
Unit was friendly, interested in a manner analogous to the
reaction Dr. Frankenstein must have had when his monster
first spoke to him. Both Lieutenant Commander Charley

Dillon and Lieutenant Commander Don Van Ness were
under constant pressure monitoring the various programs
dealing with blacks, and as human beings in Reserve officers
uniforms, and being merely two in number, they obviously
and necessarily were concerned with the programs that were
causing some flack; such as the all-black construction battalions, the labor units the National Association for the Advancement of Colored People was objecting to.

"Nice to see you," said Charley Dillon. "I'm afraid we
might have been neglecting you. But you seem to have
everything in hand."

The captain had to agree; anything else would have
been a reflection on his ship.

He told them what he had in mind.

"It's too soon to think about transferring your ship
from Eastern Sea Frontier," Don Van Ness told him.

"But this type of operation doesn't prove much. I think
we've shown that these men are capable sailors. What about
their reaction when shots come our way? . . . And mine,
too?"

Lieutenant Commander Charley Dillon smiled. "What's
your reaction going to be when winter comes? This is only
September. The North Atlantic can be rough. How do you
think you-all will do then?" He paused. "Don't kick, yet.
. . . You've got plenty of time. First, get your white petty
officers off, and then see how you do. We'll keep you in
mind for a Negro officer. Take it easy."

The captain stood by the entrance of the Naval Annex,
waiting for Lieutenant Russell Harris. It was five o'clock, and
the crowds of civilian and naval workers were streaming by,
through the door and towards the busses and the parking
lot.

Two Amazons, with beatific looks of accomplishment
on their predatory female countenances, strode by. Between
then they held fast to a skinny, palefaced male sailor, already exhausted. Their evening's future was assured.

Bayonne Sojourn

Repairing the engines took a long, traumatic time. The work was done at the Naval Annex in Bayonne, New Jersey. The ship lay alongside the dock, her deck open, her engine-room bared to the heavens, a deep, cavernous space empty; the hull a shell around the after portion of the ship.

It was a period of nothing. Men were sent on leave; a happy way of getting them out of the way. Those who remained were occupied by being detailed to various schools in the New York area—fire-fighting school, sound school, gunnery school—anything to make it appear that they were being occupied by worthwhile training.

Their feeling of uselessness, of insignificance was deepened by where they lay alongside the dock. For a few days, USS *PC 1264* was moored directly ahead of the recently completed battleship, USS *Missouri*. The vast bow of this newest and largest warship in the world towered high and beyond the length of the minuscule submarine chaser, a gigantic roof, its sheer shadowing the little ship with the arrogance of the mighty.

The ship couldn't go anywhere. There was no chance that, whatever the emergency, USS *PC 1264* would be called upon to put to sea. Nerves tightened. A lackadasicalness toward personal responsibility for conduct began to show. Discipline began to weaken. In other words, morale—that all encompassing word for zeal, hope, pride, confidence—was shot to hell.

It showed in an increasing tendency to disregard the time set for the end of liberty ashore. When a seaman neglected to return until he was four days and seventeen hours over leave, the captain decided to crack down. At Mast, he gave the miscreant the sentence of being tried at Deck Court, the next higher tribunal.

While the Deck Court was a superior court, it was still in the family. The difference was it could give a stiffer sentence. Its judge and jury was the executive officer, whose sentence would be reviewed by the convening officer, the captain.

The punishment accorded was a stiff one. The defendent was awarded—a strange phrase—solitary confinement for fifteen days and to pay $10 out of his pay. After the executive officer had pronounced sentence, it was reviewed immediately by the captain, and the prisoner was escorted to the brig on shore by the acting master-at-arms, Gunner's Mate First Class, Leland A. Young. He stayed in the Bayonne Brig only two days, being then transferred to the Tompkinsville lock-up, where he remained in durance vile for a total of thirteen days. Later a fireman received a similar judgment for a similar offense.

One of the crew was careless in his personal hygiene. The Special Unit of the Bureau of Naval Personnel was particularly interested in the statistics of the incidence of venereal disease aboard this subchaser, as a comparison with other ships of the fleet. The stereotype of the Negro's constant proclivity for sex had raised some fears that USS *PC 1264* would have an abnormally high venereal rate, far greater than the three percent generally in the Navy. Being historically a serious problem for all branches of the armed forces, the military fought it realistically through education —from constant health lectures, illustrated by graphic, soul-shattering movies, to the free distribution of prophylactics; sometimes requiring that men going ashore show the gangway watch an added credential besides his liberty card—a neatly rolled condom. "Okay, okay," was the rationale, "you don't expect to get laid. But if you get raped, or the temptation gets too strong, just remember to slip it on."

In its battle with the scourge, the Bureau of Medicine and Surgery required that if, or whenever, anyone did contract the disease, that an attempt should be made to find out how he got it. This was a responsibility of the commanding officer of USS *PC 1264* because of his additional duty as

Medical Officer. When the pharmacist's mate reported an incident, the victim would be interviewed in the privacy of the captain's stateroom. The name of his copula companion, where the idyll took place and under what circumstances, were then entered in a form to be forwarded to the Public Health Service; presumably to bring treatment to the girl and stop further spreading of the results of her favors.

The captain conducted three such interviews. The first on the day after commissioning, the second in Tompkinsville on a day in early summer, and the third in Bayonne during this time of repairing the engines.

At the second interview, the patient told of meeting a girl in a bar on 125th Street. The romance was short; a couple of whiskeys each, then a frenzied ten minutes on an unmade bed. He had known her only by the name of Rose.

The third victim of careless passion had only been recently assigned to the ship. He was young, and uncertain as he came through the green curtained doorway to the captain's cabin.

The skipper, sitting at the desk had the Public Health form before him. He motioned to the seaman to sit down, and explained the reason for the interview.

"What is her name?" he asked, and on a whim, added, "Rose? . . ."

There was no answer. The captain looked up. The sailor was sitting rigid, his hands clutching the arms of the chair, his face transfixed, eyes wide in amazement. "How . . . how did you know, Captain? . . . You must know everything!"

It was the captain's turn to be amazed, but he tried not to show it. He mentioned the name of the bar on 125th Street.

On such are reputations made. The captain was omniscent, all-knowing. He made a note on the form that apparently, Rose was still in business.

The VD rate on USS *PC 1264* was startlingly low. It

certainly was not due to extraordinary celibacy among the
crew and officers. Perhaps the educational program of the
Navy was better followed; perhaps they were more careful.
The captain liked to think that they were more particular
in their liaisons.

There was other trouble, though, they could get into.
The ship's policy was to encourage visitors to the ship; especially the families of those who served aboard. Nearly every
weekend the ship was in port, she had visitors who would
come aboard for a few hours, have lunch or dinner, and get
a better understanding of, and share their son's, nephew's
or brother's pride in the ship.

One evening, after a day of trials at sea, the ship eased
into the dock at Tompkinsville. On the wharf were two
families of three—father, mother and daughter.

When the ship had tied up, the families were brought
aboard and to the wardroom, where the captain and executive officer greeted them. Introductions were made, and the
captain asked them whom they wanted to see. It was rather
a sticky meeting, for both parents were rather stern-visaged,
the plump daughters embarrassed and shy. One father mentioned a name.

The other promptly announced that they were here to
see him too. "He's to marry my daughter," he added.

Indignantly, the other mother disagreed. "He's to marry
ours!"

George Poor cautiously edged toward the door. "I'll
find him," he said.

Vainly, the captain tried to explain that he had no control over the personal life of any member of his crew. Contrary to folklore, he had no authority to perform marriages
aboard his ship, and he was no Solomon to decide which of
these young ladies the young Romeo should wed; not that
he was asked or supposed to make such a decision. Each of
the parents reserved that right in their daughter's favor. His
main efforts were in trying to preserve peace which was in
imminent danger of disappearing as, indeed, it seemed the

object of these visits had done. His special sea detail in coming into port was on the fo'c'sle, and he had obviously recognized the situation and decided to have some urgent business ashore.

The two families did not stay for supper. The despoiler of their daughters' virtue returned furtively about midnight, and for the rest of the time the ship was in port and he had to be on deck, kept to the outboard side of the ship and could be seen to dart nervous glances continuously at anyone who might approach along the dock.

During this time of operational inactivity, there was a steady exchange of personnel. Some of the men were transferred to take their experience to other ships, for, in August, the Navy announced that twenty-five auxiliary ships—oilers, tankers and cargo vessels—would be assigned crews, twenty-five per cent of which would be Negro.

It was time, too, the captain and executive officer thought, to take the plunge of making the enlisted crew of USS *PC 1264* wholly black. On October 4, a letter was mailed, requesting seven non-rated sailors and one pharmacist's mate "(colored)" to relieve the instructors.

The eight white petty officers assigned to train the crew had done an outstanding job. It had not been easy, emotionally, for them at first. Whenever the ship was in port, they were subject to particularly virulent insults and malicious humor. But, characteristically, there had never been any Shore Patrol reports of their reactions. As with the officers, it had been an intensely broadening experience, and deepened their loyalty to the ship, which was absolute. Their selection as instructors for USS *PC 1264* was indicative of the best Navy detailing.

Their orders came during the first week of November, 1944.

The Special Programs Unit had been asked to use its influence in assigning them to the type of duty they wanted, and it did.

Work was nearly completed on the engines. On Thursday, November 9, the ship would try them out on a short voyage to Long Island Sound and back. Chief John Z. Street didn't want to leave until after these trials, so he became the last white petty officer to be detached.

The radioman, Donald C. Frazier, wanted submarine duty, so on Saturday, November 4, he left the ship for the Submarine Base in New London, Connecticut. Kidded about transferring his allegiance from a submarine chaser to the kind of boat it hunted, he explained, "Subs ride easier. When it gets rough, you go down to where it's calm. The ice-cream machine runs all the time. I'll get pay and a half for so-called hazardous duty. I'll bet the Japs are lousier anti-sub warriors than you guys . . . and how many subs have you got?"

Doc Weber, Harold Hunt, Aaron Maerowitz and Lee Young left together on Monday, November 6. Charles Phelps and Donald Briggs left the day following.

To take their places, Louis T. Ellison was promoted to Gunner's Mate First Class, Jarvis Guice became the leading signalman, Gentle Havard took charge of the radio shack and all its operations, James Brown became the senior electrician and Adolph Cork the leading quartermaster. On Sunday, November 12, Herbert W. Jones, Pharmacist's Mate Second Class, arrived in the afternoon to be the ship's doctor.

Following the successful sea trials of the ship's engines, Chief Street was satisfied and took his departure from the ship he had served so well. "The Unflappable John Z.," a Floridian by choice, had chosen to go to Boston and the Diesel Classification Center in the Fargo Building, although it was winter. A career Navy man, he personified the new breed of Chief Petty Officers—calm, quiet, knowledgable by experience, polite with a definite, no-nonsense courtesy, there was no question about his leadership in the engine-room.

New men came aboard. Emmett Caul, a young Virginian from Waynesboro, a graduate of the Navy's quartermaster school, arrived with a little black book of addresses that was to prove invaluable to his shipmates. Cleo J. Black, Radioman Third Class, from Ada, Oklahoma; five Seamen, C. Howell, L. Sanders, C. D. Anderson, H. O. Woodley, J. H. Young and a Fireman, J. E. Major, Jr., reported during this time.

The leading petty officers, with the privileges of their new responsibilities, moved their gear into Compartment A-204L, on the first platform deck, known as the Chief Petty Officers' stateroom.

Charles S. Harvey, promoted to Chief Motor Machinist's Mate, ran his practiced machinist's eyes over the deck of his new living quarters for a likely spot to make into a safe stowage for some secret valuables.

Quartermaster 3rd class Adolph R. Cork exchanging blinker messages with another ship, while Seaman 2nd class Marcus Coleman reports to the bridge by battle telephone

Five

Escorting the "Argo"

A chill, November wind was blowing through The Narrows as USS *PC 1264* backed out of the Tompkinsville slip to go to work again. Her first assignment, after so long in port, promised to be pleasant—out of the ordinary and ending up in a better climate. Her orders read to proceed to New London, Connecticut, and report for duty as escort of the French submarine *Argo* from the U.S. Navy Submarine Base to Key West, Florida.

The Submarine Force, Atlantic Fleet, headquarters was, and is today, in New London. To it came new construction from the Electric Boat Company in near-by Groton and from the Naval Shipyard, Portsmouth, New Hampshire, for shakedown. Here, too, came the officers and men who had volunteered and been accepted for training and qualification to fight this war from below the surface of the sea. And when these modern, new fleet submarines, whose living quarters were the envy of surface sailors—stainless steel galleys stocked with the finest steaks and other gourmet delights, air-conditioning, specially designed bunks and myriad comforts—had proved to COMSUBLANT that they were ready, they were routed to the Panama Canal and onward to Pearl Harbor where COMSUBPAC—the Pacific submarine commander—would send them into Japanese waters.

The fleet submarines almost invariably cruised from New London to Panama alone. This voyage was really an extension of their training, for when they left Block Island Sound and Montauk Point behind them, they had to keep as alert against attack as if they were in enemy waters instead of supposedly friendly ones. To ships and aircraft on the prowl for U-Boats, a submarine is a submarine and, without information to the contrary, fair game for destruction. Of course, the Sea Frontiers were advised when friendly submarines were passing through their territory, but there was always the chance of someone "not getting the word."

A friendly foreign submarine would have been in even greater danger. There was always the possibility, because of language differences, that she would have difficulty in identifying herself quickly to an eager, bloodthirsty airman who had been patrolling for months without ever seeing what he sought. It had happened in April of 1942, to the pride of the French fleet, the world's largest submarine, *Surcouf*, the victim of such a mistake by an Army Air Corps bomber.

No one wanted this to happen to *Argo*. So the first operational duty of USS *PC 1264*, after her many weeks of indolence in New York, was to sail together with this sub, protecting her from her allies and making sure that she arrived in Key West where she would be used by the Fleet Sound School as a "tame" submarine; to be a target for training surface antisubmarine vessels.

USS *PC 1264* left Tompkinsville shortly before nine o'clock on the morning of November 17. Out in the bay, with the wind whistling from the south, she headed towards Manhattan and the East River.

At moderate speed, she steamed through the heavy traffic of the harbor—the Friday morning commuter traffic of the ferries, the tugs charging characteristically in all directions on their errands—her course changing continuously to avoid the debris cluttering the bay.

Slowly, she made her way up the eastern shore of Manhattan, within rock-throwing distance of the workers streaming downtown on the east side highway. The waters narrowed and became more turbulent as she approached Hell Gate. Loaded barges slithered by with yards to spare; some heavy with gravel, others with garbage to consign to the ocean off Ambrose; each under tow by a tug, seemingly too small to be able to maneuver its charge, apparently caring little whether it could.

It was cold, but the captain sweated, piloting his ship through the eddies and swirls of the current. Then, at long last, City Island was off to the port and Long Island Sound stretched ahead, its shores widening to open safety. Hell Gate was passed.

"All engines ahead, standard!"

The ship took a little less than eight hours to reach Pier 6 at the Submarine Base, four and a half miles up the Thames River from its mouth. The log notes the time was 1729, one minute before the scheduled time for supper at 5:30 P.M., which must have pleased the cook, Occonar Young.

They stayed alongside the pier for twenty-four hours. The operations order called for them to leave after dark on Saturday night, in order to traverse New York Harbor by daylight on Sunday. The submarine base, though, was a busy place, and dock space was at a premium, so on Saturday afternoon, USS *PC 1264* was asked to leave her berth and anchor in the river. She was to be ready to leave with her charge at 10:30 that night.

At a quarter past five the ship got underway and slowly headed for an anchorage down river. It was twenty minutes past six when fifteen fathoms of chain rattled out of the hawsepipe.

Cork, on the wing of the bridge, peered through the pelorus to take bearings to fix their position on the chart.

"New London Ledge Light—One one seven degrees!" he called. "New London Harbor Light—Three four three degrees!"

Caul, the new quartermaster striker, marked the bearings down in the log. During the next four hours, these bearings would be checked periodically, to make sure the figures remained the same, showing that the anchor was holding firmly, and that the tide and current had not set the ship adrift.

The night was black. Only a very faint glow came from the shore and the city. New London, as did all coastal towns and seaports, maintained a semi-blackout every night; not from fear of enemy bombings, but to cut down on the reflected light against the sky above—a light that could be seen miles away at sea, and had proved to be disastrous to many merchant ships, whose hulls could be silhouetted against it to the dangerous advantage of U-Boats to seaward.

From up-river, red and green running lights slowly approached the subchaser's anchorage. A signal lamp flashed a message. *Argo* was heading for the rendezvous outside the harbor. She was right on time.

USS *PC 1264* was ready, too. All hands were at special sea detail. The executive officer had reported all departments were ready to get underway.

The captain carefully printed some words on a piece of paper and handed it to Guice.

"Send this to *Argo*," he said. "Let's go. . . . Hoist the anchor!"

He ordered a short kick ahead on an engine to take the strain off the anchor chain.

By the light of a flashlight, Guice read the message. "Captain," he asked, "are you sure . . . I mean, do you want me to send this?"

"Yes. Go ahead, letter by letter. I hope he understands it."

Guice obviously didn't. But his was not to reason why, and he promptly switched on the 12-inch signal light, swung it toward the low-lying shape passing, and slowly transmitted the letters of the words: "B . . . O . . . N A . . .

C . . . C . . . U . . . E . . I . . . L   D . . . E   PC
1264 (Guice tore through this phrase) . . . B . . . O . . . N
V . . . O . . . Y . . . A . . . G . . . E."

It took five days to reach Key West. Off Cape Hatteras
the weather became exceedingly bad, with towering waves
crashing over the two vessels. In desperation, the French
asked for permission to submerge; their boat wasn't designed
to travel comfortably on the surface, and her rolling must
have been a bruising nightmare. *PC 1264* could see her
agony and appreciate that it was far, far worse than her own.
But the orders had been explicit. The submarine was to
travel on the surface; she must be under constant sight from
the subchaser. The request was refused.

Then, past Hatteras, the more they got into southern
waters, so did the weather improve. Aboard the subchaser,
as aboard the submarine undoubtedly, appetites came back
to life. Food that had been anathema was now sought at all
hours.

Lieutenant Will Otto was officer of the deck during the
mid-watch; those lonely hours between midnight and four
in the morning, when afloat or ashore the hours seem to
pass more slowly than at any other period of a day; when
human resistance is at its lowest, the dawn being so far
away. Will Otto, as was the custom, was on the flying bridge.
His quartermaster, Adolph Cork, was below in the pilothouse. He was bored. There was still a couple of hours left
before his watch would be relieved. Midway in the mid-
watch, Cork knew why this was the time of day that death
came in hospitals; there was too much time to wait for
something to happen—for even such an event as breakfast.

Food. Ah, that was an encouraging thought.

The crew's mess and galley stores were back aft on the
lower deck, underneath the 40 mm gun. To get to the galley,
you had to go along the deck and climb down a hatchway
near the depth charges on the stern. Occonar Young protected his stores of food with a vigilance equaling, if not ex-

ceeding that of the Secret Service for the person of the President. To Young, the time for eating was the prescribed time, snacks between meals merely spoiled the crews' enjoyment of his culinary delights. Besides, indescriminate foraging loused up his accounting, to say nothing of future menus. So Young kept his kingdom locked by the heaviest padlock he could find.

To breach Young's defenses was a challenge Cork considered worthy of his talents. But there was a greater one, with additional satisfaction with success.

This was an invasion of the officers' pantry.

Every general in planning an attack weighs the pros and cons. Considering the latter, Cork knew that Officers' Country—that area comprising the wardroom, the wardroom pantry and the officers' staterooms—was off-limits to enlisted men, except upon official business and by invitation. When violated, and especially upon an illegal errand (which could be classified as "theft") could result, if he was caught, and according to the captain's whims, in anything up to and including a general court-martial. Cork's ability as a sea lawyer would be taxed under such a circumstance.

To reach his objective, the refrigerator in the wardroom pantry, would take him through highly dangerous territory. While at sea, the captain often used the wardroom as his sea cabin; when needed, he was only sixteen feet away from the bridge; moreover, the transom on which he slept was next to the door to the charthouse. To reach the pantry, Cork would have to slip by the transom without waking him.

Considering the hour, the chances were that the captain would be asleep. But commanding officers are strange creatures, with unpredictable habits at sea—they sleep at odd hours. They also are highly nervous; they are forever imagining dire happenings which are reinforced by unaccustomed sounds; not the least being a strange human being skulking nearby.

Cork, on the wing of bridge, considered these things.

Impulsively, he went into the pilothouse and called through the voice tube to the flying bridge.

"Mr. Otto."

"Yes."

"Request permission to go to the head."

"Granted."

Between the bridge and the wardroom was the radio-room and charthouse, all in one; lighted, for the ports were tight shut, so the radioman could see to type any incoming message, but more usually so he could read his paperback resting against the transmitter; his ears subliminally alert to the possibility of the ship's call sounding in his earphones. The duty radioman didn't move his eyes from the page as the lights went out when Cork opened the bridge door, accepting the momentary darkness as a mere blinking of his eyelids.

Cork paused by the wardroom door. His hand was on the knob, but he didn't turn it. Something, he felt, wasn't quite right; there was something he knew, instinctively, he hadn't considered. Then he realized what it was.

The wardroom, joined to the charthouse, and itself blacked out, would have no effect on the charthouse lights when he opened the door. Worse, when the door was opened, the light's rays would probably fall directly on the skipper's face. The effect would be worse than noise or the psychological effect of his presence. That is, if the wardroom *was* blacked out. Then Cork remembered. The captain was a fresh-air fiend. Bradford, the steward's mate, had said that he thought the reason the skipper used the wardroom for a sea cabin was really because he could sleep with the ports opened and get the fresh air denied him in his stateroom below. If that was so, then the opening of the wardroom door would darken the charthouse.

It was worth a try. Cautiously, Cork turned the knob and gently eased the door open.

Out went the lights, and Cork slipped through.

A foot away from him came the sound of heavy breathing. Steady, uninterrupted. Cork edged to the door of the pantry. Softly he opened it, and quietly moved through.

The pantry, as he closed the door behind him broke into light. There was his quarry: the refrigerator. He reached for the handle and turned it. No locks here. The goodies therein, on hand for the sporadic needs of the officers were his in all their variety—milk, sandwich spread, bologna and other cold cuts, known affectionately as horse cock, dishes covered with celophane—all were his for the taking, and all whetted his appetite by their very availability.

A sandwich would be the thing, but where was the bread? He turned to search for the bread container, and as he did, he suddenly learned that he was not alone.

Leaning against the bulkhead by door to one side of him, was the executive officer.

Lieutenant George Poor was chewing a sandwich himself. He regarded Cork stolidly, with just the hint of amusement.

Cork was shocked, but only momentarily. "Excuse, me, sir," he said blandly, "but is this the right train for Chicago?"

The executive officer considered this question seriously. "Perhaps," he finally answered. He gestured with the remains of the sandwich to the locker above the refrigerator. "You know, Cork," he said, "there's a couple of cans of mushroom soup in there. What say we have something hot?"

In the darkness of the wardroom, behind the pantry door, the captain slept heavily on.

On Wednesday, November 22, trouble developed with the subchaser's steering mechanism. It took four hours to repair. *Argo* was told to carry on; she would be overtaken when the repairs were completed.

But it took longer than expected, so, as the submarine reached the horizon and was about to slip over the rim, she was recalled—those orders to keep her in sight at all times had been emphatic.

She came back, gliding on the surface of the warm Florida sea, full of concern for her escort.

From her blinker came the message: "Shall I take you in tow?"

Messages between the subchaser and the submarine had been so far, exclusively in French. French, that is, that the captain believed he knew; *Argo*, with characteristic Continental good manners, had understood his messages. But this time, his vocabulary failed him and he answered in English, because there was a nuance he wanted to communicate; what he felt, at the moment, was lighthearted, even jocular.

"Thanks," he had the signal lamp transmit, "but as an antisubmarine ship my reputation would be destroyed. Repairs will be completed in one hour."

His joking failed. Upon arrival in Key West the next day, the French captain paid an official call to apologise for his "insult." He also brought an invitation for the officers to lunch the next day aboard his boat.

In the cramped quarters of the submarine, the subchaser's officers had a memorable meal. Nothing less, of course could be expected of the French, even under such circumstances as this, in which *Argo* found herself. Old, buffeted by the seas and by the disgrace of the Third Republic, her torpedo tubes and the barrel of her deck gun welded shut by a suspicious, newly designated ally, whom she would have to serve as an emasulated practice rabbit until her country had regained her dignity, she—*Argo*—had not lost her pride.

As importantly, she had not lost her sense of refinement, of elegance, even in the hot, poorly ventilated, diesel-scented confinement of her pressure hull.

Chilled sherry, not enough to deaden the taste buds, preceded a dinner concocted from native supplies, but prepared beyond the knowledge or expectations of the Key West commissary.

Cabbage rolls a l'orange were the appetizer, followed

by gigot—ordinary leg of lamb, but by no means plain—
with its hidden slivers of garlic, roasted with a covering of
butter and spices mixed to a paste and served the instant it
was ready. Vegetables were white Navy beans au jus, their
plebeian past submerged by the juices of the gigot in which
they simmered just before serving; chilled celery au vin,
fines herbes, which had been boiled in chicken broth and
the dry, whiteness of Chablis, then cooled.

Two dessert dishes followed. First, small cheese tarts,
baked to a delicate brown, then larger chocolate ones,
topped with whipped cream and with an almost indefinable
taste of rum; each an individual, small pie, served in its own,
fluted paper cup.

And, with the courses, there were the proper wines.

Such hospitality had to be reciprocated. The officers of
Argo were invited to board USS *PC 1264* for dinner the next
night. Occonnar Young was entreated to surpass himself
with his menu. "A typical American meal, but do your very
best."

Perhaps the supplication unnerved Young. The next
evening's meal—by U.S. Navy Regulations prefaced by no
cocktails—was an American disaster, but a tribute to Gallic
diplomacy. The dinner was simple—fried chicken, mashed
potatoes, peas, apple pie and coffee.

A French officer tried to cut his drumstick. The meat
would not take the knife. The drumstick flew from the plate,
higher than it had in life, across the table to lodge on Lieutenant Hardman's lap.

The Frenchman did not look up, but carefully pushed
some peas onto his fork. "I think," he said, "I may enjoy my
visit to the United States."

The subchaser's skipper felt he might, if he made sure
he ate aboard his own boat. He thought a little wryly of his
departure from the submarine the night before. He had
been sincere in his gratitude for the banquet, and had asked
about the food. "The last . . . the small pies we had. What
do you call them—their name?"

The French captain's face was expressionless, but there was the suspicion of a twinkle in his eyes.

"*Le Nègre en Chemise,*" he answered. "I had—how do you say?—a thought . . . a thinking . . . you would particularly enjoy them."

A Night at the Movies

USS *PC 1264* spent four and a half days practicing how to sink submarines, under the tutelage of the Fleet Sound School. Every morning before eight o'clock she would get underway, with one or two instructors aboard, and head out into the Gulf Stream to rendezvous with a target submarine.

Evenings were spent mainly in resting up for the next day's operations, for Key West had little to offer in the way of recreation, that was pleasant and free from embarrassment. Not even a government installation could be depended upon, as a group of the ship's petty officers learned, one night.

Lieutenant George Poor had the duty. The other officers had left the ship to go to the Officers Club and test Lieutenant Hardman's way with the slot machines. The night was warm, the sky clear.

Two other ships were nested between the *1264* and the dock—a landing craft, USS *LCI 875* and a frigate, USS *Nemesis.* A few of the men had decided to go to the movie at the Coast Guard station and George Poor watched them leave, checking out with Emmett Caul at the gangway; each one in his dress whites, conforming strictly with Navy protocol as he crossed the intervening ships, saluting each quarterdeck before passing.

He chatted with Louis Ellison and Jarvis Guice, who were waiting for Samuel Chadwick to join them. "What's the movie?" he asked.

"Something called 'They Live in Fear,'" Guice answered.

When they had left, Lieutenant Poor spent a few moments checking the mooring lines and then went into the charthouse and collected the letters from the mailbox and took them down to his stateroom. All personal mail had to be censored before it left the ship; this was a chore primarily of the communications officer, but to keep the mail moving, was undertaken by the duty officer in port. It was required by regulation to ensure that no secrets—ship's itinerary and operations and such—became generally known. Naturally, it was heartily disliked by all letter writers, meaning everyone.

He finished the last letter, sealed it, rubber stamped the postmark adding his initial as censor, then returned the stamp to the safe. He gathered up the letters to return them to the mailbox. As he climbed the ladder, he heard the sound of many feet on the steel deck above him, and then voices—loud, angry.

He dropped the letters in the mailbox and went out on deck. "I don't think I'll ever forget what I saw," he remembers. Lined up, packed together on the narrow deck, were twenty to twenty-five of the crew. Their eyes wide with bitterness, they had obviously experienced something together that had given them collectively a highly emotional reaction. The intensity of their feelings made it almost impossible to quiet them enough to find out what the trouble was. And when he did, it was the same, old story; certainly nothing new in the lives of these men, but uniting them even more strongly, regardless of education, upbringing, or what section of America they called home.

The trouble, basically, was one of privilege. Military organizations have a cult of caste; R. H. I. P., meaning "Rank Hath Its Privileges," is iron-bound in tradition and custom. Higher rank brings greater responsibilities, it also brings better perquisites, in enlisted as well as commissioned ranks. Chief petty officers have their own clubs, distinct from enlisted men's clubs. In gatherings, such as movies, special sections are reserved for different ranks.

So it was on the Coast Guard station in Key West. But the local administration went beyond the recognized R. H. I. P. It used the system for segregation as well; technically disguised, of course. There was a section for officers, for chiefs, for petty officers, for seamen, and one for steward's mates. The last, of course, were "colored," so, not unstrangely, there was an additional identification than rating to this section.

When the petty officers of USS *PC 1264* had paid their admission charge at the box office and entered the movie hall, Louis Ellison, Gunner's Mate First Class, Samuel Chadwick, Storekeeper Second Class, and Jarvis Guice, Signalman Second Class, seated themselves in the petty officers' section, their right and privilege. A moment or two later, a seaman told them to move to the steward's mates' section. They pointed out that they were petty officers with general ratings and were, therefore, where they belonged. The seaman left, returning almost immediately with a chief petty officer of the shore patrol, who told them that if they wanted to see the movie, they would have to watch it "along with the other niggers." In the meantime, more of the *1264*'s men were arriving and receiving the same treatment.

It was a situation that could have escalated dangerously, but quickly, Ellison told the subchaser's men to meet him outside. There, he convinced them there was little they could do now; that it would have to be settled by the skipper or the executive officer.

"So," he said, "let's get back to the ship and see what they will do."

Going back to the ship, their individual frustrations, their anger at their treatment grew and enlarged, fed by their collective fury, so that by the time they reached the ship they were, as Lieutenant Poor saw, "really emotionally upset human beings."

What they wanted was the executive officer to go immediately to the movie house and demand the seating of the men. Lieutenant Poor explained that he couldn't, as duty officer, leave the ship, but that certainly something should be done, and he promptly telephoned the captain at the officers club.

He must have relayed the feelings of the men graphically and accurately, for in only a few minutes he arrived.

He listened to their account, then asked Ellison to accompany him to the Coast Guard Station. "We'll go and talk to the commanding officer," he said.

But before they reached the administration office, Ellison sensibly suggested that his presence might inhibit the conversation. The captain agreed.

Ellison was right. The commanding officer was not there, and so the captain saw the executive officer, a lieutenant commander, whose upbringing had completely ignored his native state's reputation for politeness and gentility. He claimed the policy of the base in its treatment of "nigras" was his, and would remain so; no goddam nigra-lovin' Navy lieutenant would tell him what to do; the Coast Guard didn't have to listen to the Navy. He was reminded that this was wartime and the Coast Guard was under the operational control of the Navy and had to conform to Navy personnel policies; as executive officer, it was his duty to carry them out, or, by God, he should be fired.

It became a verbal slugfest that very nearly became more serious. The captain was shaking when he left the building and met Ellison on the corner.

They walked slowly back to the ship in silence.

"A Sunday Kind of Love"

Tuesday, November 28, was to be another day of antisubmarine exercises; the lines were cast off at 7:26 A.M. The captain was surly as he guided the ship into the channel.

"Mr. Poor," he complained to the executive officer, "we're getting too damn sloppy. We were eleven minutes late getting underway. We've been late every morning."

"The instructor was late getting aboard yesterday, Captain."

"I know, but we wouldn't have been ready, if he had been on time. From now on, I want us to be ready to go at the exact moment I've planned."

Actually, there was no need to worry about being late for the rendezvous, this morning. They had just cleared the harbor when a message came from the base, ordering her to return. Within an hour of leaving the dock, she was back again. The captain climbed up the hill to the operations office to find out why.

The reason was explained in an OP—an operational priority—message from Eastern Sea Frontier: ". . . Report Commander Task Unit 02.9.8 as additional escort KN 353 departing Key West 29 November." The rest of the day was spent in loading stores and pumping aboard 9,756 gallons of fuel oil and 220 gallons of lubricating oil.

"Tomorrow morning," the captain said, "we're going to take off at seven o'clock sharp. Not seven-o-one, or six fifty-nine. *Seven*. Pass the word to the crew, George, that I mean it this time. No excuses. If a man is not aboard at seven, he'll get left behind. By God, George, for once we're going to leave on time."

Reveille was set for 5:15. Breakfast was early. By six forty-five, all preparations had been made; every man was at his station; the captain on the flying bridge, ostentatiously checking his wristwatch. To kill time, Lieutenant Poor spaced his reports of departments "ready for sea." The men of the deck force shifted from one foot to the other, glancing at the flying bridge.

The second hand of his watch swept toward the moment of the hour. The captain leaned over the bridge screen and called to the fo'c'sle: "Cast off three, four, five and six. Hold two. Take one to the winch."

The men acted. The lines were hauled aboard. The bowline was led to the winch.

By the bow, Henry Perry cupped his hands to his face, and shouted towards the bridge, "Captain! Captain! Wait!"

What was it this time? Determined, the captain ignored him and turned his back to look aft at the swinging out of the stern.

"Captain!" Perry yelled. "Gismo's not back yet! He's still ashore!"

The captain sprang around. "My God!" he screamed. "Get those lines back ashore! . . . Where's that damn dog? . . . Perry, get a search party going! . . ."

Gismo, Ship's Mascot First Class, had heretofore a seemingly occult sense of time. As fond of liberty as any of his shipmates, he was usually the first ashore in port. Somehow, he had always known when the ship would leave, and always managed to return in time, even after a period of days. As ship's jester, this day, he could have wanted to show the captain up, for, six minutes after seven he trotted down the dock and jumped aboard, apparently oblivious to the embarrassment of his commanding officer and to the undisguised enjoyment of his shipmates.

"Mr. Poor," roared the captain. "Bust Gismo to Second Class, effective immediately! Now, let's get the hell out of here."

KN 353 was the name for four merchant ships and their protection from Key West up the East coast to New York. Only one of them, the British freighter, S.S. *Nyanza,* was destined for the final port. The Panamanian S.S. *Moldova* would be detached to go to Baltimore, the other two— S.S. *Merida* of Honduras, and an American, S.S. *Lake Freeland*—would break off for Philadelphia. The escorts, as well as USS *PC 1264,* were two Coast Guard cutters, USCG *Icarus* and USCG *Galatea.*

Early in the afternoon of their departure from Key West, the subchaser's crew was increased by two signalmen second class.

The convoy commodore, Commander Rowland D. Hill, USN (Ret.), had found that the S.S. *Nyanza*, the only ship going all the way to New York, couldn't accomodate him and his staff, so he had to set up his command in the escort commander's ship, *Icarus*. This cutter didn't have enough room for all the commodore's staff, and as she had sufficient signalmen to handle the commodore's traffic, two of his signalmen were assigned to travel in USS *PC 1264*.

They were transferred by small boat to the subchaser cruising off the convoy's starboard bow. As they came alongside and passed their seabags to the deck of the ship they would ride for the next five days, they were two surprised young men.

But their initial misgivings about being a racial minority of two, became immediately unimportant. This was their first experience of life aboard an escort ship; up to now, their sea duty had been exclusively aboard large, heavy freighters. Until USS *PC 1264* reached Tompkinsville on December 6, they were continuously and agonizingly seasick.

The first four days of the voyage were uncommonly pleasant for winter; Florida Chamber of Commerce weather. The days were warm, with a balmy 78° temperature. As Cape Hatteras was approached, the promise of its historic, angry reputation became a certainty. The winds increased to Force 6 on the Beaufort Scale—the measure of strong breezes over 25 knots. Whitecaps were everywhere, spraying from fifteen-foot waves in streaks across the gray roughness. The *PC* rolled and pitched. The guest signalmen, and some of the host crew, if they could feel anything at all beyond their misery, felt deep envy of the merchant ships, plowing through the waves with no apparent, untoward motion.

But the first few days were as comfortable as any a subchaser could enjoy. Visibility was good, the air warm, and USS *PC 1264* patroled the starboard bow of the convoy, slowly and methodically in broad sweeps across her base course line, her speed of advance the steady, slow eight knots of the merchantmen.

In the wardroom, the captain lay comfortably on the transom, his shoes off, leafing through a magazine, undecided to read or take a nap. The ports were open, letting the warm, fresh southern air in. Muted, from the signal bridge came the sounds of a trumpet. The executive officer was practicing, and undoubtedly being accompanied by a self-appointed drummer—usually Willie "Chico" Hawk— using the semaphore flags as sticks, on an ammunition ready box.

The captain may have been dozing, for he didn't see Ensign Stanley Rhodes come through the door from the main deck. When he was conscious of his presence, the communications officer was standing by the coffee urn, pouring a cup. "Getting to be time for your watch?" he was asked, more for conversation than anything else.

"Just came off, sir. Mr. Otto relieved me."

"It's later than I thought." The captain glanced at the clock. The hands on the twenty-four-hour face marked 1605. I'd better start thinking about writing the night orders, he thought.

"Captain. Do you know anything about song writing?"

"Good Lord, no. Why?"

"I . . . I mean, if someone wrote a song. . . . How would he sell it? You know, to a publisher?"

"You've got me, Stan. All I've heard, isn't good. I mean, I'm told it's the dirtiest business of all to try and break into. Beginning writers get their throats cut and their songs stolen." He paused, then went on, "Have you written one?"

Ensign Rhodes nodded.

"Well. . . . A successor to Irving Berlin. What kind of a song is it? Ballad? Romantic? . . . Have you shown it to Mr. Poor? . . . He's our musician aboard."

"I haven't got it all written down yet. George—Mr.

Poor—is trying to show me how to do it. I guess you'd say it's only in my head right now. And I guess, too, that it's a romantic song—a kind of love song—dance music." Then, eagerly, "Would you like to hear it?"

The captain grinned. What could he say, except, "Why, sure, Stan. Go ahead."

Ensign Rhodes, an unconscious performer, moved to the middle of the wardroom deck, his backdrop the gray bulkhead, and stood between the two portholes; in his mind, perhaps translating it into the floor of a nightclub, and he, the emaciated current idol of swooning, screaming and fainting New York teenagers.

There must have been a difference, however, in the voices. Somehow, the communications officer's voice failed to communicate the tune; it could be, of course, the captain decided, that Ensign Rhodes couldn't carry a tune.

But there were lots of words strung together that went up and down in nasal intensity. Words such as "love," "Saturday night," and "keep me warm on" something; at least, "moon," and "June," were missing.

At the very least, politeness required that some sort of critique be given the young composer. The captain was concentrating so hard on what he might be able to say that he was now sitting up and leaning on the table, watching the troubadour intently.

A movement at the left-hand porthole caught his eye. Someone had passed along the deck, going forward. Like waiting for the other shoe to drop, he waited for the head to pass the second port. It didn't, and his interest as suddenly switched. He watched.

Ensign Rhodes' serenade was reaching the heights of musical passion. Slowly, carefully, a face moved into the porthole. A face with eyes wide with the astonishment of Henry J. Perry, Coxswain and acting Boatswain's Mate and Master-at-Arms. The face of a man hearing an officer sing a love song to the captain.

The captain at the time didn't appreciate the musical talents of Ensign Stanley Rhodes. But a music publisher eventually did. With the assistance of collaborators, his song was published, made the hit parade, and is still heard today. It is called "A Sunday Kind of Love."

Christmas Holiday

Shortly before midnight on December 5, 1944, with S.S. *Nyanza* safely in the swept channel to New York harbor, Convoy KN 353 was ended. Lieutenant Commander W. D. Stevens, USCG, the escort commander, released his escorts to proceed independently to port. At 1:30 A.M., USS *PC 1264* tied up to her sister ship, USS *PC 1265*, alongside Pier 7 of the U.S. Frontier Base, Tompkinsville, Staten Island. She was home again.

She stayed at home for a month. The reason for this extended holiday was the usual one: trouble with the engines. Particles of metal had been showing up in the oil. The previous lengthy work by the Navy Yard had been a great deal less than satisfactory; it was found that when the engines had been replaced, neither they, nor the reduction gears had been aligned properly; moreover, there had been faulty welding of the lubricating oil piping. So, on December 10, the ship had to be towed back to the Naval Annex at Bayonne, to give the yard engineers another try at repairing them.

For the ship's company, it was no hardship; Christmas and New Year's Day were included. Moreover, Bayonne was closer to Jersey City than Tompkinsville.

Jersey City was becoming as popular a liberty town as Harlem. This was due entirely to the arrival, one month before, of a quartermaster striker named Emmett C. Caul.

Emmett Caul had been born, and spent most of his twenty years, in Waynesboro, Virginia. He was no country lad, although he did give the appearance of being more reserved and quiet than others of his age. Before coming to the ship, and following his training at Great Lakes, he had been assigned to New York. In these six months, he had become acquainted with, and, as an embryo quartermaster, duly recorded the names and addresses of a number of very attractive young women; some of whom lived in Jersey City. In the Southern tradition, he generously helped his shipmates plan their liberties.

Indeed, Caul's taste in beauty could break class barriers. Ensign Stan Rhodes, Duty Officer one evening in Tompkinsville, was so taken with the young lady Caul had brought to visit the ship and have dinner aboard, insisted —contrary to Navy custom and the sanctity of "Officers Country"—that Caul entertain her in the wardroom, instead of the crew's mess.

It was a policy of the ship that friends were always welcome to visit during off-duty hours. Unfortunately, there were cases where the welcome didn't extend to the Navy Yard gate. As in Miami, during shakedown, there were cruel and embarrassing incidents. After one such occurrence, when Lieutenant Otto had learned that a group from one of the crew's church was prevented from entering the yard, had quickly gone to the gate to escort them in, and had experienced the bitter rudeness of the Chief Petty Officer there. Walking back to the ship, he had tried to apologize.

"Don't think anything about it, Lieutenant," the pastor said gently. "We are used to it."

During this month, Lieutenant George R. Poor, the ship's first executive officer, received orders to take command of USS *PC 1218*, a subchaser also based at Tompkinsville. It was a well-merited promotion and, from the standpoint of his qualifications, long overdue; from the beginning, his experience as a seaman and an administrator surpassed that of the majority of Donald Duck Navy skippers. For the launching of such an experiment as USS *PC 1264*, he was without peer. Executive officers, by the very nature of their positions as primary supervisors of ships' crews, have to be realists—supposedly hard-nosed characters. George Poor, though, maintained discipline naturally, for he was a natural leader. Committed to the success of the program that was the reason for USS *PC 1264*, he set the tone that was followed by each successive executive officer. His was a personality that did not need to be bolstered by rank or position.

Wilbur F. Otto, recently promoted to senior-grade lieutenant, "fleeted up" to take his place.

Two days before George Poor was detached, a new junior officer reported. A copy of his orders had preceded him, so his name, his rank—ensign—were known, but nothing else. When he arrived in the early afternoon of Saturday, December 16, the captain felt that an interesting new dimension to the ship's complement had been added.

Benjamin Shanker, born twenty years before in St. Louis, Missouri, was a Southerner. Raised and educated in New Orleans, he had completed pre-medical training at the University of Texas, before being commissioned in the Naval Reserve the previous September. It would be interesting to see what his reaction to serving with this crew would be—and to see how the crew would react to him. Would he confirm the widely held theory that blacks respond more readily to the leadership of southern officers, because "They know better how to handle 'em"?

But what was particularly intriguing was that Ensign Benjamin Shanker was not only from the south, but himself a member of a minority group. Being a Jew, would this have any bearing on his relationship with a black ship's company? Gunnar Myrdal in his study, *An American Dilemma*, drew attention to the phenomenon that injustice doesn't mean more tolerance among those suffering themselves under bias; that the Jew has been charged with equal, if not more, prejudice against the Black as any southern cracker. Now, one of the officers assigned to this subchaser was both a southerner and a Jew.

But this, itself, proved to be a stereotype. The men, at first, were guarded and suspicious of him. "It didn't take us long, though," Emmett Caul remembered many years later, "to find he was a real good Joe. He was quieter on watch; more reserved and stern-looking. It took us a while to figure him out."

Ben Shanker became the gunnery officer. Louis Ellison, the leading gunner's mate, found him to be a perfectionist; eager to know all that he could of the weapons, the ammunition, and the procedures of his department, and not a bit hesitant to acknowledge his inexperience and learn from Ellison and Bennett the practicalities of his department. So, acceptance came soon enough, and preconceptions based on geographic origin were forgotten.

As the most junior officer, Ensign Shanker was stuck with most of the holiday duty. As many as could, officers and men, took Christmas leave. For those who stayed aboard, a Christmas Eve service was held in the crew's mess hall, conducted by a chaplain from the base, the Reverend Lacour. He and his wife had brought with them a portable organ which Mrs. Lacour played, and three very attractive young ladies who had no trouble at all in leading the ship's congregation in carols. Fireman First Class Howard R. Carter's professionally trained baritone sang a solo. The generous Lacours had also brought Christmas presents with them, a variety of goodies—from cigarettes to hand-knitted watch caps, bought or made by two Bayonne organizations, the Junior Red Cross and one called "Bundles for America."

And the next afternoon, the Lacours were back again with a group of about thirty young singers, who sang on the fantail—the afterdeck of the ship. Snow lightly fell, adding to the sense of Christmas. Soon, the dock was crowded by sailors from the other ships in the yard, joining in the well-known carols. "It broke up the Xmas duty rather nicely,"

Will Otto reported in his diary.

The new executive officer shared the holiday duty with the new gunnery officer. Lieutenant Otto had the watch on New Year's Eve, after the ship had returned to Tompkinsville.

It is a custom in the Navy that the first entry in the log on the first day of a new year be poetic.

Will Otto's tour de force, hitherto unpublished, described the state of the ship between midnight and 0400 hours, January 1, 1945, thus:

> Moored fast are we
> Port side to quay
> Outboard the 1265
> PC is she
> And so are we
> With a crew that looks alive.
>
> This side of heaven
> North Side Pier Seven
> United States Naval Frontier Base
> The Island of Staten
> Close to Manhattan
> In the State of New York is our place.

It was quiet in Tompkinsville that night, but there, and in all parts of the country there was hope that perhaps before the next new year came around, it could more happily be celebrated, that the toasts to a brighter and peaceful future be made with greater certainty.

Signalman 3rd class Jarvis E. Guice running up a flag hoist

Six

Buzzbomb Alert

The new year was eight days old. In Norfolk, Virginia, at his headquarters, the commander-in-chief, U.S. Atlantic Fleet held a press conference.

Admiral Jonas H. Ingram was a bluff, burly Indianan, whose prowess on the football field—first as a midshipman and later as a Naval Academy coach—had started his reputation as an aggressive, colorful character. Duty as a Navy public relations officer in the 1930's had taught him that newspapermen were usually not the ogres senior government and military officials consider them to be, but can be a very useful tool—indeed, sometimes the only one—in getting support for something from the public.

From July until December, Eastern Sea Frontier had been relatively quiet. But on December 3, a snorkle U-Boat sank a Canadian ship, the S.S. *Cornwallis*, with the loss of all except five of her crew. Despite an intensive hunt by Eastern Sea Frontier and Atlantic Fleet forces, the submarine got away.

She was *U-1230*. Five days before sinking the Canadian, she had scored another success. Undetected, she sailed silently into the deep, rocky waters of Frenchman Bay and near the popular Maine summer resort of Bar Harbor disembarked two German spies in a rubber boat, and left as quietly as she had come.

157

The spies were not as successful. The F.B.I. arrested them in New York City and, under questioning, said that German submarines were being fitted with rocket launchers which would enable them to fire robot aerial bombs, such as the V-1 and V-2 that had caused such havoc on London, from far at sea. Boston, New York, Philadelphia and Washington could expect them.

This intelligence supported some fragmentary reports from Allied agents in Europe. Admiral Ingram decided to take steps to meet this possible threat. One of them was to alert the public—it might lessen future panic if such attacks did come; more immediately, it might make the coastal cities enforce the "brownout" regulations more strictly. With the apparent lessening of U-Boat activity off the east coast, the cities and towns had become complacent about their nightly dimming of lights.

Another step the admiral took was to regroup his forces.

Two and a half days before Admiral Ingram talked with the press on Monday, January 8, USS *PC 1264* left New York with three other escort ships and a convoy to Key West—her three fellow protectors were two coast guard cutters, *Galatea* and *Icarus,* and USS *PC 1218.*

Plowing steadily southward, they had reached the waters off Cape Hatteras on Sunday afternoon. Rolling and pitching in the typical Hatteras seas, the frigid January spray numbing the lookouts' faces, with only the hope that ahead lay Florida, when suddenly their fortunes changed. A message chattered over the radios detaching *Galatea,* USS *1218* and USS *PC 1264* and directing them back to New York. *Icarus* was left to shepherd the convoy on.

Shortly after noon the next day, Monday, when they were approximately one hundred miles offshore of Atlantic City, the two subchasers were told to proceed independently. Seven and a half hours later, USS *PC 1264* tied up to a Tompkinsville dock.

The ship couldn't realize it then, but her operational

life had changed. Before the war was over, she would escort only one more convoy from start to finish. From now until then, she would conduct mainly independent antisubmarine duty. It came to be called "Anti-Buzzbomb Patrol."

First Patrol

The Navy took the threatened U-Boat offensive seriously.

As soon as USS *PC 1264* docked in Tompkinsville, workmen came aboard and installed an additional radio in the pilothouse. Unlike the TBS—the short-range "Talk Between Ships"—this transmitter was capable of carrying a voice message over several hundred miles. Its frequency was continually monitored by three shore stations: Eastern Sea Frontier Headquarters in New York City, the Naval Lighter-Than-Air Station at Lakehurst, New Jersey, and the Army Air Corps bomber command in Mineola, Long Island.

The idea was, that when a contact was made with an enemy submarine, the watch officer would grab the microphone and report it, giving his position. Instantaneously, all three shore stations would be alerted and—according to plan —Eastern Sea Frontier would dispatch a hunter-killer group of destroyer-escorts; blimps and bombers, armed with depth charges, would take off from Lakehurst and Mineola to join in the attack.

It was an imposing instrument set against the bulkhead next to the door leading to the starboard wing of the bridge. It made the pilothouse even more cramped, but its newness, its appearance of efficiency and the knowledge of its purpose made it welcome.

By noon the next day, this new gear had been tested and pronounced operational. An hour and a half later, USS *PC 1264* put to sea.

For eight days and nights, together with the Coast Guard Cutter *Might* (*PG 94*) and two PCs—the *1175* and *1219*—she patrolled the Atlantic from the tip of Montauk Point, Long Island, as far south as Cape Charles, the entrance to Chesapeake Bay.

They patrolled in formation, practicing co-ordinated attacks on imaginary submarines, and techniques in finding one again that might have been lost after an attack.

The Officer in Tactical Command (OTC) was the commanding officer of *Might*, a dark-haired, bushy-browed Coast Guard lieutenant commander, whose thick Slavic accent compounded with the static of the TBS to make his commands almost incomprehensible. He was promptly dubbed, "The Mad Russian."

The second night out was cold and dark. The winter sky was closed by heavy, low-lying clouds. The ships rolled in the off-shore swell, some forty miles south of Long Island, the Mad Russian's flagship leading the subchasers like a mother duck followed by three ducklings.

The TBS crackled. When the pronunciation was sifted from the static, it was an order to conduct a box search. This was a tactic to find a suspected submarine, or a lost one, by steaming according to a fixed plan, each ship sweeping with its sonar along courses that boxed in an area of ocean; a box that increased in size with the completion of each circumnavigation. Through the night the small armada sailed around the sides of the enlarging boxes; the OTC growling each change of course.

Well before dawn, the captain of USS *PC 1264* was in the charthouse, leaning over the chart, watching Emmett Caul plot the line of the next change of direction. Operating under such a fixed pattern, Caul could anticipate the next course change by keeping an eye on the stop watch.

In a few moments, the order would come. It would be acknowledged by each ship in the order they steamed behind the *Might*. As last in line, USS *PC 1264* would be expected to "willco"—meaning, "will comply"—last.

Caul drew the penciled line northward on the chart. He looked quizzically at the captain, his eyebrows raised. The captain reached for the dividers, took a measurement and went to the TBS.

The order came—a ninety-degree turn to the right. *PC 1175*, then *PC 1219* acknowledged. The skipper pressed the button on the mike.

He gave the ship's temporary code name, then, "Roger," he said. "Request permission to break formation."

There was silence for a moment, then the OTC's voice shouted through the atmospheric disturbances, demanding a reason.

"According to my plot," the captain answered slowly and distinctly, "this course will put us on Westhampton Beach in twenty-two minutes."

The Mad Russian must have pushed his mike button in agitation. His roar, calling for his quartermaster, his OOD and an assortment of deities, filled every pilothouse of his command. Then there was silence.

Thirty seconds later came the order turning the fleet away from the deserted holiday beaches of southern Long Island.

Stamford Nights

All hands had finished breakfast on Wednesday, January 17, when the ship entered The Narrows of New York harbor and headed for her berth on Staten Island.

But she would have no rest. By one o'clock in the afternoon, she was underway again; this time to go to the Naval Ammunition Base at Leonardo in Sandy Hook Bay.

The reason was to unload her ammunition. The time had come to clean her bottom and give her underwater hull a fresh coat of paint. This would be done by the Luders Marine Construction Company in Stamford, Connecticut; a yard noted for the civilian yachts it built.

Ensign Ben Shanker and his leading gunner's mate, Louis Ellison, had worked out a smooth, orderly and speedy transfer of the shells, depth charges and rockets, ashore. After an almost unbroken thirteen days at sea, to leave again tomorrow morning for an unknown port in Connecticut and the possibility of a patrol immediately from there, the crew was anxious for New York tonight. Rank had no privilege; meant nothing under these circumstances. Petty officers from every department toiled alongside seamen and firemen, passing the ordnance, hand to hand, from the magazines below and the ammunition ready boxes on deck, to the trucks waiting on the dock.

Even though the ammunition was discharged in record time, it was dark before the ship returned to Tompkinsville. Again, a record was made—by the liberty section in changing into their dress uniforms and catching the ferry to Manhattan.

Stamford may have been unknown to USS *PC 1264*, and vice versa, until Thursday, January 18, 1945, but in the three days the ship was there, each got to know the other. Some firm friendships were made, which is remarkable, considering the reputation the Friday liberty party nearly made for the ship. But the ship herself made retribution and the wholehearted, generous hospitality of some Stamford residents, especially a Dr. and Mrs. Corwin, made this ship's visit a memorable one.

Friday night could have been disasterous. Shortly after the ship arrived on Thursday morning, the United Services Organization Center in the Negro section of the city, invited the ship to a party the next night. It was to be a party for the crew of USS *PC 1264* alone, which was probably the cause for the Donnybrook that followed for, with the party well underway, it was invaded by some black sailors from the Submarine Base in New London.

How the fight started in the room where refreshments were being served is unclear. It may have been caused by the New London sailors who were steward's mates and resented the general rates of the subchaser's men; it may have been the boastful pride of a seagoing sailor over a shore-based one, or his disparagement of the rating that until recently had been the only one open to his race. More probably, it started over a girl.

Whatever the cause, such a noise erupted from this room, that Lieutenant Otto, the senior officer there, dispatched Henry Perry, Boatswain's Mate and Master-at-Arms, to quiet it down.

Perry got to the door and opened it. A chair sailed through, followed by some struggling bodies. The men in the outer room immediately joined in. The melee became general. The officers tried to round up the hostesses and get them through the front door; they all made it on their own. At one point, Perry was struck painfully on the side of his head; in rage, he turned to find his assailant was Lee V. Miller, a seaman first class and gunner's mate striker. "Hey! What do you think you're doing?" Perry demanded.

"Sorry, Boats!" Miller yelled and moved on.

Subchaser efficiency shortly took over. Four men were stationed by the front door. The invaders from the Submarine Base were passed to them and heaved into the street.

Then quiet returned. Although there had been a frenzied few minutes, very little damage had been done and no one seriously hurt. The following morning a detail from the ship returned and repaired and cleaned the center thoroughly.

The fracas didn't disturb Dr. and Mrs. Corwin, who lived nearby the center. Dr. Corwin, a dentist, and his wife invited the ship's liberty party and officers to their home the next night. A private residence, there were no gate crashers, so the evening was calm. That one of the Corwin's guests was an F.B.I. agent, Lieutenant Otto thought, could have had a sobering effect. Not so the agent's sister, a highly attractive, talented and winsome eighteen-year-old. How many letters she received with a USS *PC 1264* postmark in the months ahead, only she could know. Later, when a ship's paper was produced, she wrote for it, contributing some excellent poetry.

David and Goliath

German submarines—the enemy USS *PC 1264* was built to combat—had undergone various changes and improvements in the course of the war. Measures and countermeasures, the competition to find better weapons, better offensive and defensive tactics, was a constant goal of both sides.

When the *PC* class of ship was on the drawing board, submarines were slow-moving vessels; rarely able to move faster than five knots under water, and perhaps twelve on the surface. Underwater, they could run only on electrical power, which meant that for an average period of about four hours a day they would have to come to the surface to recharge their batteries by their air-gulping diesel engines. Invariably, they would do this at night, when the darkness gave them some measure of protection. But with the advent of radar, they became particularly vulnerable against aircraft and surface ships. And, when found below the surface by a subchaser's sonar and contact was maintained, even if she escaped damage from depth charge attacks, there would come a time when the U-Boat would have to surface or suffocate.

The shallow draft of a subchaser was considered a protection against torpedoes, and her surface armament of a 3"50 caliber gun forward, three 20 mm machine guns on the superstructure, and a 40 mm rapid fire gun aft, was considered sufficient to take care of any surfaced submarine. Her top speed of twenty knots was faster than that of any *unterseeboot*—in 1942.

By the end of 1944, greatly improved enemy submarines were roaming the seas. The Schnorchel (or snout), a Dutch invention captured by the Germans in 1940 but not developed until four years later, enabled a U-Boat to travel on its diesel engines at periscope depth and to charge its batteries without surfacing. Abbreviated by the British to "snort," and by the Americans to "snorkel," it was a mast, consisting of an air induction trunk and a diesel exhaust pipe, that could be raised above the surface while the rest of the submarine hull remained below water.

Thus, a submarine could remain hidden, with little chance of visual sighting, almost indefinitely.

U-Boat speed and armament were improved. Their pressure hulls were strengthened so they could dive deeper, increasing their ability to evade the slow-dropping depth charges.

By January 1945, the *PC* was outclassed. But Goliaths can be defeated by Davids. During the next three months, after her beauty treatment in Stamford, USS *PC 1264* never doubted that if she could come across one of these craft on her anti-buzzbomb patrol, the Biblical story would be re-enacted.

She may have had her chance.

Action at Buoy Able

During the three months of her patrolling, USS *PC 1264's* usual responsibility was a line running north by east for twenty miles from Buoy "Able," the farthest seaward buoy marking the mine-swept channel into New York— forty-five miles away.

Sometimes the routine varied. For two days in March, she took a group of scientists and Atlantic Fleet antisubmarine experts up Long Island Sound to Block Island, to observe the operations of a snorkel-fitted submarine. They were trying to figure out a way to detect such an elusive target. On another day, she was ordered to leave her station for a day to join the Mad Russian again in his favorite activity, conducting a search pattern. But usually she went back and forth on her patrol line, sometimes alone, sometimes in company with Lieutenant Russell Harris' USS *PC 1209*.

Despite the wintry weather, the conspiracy of wind and cold that angered the sea, it was as pleasant a duty as could be hoped for at this time of the year. It fell into a routine: seven days out, five days in port . . . seven days out, five days in. . . . "Darling," the captain was able to say to his wife, "see if you can get the Officers Service Committee at the Hotel Commodore to spring a couple of tickets for 'Oklahoma,' two weeks from tomorrow. I hear it's a damn good show."

And there was always much more satisfaction in operating alone. Plodding back and forth on this twenty-mile line was not as boring as might be thought. The sea was the sea, continually changing in pattern and shape, empty to the horizon on all sides, wherever you might be. And always at one end of the line was the great, swaying black and white light buoy, its gong banging its deep, mournful note, telling you where you were exactly at every round trip; checking the accuracy of the navigator and the helmsmen. And, telling you too, that you weren't really alone: to the east, forty-five miles away, was home.

Buoy "A" was helpful in another way. Its huge bottom and mammoth chain, keeping it anchored to an exact spot on the ocean floor of the continental shelf, reflected well the beams of the sonar—the supersonic echo-ranging device—with which the ship could search for and hopefully find its underwater enemy. So, often it became the target for a drill.

One afternoon, the weather was strangely mild. Officially, spring was still a few months away, but it seemed almost at hand. Tomorrow would prove it but a titillation, but today the sea was calm, the sky blue, the sun's brilliance yellowing toward the evening's red, as it started its slide to the west.

The first section was on watch. The executive officer was OOD, Adolph Cork doubling as quartermaster and signalman, Paul Rhinehart both watch gunner's mate and lookout. They were on the flying bridge. The captain climbed the ladder to them and settled himself in the chair to the left of the 20 mm gun mount. He raised the binoculars around his neck to his eyes.

"How long, Will," he asked, "before we get to the buoy?"

"Twenty minutes, captain. We ought to be able to see it—yes, there it is."

The ship was cruising at two-thirds speed. Faintly, halfway to the horizon, about three miles away, the spindly outline of their marker could be identified.

"On the nose, again," the captain said. "Will, let's scare hell out of her again. Pass the word, 'Man your battle stations!' A drill. We're going to disable 'Able.' "

The klaxon scream for battle stations was reserved for the real thing, as was the phrase "General Quarters!" Drills were known for what they were, by human warning. The word was passed from the bridge talker to the gun crew on the after 40 mm. They, in turn yelled, "Battle Stations!" that was repeated by everyone in earshot, above decks and below. Bodies streamed up from the compartments; when relieved, the present watch standers hurried to their Condition One stations.

The captain and executive officer climbed down to the pilothouse. Will Otto turned the power on the recorder.

"Target, dead ahead," the captain told the sonarman, Henry James.

"Aye, aye, sir," he said. "Got it. Target bearing dead ahead. Stationary. Range four thousand yards."

Richard Bennett, the bridge talker, relayed the reports from the stations around the ship. All were manned and ready.

"Range three thousand. Bearing steady."

"Very well," the captain answered. There really wasn't any need to carry on with this drill. The men had responded quickly and smoothly, reaching their stations. Concentrating the sonar on this innocent victim meant relinquishing temporarily the general sound search through the waters all around where a less innocent object could be lurking. Oh, what the hell, we might as well carry it on to twelve hundred yards, when, with a real attack, we would speed up to fifteen knots to prevent the depth charges from blowing off our tail. "Bennett," he said. "Tell depth charges to simulate a shallow pattern."

"Range two thousand, bearing steady," James reported.

"Depth charges simulated for shallow pattern," Bennett advised.

"Very well." The captain watched the buoy looming steadily larger ahead. In a few moments, he'd order the helm over to take an attack lead angle and bring the ship up to standard speed.

"Range fifteen hundred. Steady. Range fourteen . . . thirteen . . . twelve!"

"All engines ahead standard!"

Bennett rang the telegraph. The diesels below rose in a heavier roar. All felt the stern settle as the propellers bit deeper.

"Right ten degrees rudder!"

As the captain gave his order and before Paul Davis, the helmsman, could repeat it, James yelled, "Target bearing left rapidly!"

The captain froze. Davis had started to swing the ship right. "Repeat!" He swiveled to the sonarman.

"Bearing went left . . . disappearing!"

"All engines ahead one third. Hard left rudder."

There was only enough room to turn inside the buoy, but only just. James was cranking his sonar dome wheel from side to side frantically.

"Steady on zero eight zero, Davis," the captain ordered.

"Steady on zero eight zero, sir," Davis repeated.

"Target bearing zero seven seven," James announced. "Down doppler."

"Range?"

"Thirteen hundred yards. Bearing going left. Zero five eight. Doppler up . . . I think!"

Doppler is the name given to the change in pitch of the returning echo. An up Doppler means a higher tone, signifying the moving object is coming nearer; even as the scream of an approaching train's whistle rises in tone as it nears, then dwindles down after it passes and disappears down the track. It is an indication of relative movement. Whatever the target was James had caught on his sonar, it was coming relatively closer; probably because the ship was gaining upon it.

"Come left to zero five five. Sound the general alarm. General Quarters!"

I think I've got one, the captain thought. German submarine captains were known to lie doggo next to known wrecks, feeling secure that the sonar echoes from his hull back to a snooping surface ship would be ascribed to the sound waves bouncing off the wreck. Where better could he rest than next to the seaward buoy of New York's swept channel? What better vantage spot could he have, lying in wait for any one of a number of convoys which would have to pass closely?

The captain was sure that, at long last, he was meeting the enemy. As he saw it, the submarine he was now tracking, had indeed been sheltering under the buoy, unconcerned by the "pings" of the subchaser's sonar. He may have been there for a day or two, unworried as the small patrol craft on schedule came near him. He may have been there long enough to learn what this schedule was, and at night, during the three to four hours it took for the subchaser's round trip, carefully blown his tanks and come to the surface to give

his crew some fresh air, making sure that he floated alongside his protecting buoy, so radar reflections would similarly
be blamed on "Able."

Then what had happened? . . . Today, he had been
lying there, feeling secure in the mud. From the distance
he could hear, through his hydrophones, the noise of the approaching *PC*. Then something began to worry him. He
noticed that the American's sonar was concentrated on the
buoy. . . . Was it the buoy, or was it, perhaps, upon him?

He waited and his worry grew. The sonar echoes pinged
off him regularly. The surface ship was acting exactly as
though it was performing the preliminaries to an attack.
Steadily, it approached. If, indeed, she was attacking, she
would soon have to come up to attack speed. And if so, the
German knew that with the depth of ocean here only 135
feet, the blast would be concentrated. His own maneuver-
ability because of this shallowness was severely limited.

When he heard the subchaser's engine revolutions increase, he must have been suddenly, frighteningly positive
he had been discovered. Frantically, he got underway; desperately hoping to be able to reach the deeper waters off the
continental shelf. He probably felt it was too late; in seconds,
the depth charges should explode.

But they didn't. Instead, the vessel turned away. The
pinning was lost in the turbulence of her screws.

The *PC* slowed, then sharply turned back. The sonar
echoes found him again.

At this moment, the *PC*'s skipper thought, the German
must be cursing himself. He'd given himself away. And now
James had latched onto him again. This time there'd be a
real attack.

"Set the Mousetraps! . . . Prepare to fire by recorder!"

On the bow, Ellison quickly readied the "Antisubmarine
Projectiles, Mark 22," on their two launching racks. Fired by
rockets, their TNT-filled bodies exploded on contact. Fast
traveling and fast sinking, they were more accurate than the

classic "ash-can" depth charges, for their firing did not require the ship to take a lead angle to offset the sinking of
the charges.

The recorder, watched by Will Otto, was tied in with
the sonar equipment and, by a stylus marking the outgoing
and returning signals, gave a visual graph of the target's
range. When the range coincided with the known trajectory
of the Mousetraps, the executive officer pushed the firing
button and sent them on their way.

The captain suddenly remembered his new radio. After
this run, he thought. Maybe we can give them a fait ac-
compli, and save the blimps and bombers some gas.

USS *PC 1264* tracked her quarry, keeping her bow on
it. Then, "Whoosh . . . whoosh. . . ." the series of rockets
left their racks and sped in a low arc over the water and
dived. Will Otto clicked his stop watch.

"Right full rudder!"

The ship heeled to avoid the hoped-for explosion.

And it came, in one mighty cataclysm—a boiling blast
of water thrown upwards. As mighty a cheer came from
everyone topside; a Mousetrap explosion, set off by a contact
fuze, meant a positive hit.

But it doesn't necessarily mean hitting a submarine.

"What was the time, Will?"

"Five seconds."

The captain's exultation dropped to the depth of the
ocean bed he'd wounded. "Maybe we hit the earth," he
said. "Davis, steady on the last attack course. James, find
her again."

"Captain." It was Bennett, the bridge talker. "Caul,
back aft, says he saw the sub!"

The captain rushed out on the bridge wing. He was not
alone. The temptation must have been overwhelming, but
Davis stayed at his helm, and James at his sonar, trying to
pierce through the disturbance of the sea for that which—
it was now claimed—had been seen.

The waters were still troubled as the ship sailed through them. There was no sign of wreakage, of oil, or of any tangible indication that a submarine had been there.

"Bennett," the captain said. "Find out what they saw back aft." He reached for the microphone of the radio that now would inform the awaiting forces in New York, Lakehurst and Mineola, that a probable conning tower of a submarine had been seen.

Eastern Sea Frontier, however, was skeptical. Instead of the waves of bombers, the flocks of blimps, the fleet that would steam to give battle, only USS *PC 1149* and a small district ship was assigned to assist. Later, the Coast Guard cutters *Thetis* and *Icarus* joined in.

Contact was regained following the initial attack, and two more were made. Hopes rose with the discovery of a thin, though widely spread oil slick. But, by the time the assisting ships had arrived, the contact had been lost. Until late at night the search continued without success, and was finally broken off to allow the ships to return to their assigned patrols.

Emmett Caul and Adolph Cork both claim they saw the conning tower of a submarine rise momentarily then sink back into the turbulence. The disbelieving headquarters of Eastern Sea Frontier, however, considered it to be either a whale—admittedly a possibility—or the wreck of the *Lillian,* a vessel sunk three and a half miles south of Buoy "Able." If the latter, it could only prove that ghost ships do exist to move forever below, as well as above, the seas.

The crew of USS *PC 1264* prefers to think her quarry was *U-866,* a damaged submarine sunk two weeks later off Sable Island, east of Nova Scotia. Navy records show that this submarine was damaged during a bombing raid on Bremen, before she left on war patrol. Perhaps. . . .

In the daily War Diary of Eastern Sea Frontier there is a notation in the entry for February 28, 1945, concerning this incident: "RHIND (DD) en route New York to Casco, volunteered assistance; but considered the other vessels adequate and continued en route. . . ."

This new destroyer, on her way to shakedown in Maine, came tearing by in her fresh, new paint, with the cockiness of being the newest unit of the fleet, possessing the most modern, sophisticated equipment so far developed. With the self-importance of an academic professional, she informed USS *PC 1264* by blinker light, categorically, there was no enemy submarine in the vicinity. She implied it was far more important for her to be elsewhere.

Jarvis Guice flashed a disgruntled *PC's* reply: "Your moral support was magnificent."

Movies and a Race

In the lineal list of the United States Naval Reserve, the captain of USS *PC 1264* was senior to the commanding officer of USS *PC 1209*. Automatically, then, whenever these two ships operated together, the former was Officer in Tactical Command—the OTC. The principal advantage to *PC 1264* was that on return to port, she could ensure obtaining the better berth by the dock for herself.

They were sister ships, both built by Consolidated Shipbuilding Corporation, and were commissioned a week apart. Their duties were similar in every respect, so of all the subchasers assigned to Task Group 02.9, based at Tompkinsville, these two performed more missions together than with any others. Thus, a comaraderie was established from the beginning of the ships' lives. It was reflected in many ways, none peculiar to these particular crews, but common to small groups of people, living or working together; whether military units or neighbors in a housing development. Samuel Chadwick, the tall, calm schoolteacher from North Carolina and temporarily, for the duration of the war, storekeeper for USS *PC 1264*, early established his reputation as the best procurer of supplies—allowed or otherwise—in the New York branch of the Donald Duck Navy. When the interests of his ship were fulfilled, his talents were available to USS *PC 1209*. Similarly, whenever the storekeeper of the *1209* could latch onto something to help the *1264*, the favor was reciprocated. It was a profitable arrangement.

It may well have been Lieutenant Harris' charm with the WAVE film librarian that gave the ships the best available movies to show when at sea. Whatever the reason, it was successful, so it was his responsibility to obtain the reels before leaving; dividing them. Halfway through the voyage, the ships would come alongside each other and exchange the canisters.

At the start of one patrol, when getting underway, the captain of USS *PC 1209* announced loudly to his OTC, so the crew of the *1264* at special sea detail could hear, that he doubted if he would be able to exchange one film he had obtained. As the ships separated from their berth, he was asked the reason for such an ungenerous, bordering on mutinous, suggestion. Lieutenant Harris leeringly replied he had managed to obtain a print of "Ecstasy," the notorious movie showing Hedy Lamarr in all of her seventeen-year-old beauty.

That there might even be a possibility, anticipation by the men of USS *PC 1264* convinced them, despite the arguments of their captain who argued that by now they should know the character and humor of their sister ship's skipper. But he was unavailing, and until the scheduled transfer of the films, their talk was of little else.

When the ships came together halfway through the patrol, even the off-duty sections were on deck to watch the exchange. It was Henry Perry who leaned across the lifelines and gathered the cans of reels. He looked through them, grabbed one and held it aloft toward the bridge.

"It is true, captain," he yelled. "Here it is!"

Russell Harris grinned across the few feet separating the two flying bridges. "I still don't believe it," his OTC replied.

Triumphantly, Perry carried the cannister up to the flying bridge. He showed the label.

Sure enough, the printed label said: Hedy Lamarr—ECSTASY.

"I still don't believe it," The captain said.

The first showing that evening for the off-duty sections was packed to capacity. The duty section was morose and envious.

They needn't have been. The film in the container with such a pleasurably exciting title printed by special order at the Base Print Shop, was a relic from the old Videograph, so bad that its name was soon forgotten.

Another Harris ploy in the continual gamesmanship between the two ships, followed an accident to USS *PC 1264*. A few days before she was to escort a convoy, while creeping up the ship channel in a thick fog, she bumped Buoy "15," and damaged one of her propellors. USS *PC 1209* was assigned to take her place as an escort to the convoy. Two weeks later, upon her return, there was a ceremony, during which the captain of USS *PC 1264* was presented with a model of the buoy. The *1209*'s skipper drew attention to the hazards caused by an ignorance of piloting and expressed the hope that this replica would remind the captain-navigator of USS *PC 1264* what a buoy looked like.

The recipient accepted it with gratitude. He remarked that it would be a constant reminder of the *1209*'s capability in the art. The replica was indeed a very exact model in shape of the nun buoy he had unfortunately struck. It was also correctly numbered "15." But, strangely, it was painted red—odd-numbered buoys moored on the right of a channel when leaving a harbor, are invariably painted black.

Captain Harris, joining in the general laughter that

swept both ships, quickly grabbed the cone-shaped model. Later, he quietly returned it, privately, its identification correct.

At the conclusion of one of their joint patrols, USS *PC 1209*, anxious for once to get back to Tompkinsville first and get the better berth, challenged USS *PC 1264* to a race, wagering a keg of beer.

The challenge was accepted, but the finish was set at the passage through the submarine nets at The Narrows. Charging at flank speed through the lower harbor to the Tompkinsville piers might have raised the eyebrows and undoubtedly the ire of Eastern Sea Frontier brass. As it was, their passage up the swept channel was hair-raising enough, especially as a trans-Atlantic convoy was threading its way to the sea.

It was a challenge of engineroom gang against engineroom gang, and strange and wondrous things were accomplished by Chief Harvey and his men. What they did to make their ship draw gradually ahead, her wake raising great waves that spread to crash against the gargantuan sides of the freighters stolidly coming down channel, bringing the pilots and merchant skippers to lean from the bridge wings and shake their fists at the tiny warships, will probably always remain a secret with the black gang. It has been told that Gibson and Turner, and Randolph and Vanderhoop together got their combined bulk to hold down the governor. At any rate, USS *PC 1264* was ahead by a few yards of USS *PC 1209* going through the narrow opening between the heavy meshed submarine net guarding The Narrows, the wash from their sterns rocking the net tenders and, again, causing, the crews of those anchored vessels to come out on deck and scream unheard imprecations at the crazy Donald Duck sailors.

Past the net, USS *PC 1264* slowed down, her captain relieved that the engines had held; sharing with everyone abroad the exhiliration of victory. USS *PC 1209* maintained her speed longer . . . enough to ensure her choice of a berth at the Tompkinsville Frontier Base.

USS *PC 1264*'s last anti-buzzbomb patrol with her sister ship ended on Wednesday, April 25.

Five days before they left, copies of two officers' dispatch orders were received. One of them brought long-awaited news. Dated that day, April 18, it directed an Ensign Samuel L. Gravely, Jr., USNR, to report aboard for duty, when detached from duty under instruction at the Submarine Chaser Training Center, Miami, Florida. The Special Programs Unit of the Bureau of Naval Personnel had finally come through. Another phase of the experiment would soon begin. USS *PC 1264* had, at last, been assigned a Negro officer.

The other orders were for Lieutenant Will Otto. Well-qualified for his own command, he would now get it, in an exotic setting: USS *YF 1142*, a wooden-hulled New Zealand-built supply ship that carried a variety of commodities between the islands and atolls of the Marshalls in the central Pacific. Until the end of the war, and for six months after, he and his crew of twenty-four—eighteen of whom were Marshallese—would provide the only link in the development by the Foreign Economic Administration of many of the little known islands of America's new United Nations trusteeship.

With Lieutenant Otto's leaving, Lieutenant Ernest V. Hardman would succeed him as executive officer. A trained engineer would therefore be needed to replace him. So, a few days later, the Bureau of Naval Personnel prepared orders for an Ensign Donald G. Morman, USNR. With the arrival of the two new ensigns, the ship would have been overloaded with officers, so, to make room, Ensign Stanley Rhodes would be detached and assigned to the Third Naval District.

During this week in port, the ship also lost Arnett E. Gibson, the ex-Army trooper and motor machinist's mate, who was transferred to shore duty at Lido Beach, Long Island. Older than any of his shipmates, his maturity was a steadying influence, especially as most of the men were in their very early twenties. By custom, the name "The Old Man" belongs to a ship's skipper; at 45, Gibson was "The Ancient Mariner" of USS *PC 1264*. He would be greatly missed.

On Monday, April 23, USS *PC 1264* left Tompkinsville for her last patrol. As she steamed down the channel, through the morning mist, her crew had no inkling that this would not be another routine assignment; seven days from now they should return as they had before, with nothing out of the ordinary to expect, except to welcome some new faces among the ship's company.

She would be gone a little longer. She would go a little farther than the patrol line toward which she now was steaming. She would do a little more than sentry duty on this cruise.

Charleston to New York

The patrol, USS *PC 1264* was assigned, had the code name "Zed." It was the one she had guarded often before, leading north by east for twenty miles from her old friend Buoy "Able." If any German submarine was skulking there when the subchaser reached it at 2:30 that Monday afternoon, she remained cosily nuzzled beside the large marker.

The weather that spring of 1945 was beautiful. As April merged into May, the wind was generally from the southwest, with warmth as gentle as the air that brought it, keeping the waves constant, unbroken. Weather ideal for the comfort of a subchaser with her narrow beam and shallow draft and a coltish tendency to skip and jump in any weather at all. It was ideal, too, for the quarry she hunted; for the clear nights brought a waxing moon, whose fullness would be reached on Sunday, the 29th.

Convoys abhor the full moon on a cloudless night. "Submarine nights," they were called, for the U-Boat had an added advantage: low in the dark water, they were hard to spot visually in the gloom, while the slow, lumbering merchantmen and their guardians were silhouetted sharply against the moonlit sky.

Such nights, though, were pleasant for the USS *PC 1264* on patrol; she had the same danger, but concern only for herself. The calmness of the sea, the brilliance of the sky, the warmth, the knowledge that routine called for seven days on station and five days back in port, made this a yachtsman's holiday at this time of the year. After supper and the movie, the off-duty sections would be on deck; some to sleep in fresher air than in their constricted, blower-ventilated compartments; some to sit and lie on deck and talk; some to join the captain on the signal bridge, and with him mark the stars and name them.

So it was, on this night of Wednesday, April 25. Then, shortly before midnight, the fortunes of USS *PC 1264* changed.

Fifty miles away, a radioman in the headquarters of Eastern Sea Frontier at 90 Church Street, New York City, tapped a message. Simultaneously, the radioman on watch in the PC's radio room recognized the ship's call signal, and began to take down the coded letters.

Ensign Ben Shanker was the officer of the deck. When told of the incoming message, he promptly notified the captain and the communications officer. Ensign Stan Rhodes was awake and dressing, when the messenger came to his cabin, for he was due to relieve Ben at midnight. This would be delayed, because now he would have to break out the ECM—the Electronic Coding Machine—to decode the jumble of letters that Gentle Harvard had interpreted from the stream of staccato dits-and-dahs in his headphones.

Ben was still in the pilothouse when Stan stumbled up the steps with the decoded dispatch. After midnight, with the new watch on duty, the captain had offered to relieve him so he could turn in, but Ben's curiosity was too strong. Incoming messages were a rarity, and certainly meant something out of the ordinary. Ben wasn't about to miss out on it.

The previous watch section felt the same way. Navy custom calls for a man relieving the watch to show up at least a quarter of an hour ahead of time. Not only is it a polite, compassionate gesture, but a practical one, too. It ensures continuity, so he who takes over knows what is going on then, and what can be expected during the next four hours.

The message started coming in, before the change of watch had begun; when the new section came to take over, their strongly curious predecessors remained, cluttering the pilothouse until they were ordered away.

The captain took the English translation from Stan, and left the darkened bridge for the lighted charthouse.

This pleasant, easy patrol was, indeed, over. The penciled words on the scratch pad read: PROCEED IMMEDIATELY CHARLESTON NAVAL SHIPYARD X REPORT PORT DIRECTOR FOR INSTRUCTIONS AND ROUTING OF CHARLESTON SECTION CONVOY KN-382 X ASSUME COMMAND ESCORT GROUP THIS SECTION.

He reached for a pencil and the dividers, and looked at the chart spread across the table. This chart couldn't be used; it was large scale and took in only the waters off New York, Long Island and Northern New Jersey. He spoke into the voice tube to the bridge: "Mr. Shanker, ask the quartermaster to come here, please. And is our course still One Nine Zero?"

Ben's affirmative answer coincided with the automatic blackout of the chartroom, as the door from the bridge opened. Emmett Caul came through. He banged the door shut, bringing the lights back on.

"Caul, I'll need a chart covering the coastline from at least New York to northern Georgia." He turned to the voice tube again. "Ben, check the rough log and see what time we changed course to the leg we're now on."

There was a pause, then Ben's southern voice, sounding almost breathless with anticipation: "Twenty-two, thirty-six, Cap'n." He couldn't help adding, "Where are we going?"

Ben Shanker, affable, good-natured, an easy mark for wardroom humor. The captain was tempted to say, "Londonderry, Ireland," but caught himself in time, realizing other ears were listening. "Charleston, South Carolina, Ben. Nearer your part of the world."

Caul had pulled another chart out of the long table drawer, and transposed the patrol line on it. Quickly, the captain estimated the ship's present position and with the parallel rule, drew a course line from it toward the jutting hump of Hatteras.

Back to the voice tube. "Mr. Shanker, change course to Two Zero One."

"Two Zero One. Aye, aye, sir."

Almost imperceptibly, the ship leaned to the turn.

"Mr. Shanker. All engines ahead standard."

"All engines ahead standard. Aye, aye, sir."

The ship shuddered and subsided with the increase in speed. The captain looked at the clock. It was seven minutes before one A.M.

At the change of course, the ship was almost at the southernmost tip of her patrol line. Steadily she headed through the calm seas, her diesels driving her at fifteen knots. Watch followed watch in uneventful routine, but there was a new feeling among the crew. Patrol was great— a week out and five days in port made it easy to plan for liberties ashore—but it was routine, as indeed nearly everything was routine, even this upcoming convoy. But now, there was a difference. Before, USS *PC 1264* was only one of an escort group. This time she would be the boss of other escorts and the convoy. USS *PC 1264* would give the orders, plan the strategy. Escort commander was her temporary title. But what did that really mean?

Lying on the transom in the wardroom—his sea cabin

when underway—the captain wondered about this. "Charleston section convoy KN-382 . . ." the message read. KN signified a convoy from Key West to New York. The ships now waiting in Charleston would join up with it somewhere, if he got them there safely. *I wonder how many of them there are?*

One?

My God, he thought, *maybe there's only one old tub, and my escort group will consist of USS PC 1264, alone. Some command for the first time as escort commander! . . . Well, what the hell, we'll find out all the details at the convoy conference in the Port Director's office when we get there.* He pulled the blanket up to his chin.

The convoy conference turned out to be a discussion over drinks in the officers' club. The ship had reached the entrance to Charleston harbor at twilight and made her way slowly up the channel, beyond the city to the Navy Yard, past the anchorage where tankers and freighters were lying, bows pointed against the ebbing tide. No indication came from the shore where she should dock and, in the darkness, like a bird ready to nest with its own kind, eased herself alongside two subchasers, moored together to a wharf, and tied up. Her homing instinct was right; this was where she was supposed to be.

A chief petty officer on the deck of the outboard PC called for some of his men to come topside to handle the lines of the incoming ship. "Hurry up, you guys," he yelled. "Here comes a ship full of cooks!"

These two, USS *PC 1149* and USS *PC 1547*, would be the other escorts for the convoy, the captain learned from the duty officer of the *1149*. The convoy conference with all the captains of the merchantmen had been held that morning, and right now an assistant to the port director and the skippers of these two escorts, were waiting for the tardy escort commander, to brief him at the officers' club. "They've been there a couple of hours, Captain," he was advised. "Better get there quick, before they get too sloshed to remember what you ought to know."

"How many ships are we taking?"

"Dunno, exactly. About thirty, I think. They're sitting down there in the stream, waiting. You passed 'em, coming up."

USS *PC 1264*'s assumption of responsibility for an ocean convoy in time of war, was taken in uncustomary informality. At a small table in the farthest corner of the bar, the port director's assistant, a lieutenant commander, transferred a thick Manila envelope. "All the dope's there," he told the neophyte escort commander. "Names of ships and masters, call signals, and rendezvous point for the main convoy."

The other two skippers, Lieutenant J. M. Sheehan of USS *PC 1149*, and Lieutenant Francis H. Brooks of USS *PC 1547*, had attended the convoy conference that morning. It had been cut-and-dried. Nothing much had been reported by intelligence; there had been some submarine activity well north of their course line, but it shouldn't bother this convoy. You never knew, of course, but the possibility was remote. Remote enough for Convoy and Routing to be willing to entrust these thirty merchantmen to the care of only three subchasers. For, God knows, three escorts couldn't put an adequate antisubmarine screen around this number of ships.

The meeting ended with a last bit of advice. "The ships will get underway from the anchorage on a schedule starting about oh-three-hundred. The convoy commodore wants them formed up no later than noon."

Walking back to the wharf with the other two subchaser skippers, the captain knew he wouldn't get much sleep tonight. The ship would have to be underway by seven o'clock; that meant reveille at 0530. It was now after nine o'clock, and there was all the material in this thick envelope to read, digest and remember. He would have to prepare orders for his escorts, basing their positions for maximum protection on the conformation of the merchant-men. No sweat, though; the doctrine was all there in that thick Convoy Bible, locked up in the safe. With thirty ships, they'll probably be formed into a wide, rectangular box of eight columns, with four ships in seven columns and two in the eighth. As escort commander, he thought, I'll cover the advancing line, and place the other *PCs* to screen the port and starboard flanks. And, God, don't let me foul up!

Dawn on Friday, April 27, 1945, was clear and cool. Even before the streaks of light began to outline the head-lands guarding the harbor, the sound of grinding chains, of sudden, indeterminate noises, disappearing as soon as they were made to be succeeded by others, floated across the water from the anchorage. Then, through the gloom was movement; an indistinct, amorphous mass would shift. A hoot, then an answer, cut the still air, spread over the calm water, and another shape would take its place. And with the growing light could be seen the torturous preliminaries of getting so many ships underway, out of safe harbor to the openness of the dangerous sea; there to be formed together into a bloc for their protection—not from nature, but from man.

Charleston harbor is a beautiful refuge, but in common with every seaport in time of war, never seemingly large enough for the simultaneous sortie of the cargo ships, the tankers, the freighters of various sizes and shapes from their safe haven. There was something wondrous about them: their freeboards lowered by the weight of supplies in their bellies, the draft markings on their bows and sterns showing how far below the surface lay their keels; a depth that made an easier mark for only a single torpedo or, if the master and pilot were a wee bit careless in early morning, cause an equally disasterous grounding before they even reached the sea.

The departure of a convoy was the high point of a

voyage. There could be moments of beauty later, when, if the weather was fair and the decks dry, the sight of these ships spread across the water, each placidly plowing ahead through the waves, expressing by their formation the importance of their mission, gave the men on the escorts a sense that what they were doing was really worth while; that their effort to ensure the safe delivery of these cargoes was as important a contribution as anyone could make. And they were doing it.

But these moments were not usual. On a *PC* at sea, there were other considerations of a strictly personal nature: the continual muscular strain of meeting the movements of the ship, the steady pitch and roll. The routine of the watches, the emptiness of the space to the horizon, and even the constant changing of the waves had a dulling sameness, day after day.

The beginning of a convoy voyage, however, compressed into the few early morning hours the drama a young crew expected of a sailor's life. Underway, getting something done. Starting something new. Casting off your own lines from the shore, a gesture of freedom, and with the impudence of a small manueverable vessel, sailing by these squat behemoths, your wake splashing against their sides, leaving them astern to bumble in order down the channel and through the antisubmarine nets at the entrance to the sea.

Yet, there was high romance, too, in these rust-streaked merchantmen. In Charleston, on that morning in April, less than three weeks before the Germans would capitulate in Europe and the Atlantic, were ships from four nations. Eight flew the Red Duster of the British Merchant Navy; there were four Norwegians, one Dutchman and seventeen Americans. One of the Britons, with the name *Empire Chief*, was loaded with high-octane gasoline for her country's Royal Air Force and our own Eighth Air Force; another, the *Fort Lennox*, was destined for Algiers. Others were listed for such places as Naples, Southern France and the Azores. But

now their destination was "North of Hatteras," meaning in
the main, New York, where they could expect to wait again
to be shepherded across the ocean. There was growing hope
that this might be the last. Time was running out for Hitler
in his Berlin bunker, but there was yet no assurance of surrender in his homeland, nor by his kriegsmarine. And there
was still this voyage to complete.

By one thirty in the afternoon, the convoy had formed,
and Commander B. J. Shinn, USN (Retired), the Convoy
Commodore, had signaled from his flagship, the cargo ship
S.S. *Lucius Fairchild*, that all was in order. Base course was
set for the rendezvous point at 32° 28′N., 77° 01′W.; speed
was to be 8 knots. Scheduled time of arrival, to meet the
nine ships from Key West, was noon the next day.

For the next seventeen hours, the Charleston section
of KN-382 headed almost due eastward, USS *PC 1264* patrolling back and forth ahead of her advancing charges, cours-
ing like a foxhound, her sonar pinging a hopefully protective
shield. The air was a warm, pleasant sixty-eight degrees, the
waves were gentle, and the throb of the diesels were even,
throaty, almost musical.

Watch followed watch in orderly routine. The weather
was so fair, the realization that in three days they would be
back home in New York, that all the radio news was hinting
broadly that any day now the Germans would capitulate,
brought an obvious euphoria to the crew. It was noticeable
on the watches, where conversation was officially taboo—
watch standers should concentrate on their jobs. But there
was chatter, and it dealt with the future. Not the immediate
future, the next liberty and the brave plans for feminine con-
quest, but farther on: when the war was over completely,
and each one of them could go home and determine his own
future, his temporary duty to the nation fulfilled.

None felt that life would be the same. It couldn't be.
Look at all the inventions developed under the stress of
war—radar, sonar, the faster aircraft, a host of things; all

would have peaceful, commercial uses, bringing new industry, new opportunities. And look, too, at the numbers of Americans who had had the advantage of training in the military, who could break away from the narrow borders of their prewar lives and constricted chances for betterment. They had learned more than to run a machine, to fire a rifle, to navigate, to speak in code, to tie a knot. They had met and lived with men they otherwise never would have known, and learned their worth.

They were changed and they knew it. They could never settle for the past. Yes, life was good. This war had been terrible—in agony, disruption, ruin. But good would come from it, too. Understanding, tolerance. How could it be otherwise, from so much experience?

Through the first night out of Charleston, under a nearly full moon, the convoy with its three small escorts steamed slowly across the Gulf Stream toward their meeting the next day. Ernie Hardman, the chemist, speculated about the strange new substances wartime research had developed and how it would affect his profession in a peacetime economy. Chadwick mused about the training devices that could change educational methods radically. "Me . . ." said Herbert Jones, Pharmacist's Mate 2/c, "I'm going to medical school." There was much promise in the future.

At dawn, a position report of the Key West section showed it was making better time than expected toward the rendezvous, so, shortly before 6 A.M., the Charleston section made a twenty-five degree change of course to the left to intercept. Four hours later, the "main" convoy of nine merchantmen, escorted by three frigates—USS *Natchez* (PF-2), USS *Poughkeepsie* (PF-26) and USS *Evansville* (PF-70)—USS *PC 1084* and two 110-foot subchasers—USS *SC 1017* and USS *SC 1340*—came over the horizon from the south.

Signal lights blinked across the waves. USS *PC 1264*, her present mission completed, reported to the assigned escort commander for the remainder of the journey. The message was acknowledged with a welcome from Lieutenant Alling Woodruff, USNR, the commanding officer of USS *PC 1084*, and USS *PC 1264* was assigned to patrol the starboard beam of the joining convoys.

Leaning on the Venturi screen of the flying bridge, the captain pondered the vicissitudes of Navy orders, assignments and strategy. Those nine ships that Alling Woodruff had brought from Key West must really be carrying something hot. Nine ships with six escorts!

The same thought occurred to Jarvis Guice, but he put it better. "I guess that shows how good the *PC 1264* is," he said. "We can take care of thirty with three escorts, and *PC*s at that. If we charge off the *PC 1149* for the *1084*, and *PC 1547* for the two SCs, then that makes us better than three frigates!"

In reality, the scheduling of escorts for KN-382 had been governed by many considerations, none of which under wartime operations could be made known to those actually charged with the physical protection of the convoy. All the plans, the orders, the transfer of USS *PC 1264* from her patrol off New York, the *PC*s *1149* and *1547* from other convoys, had been pointed toward the successful meeting of these thirty-nine ships and their forming up for the more hazardous segment of the trip around the hump of Hatteras and the waters off the Virginia and Delaware Capes. Even now, as the thirty ships from Charleston slowly made their way to positions with the nine from Key West to make a larger rectangle on course 060° True, the dispositions of the escorts changed again.

With the arrival of the *PC*s from Charleston, the SCs were detached and sent there. Now the thirty-nine merchantmen were ringed by seven escorts, and would be for another day. The next afternoon, two of the frigates—*Evansville* and *Poughkeepsie*—would themselves leave, and Alling Woodruff would have to rearrange his screen; as he thought then, for the last time.

Aboard USS *PC 1264,* that Saturday afternoon of April 28th, twenty-four minutes were spent in exercising emergency drills. Each hour brought the convoy eight miles closer to its destination, and, unknowingly but inexorably, closer to the event that would mark this convoy in the history of the Atlantic War.

On Sunday morning, with Hatteras safely past, the convoy's course was changed to 352° True, to head for Ambrose Light, three hundred and fifty miles away.

KN-382 was on its last leg of its journey. As the hours passed on Sunday afternoon, April 29, 1945, there was no reason to believe that this would not be as many other convoys had been, and that in two days, USS *PC 1264* would be tied up alongside a berth in Tompkinsville, another routine convoy over, to be forgotten as the others were.

After supper, and before dark, the captain stood in the charthouse, leaning against the chart table writing the night orders in the book kept there. This was an evening ritual for him, as it was for every watch officer during the night to read his words before taking over the duty. These night orders listed everything the captain could think of that the Officer of the Deck should know and what to expect: any prearranged course changes, for instance, or lighted buoys that might be seen. And always his dissertation ended with the admonition that he, the captain, should be called whenever he, the OOD, was unsure about anything that was happening, or if anything not routine was experienced, such as radar sightings of unknown objects, messages and the like. For while the OOD was responsible for his watch, the captain was ultimately responsible for the ship and all she did and happened to her.

The captain finished writing the page for April 29, signed his name and closed the green, cloth-covered notebook. It was approaching sunset and time for him to take his evening star sights. He expected to get some good ones tonight, for the sea was calm and the *1264* was riding through the water as steady as a limousine on a paved highway. The sky was clear, so there'd be a number of stars to shoot. He took the sextant from its mahogany box, cleaned the lens and filters with tissue, then made his way to the signal bridge.

Except in very cold, wet or stormy weather, the watch officer on a subchaser directed the ship from the flying bridge, directly above the pilothouse, giving his commands to the helmsman below through a voice tube. With him would be the lookouts, who doubled as the forward 20mm gun crew, and the duty signalman or quartermaster, ready to man the signal lamps or signal flags if needed. Signalmen and quartermasters were interchangeable on small ships such as this for signal watches. Each of these ratings required proficiency in sending and receiving Morse code.

Emmett Caul, the duty quartermaster, when he saw the captain's head appear above the deck, reached down and took the sextant.

When the captain finished his star sights, he had shot six of the brightest. The horizon had merged into the gloom of the night, making sea and sky one, although shortly the rising moon, in all its fullness, would make the separation clearer again. But six were ample. Three were enough for a fix, if accurately taken. With Caul, he clambered down the ladder to the charthouse to translate the figures of altitude and time to lines on the chart and a position.

When he had finished his computations and drawn the six lines of position on the chart, he was very pleased with himself. Even smug, though tempered with his usual surprise and disbelief that they had worked out at all. The lines met closely enough that he could be somewhat sure of his ship's position. The point he marked on the chart showed that the convoy was keeping pretty much to schedule. He drew a small circle with a pencil around the fix and marked the time.

Admiring his handiwork and savoring the accomplishment, it was perhaps his self-satisfaction that put him into the humor to do what no captain should ever do.

Marking the time of the fix on the chart, reminded him that it was not long before the change of watch. In a few minutes, Ben Shanker would be in this charthouse, to read the night orders, look at the estimated position of the convoy on the chart, and be ready to relieve Ernie Hardman of the deck, and take over the eight P.M., to midnight watch.

Ben, the good-humored fall guy of the wardroom. It was a natural, spur-of-the-moment thing for the captain to do.

With a pencil he marked a small *x* a short distance from the charted course line of the convoy, and drew a dotted line from it to intersect the course line at a point where the convoy should be at 9:30 P.M., almost halfway through Ben's watch. Next to the *x* he wrote the letters "SS"—the abbreviation for submarine.

Then he waited.

At 1945—quarter to eight—on the nose, Ben came into the charthouse, prepared, if not for what the captain had for him, certainly for any change in the weather. Under his arm he carried a thick, woolen sweater and his oilskins. Dumping the sweater and the foul-weather gear on the end of the chart table, he reached for the night order book, with just a short, "Evening, Captain."

The captain grunted, absorbed in a corner of the chart, working his peripheral vision to watch Ben who, with customary thoroughness was studying the page for the night. Finished, he closed the book and carefully put it back on the shelf and moved over to look at the chart.

Here was the moment of truth, the captain thought. He could look at Ben more directly for the reaction that must come. But Ben merely ran his eyes over the sheet, turned and headed up the steps to the pilothouse, grabbing his clothes into a bunch under his arm.

My God, thought the captain. He didn't even see it! An automaton, he's still asleep. But he was wrong.

Ben may not have fully awakened from his pre-watch sleep, but as he reached for the handle of the door to the bridge, his reaction was better than could have been hoped for. It was the ultimate in double-takes.

He stopped suddenly, remained rigid facing the door for at least three seconds, turned, dropped the paraphernalia he was carrying, and came back to the chart table so swiftly that there seemed to be no intermediate motion. He was at the door, then simultaneously he was back at the chart, glaring at it.

His finger rigid on the chart, eyes wide, he demanded, "What's this?"

The captain shifted his weight on the stool and leaned over to have a better look. "What's what, Ben?" His voice was studiously calm.

"This . . ." The finger poked the circle off the course line.

"Oh . . . that!" His voice was indifferent. "That's just something CNO put out this evening on the Fox Schedule. Probably nothing."

"Fox schedule? . . ."

"Continuous radio from Washington. Ships guard the frequency and take down anything that affects them. Don't have to break radio silence to acknowledge."

"And this Fox thing says we have a sub here now?"

The captain hesitated. "There probably isn't," he said honestly, "but there is a *possibility* that there is."

Ben pondered that. There wasn't any evidence of anxiety on his placid face, but when he spoke, his voice betrayed his looks. "When do you want me to call you?" he asked.

"Call me? What for?"

"The submarine. . . . It says 2130, right on that chart."

The captain straightened up, arms outstretched on the chart table, a careless mini-pushup, saying without truth, "It's been a hard day, Ben. I'm going to turn in and have a good night's sleep. You know what to do, if you pick up that sub. Sink it." Then, as an afterthought, "Perhaps, it would be a good idea to notify the escort commander. Just to let him know what you're doing."

The Old Man's had it, Ben was now positive. What the hell do you do when the skipper goes off his rocker? . . . *Navy Regs* ought to have something on this. . . . Ernie should know. Thank God I am relieving him, I can ask him. But I'd better do it where the men can't hear . . . out on the bridge wing, maybe. . . . Ben slowly turned and made for the pilothouse. He was reaching for the doorknob when the captain stopped him.

"Ben!"

He looked back. The captain was grinning like the idiot Ben now knew him to be. He had an eraser in his hand and was vigorously rubbing it on the chart. "Never mind," he said. "I've just killed him, myself."

For a moment, Ben's premedical training made him wonder what the next stage of the captain's lunacy would be: a form of dementia . . . a possibility of violence? Then he realised the truth. Goddam, he thought savagely, I've been had again. He felt a quick surge of anger that ended as it always did, almost immediately, with the relief that there was no problem at all. He opened the door and went through.

Later that night, the two of them were on the flying bridge. The bright, full moon cast a silvered path from the *1264* to the starboard flank of the convoy, the gently rolling waves in constant change of speckling sheen. The bow of the *PC* cut the water, throwing it aside in luminescent folds of phosphorescence. All the ships—escorts and merchantmen —showed no lights, but tonight the wartime necessity of darkened ships was useless as protection. To the westward, where the frigate *Natchez* and USS *PC 1149* guarded the left side of the convoy, an overcast was building up, but from USS *PC 1264*, each ship within view stood clear and sharp in the moonlight against the bright ocean and starlit sky. Two miles ahead, USS *PC 1084,* the escort commander, zigged and zagged on station. Two or three miles astern of the merchant ships, USS *PC 1247* protected the vulnerable rear of the slow-moving phalanx.

The captain always spent a lot of his time on the flying bridge. He liked being there, because it was the center of control of the whole ship. He tried to leave the running of the ship to the Officer of the Deck, but he felt less useless there; he had the sense he was doing something.

He knew that his presence probably inhibited the rest of the watch, for there was much less desultory chatter among the watch standers. Although he knew that discipline called for silence on the bridge to maintain alertness to the individual jobs, he often wished that the historic aura that envelopes the commanding officer—on however small a ship—could be dispelled, so he could better know the men who served with him. The junior officers could do this, and profited from it, as did the men, in understanding, awareness.

The position of captain fostered hesitancy. He sensed the gap and regretted it, but there was nothing he could, nor would, do about it. He was older than they, too. And this increased the gap. But somehow, at night, the daytime protocol was lessened. With evening darkness, inhibitions were also weakened and talk was freer.

"It's about the time," said Ben.

The captain swiveled around on his stool. "Time? What time?"

"For your submarine to show, captain." Ensign Shanker stuck out his arm, showing his wristwatch. "It's 9:30."

The captain grunted. "You know, Ben, that was a hell of a thing for me to do. God knows, I'm Irish enough to know better. Tempting fate, it is." He paused, remembering. "In Ireland, where I went to school, the little people—the leprechauns—delight in casting a spell to make things happen you hope won't."

Ben laughed. "And how long does the spell last?"

"Not long, I hope. Hey, I'd better not say that. I should say a long time, and then the leprechauns will make it short."

But it wasn't long. The Fates, leprechauns, little people, took their revenge.

Five minutes later than the time predicted and marked on the chart of USS *PC 1264*, a German submarine did appear on the course line of KN-382. Specifically, the *U-548*, a 750-ton snorkle-fitted unterseeboat, commanded by Kapitanleutnant Gunther Pfieffer.

To the startled eyes of lookouts on the Coast Guard frigate *Natchez*, patrolling the forward-left quadrant of the convoy, came the sight of a periscope feathering the surface of the sea off their port bow.

Six miles to the eastward, on the other side of the convoy, the watch on USS *PC 1264* saw a white flare burst, and heard the voice of the frigate's OOD splutter over the short-range radio, the TBS: "Submarine sighted off port bow. Am attacking." And the thunder of depth-charge detonations rolled toward them.

Ben Shanker, feeling strangely vindicated, shouted, "You called it, Captain! You called it!"

"Sound general quarters!"

The TBS came alive again. Alling Woodruff, the escort commander, promptly ordered a forty-five degree change of course for the convoy to the right, following the doctrine of turning the convoy away from the danger. *Natchez* was ordered to continue her attacks, and as she was left behind, Woodruff's *PC* steamed to cover her sector, passing the word to USS *PC 1264* to take her place on the starboard bow of the redirected convoy.

At flank speed USS *PC 1264* moved up to her new station. It takes time to move the heavily laden merchantmen of a tightly grouped phalanx onto a new course. And it wasn't until after ten P.M., that they were headed northeast, away from the submarine that had exposed her position.

By then, two hours before midnight, the escorts had regrouped. USS *PC 1084* was screening the convoy's left bow, and USS *PC 1264* was protecting the right. USS *PC 1547* had moved up to the starboard beam in place of *1264*, and USS *PC 1149* had dropped astern.

All the activity was taking place on the port side of the merchantmen, so the *1264* felt rather out of it. She was still at general quarters; her stations were fully manned. Before much longer, she could expect to go back to her regular war cruising condition. But there was something odd about this action—why it had taken place the way it did.

An enemy submarine had been discovered off the bow of an escort vessel. The TBS report had said it was "sighted"— a visual contact, rather than by sonar. The captain and Ensign Shanker took this literally, understanding it to mean the submarine had surfaced. Why? . . . Why had she surfaced close-by the most lethal escort of this convoy, a frigate?

Ben asked the captain. "Damned if I know," was his answer. "All I can think is, the kraut captain wanted to come to periscope depth to take a final look to aim his torpedoes, and his engineer blew too much air into the ballast tanks. So he came up too much."

They thought about this as their ship sped to her new position. It seemed logical, and damn lucky for the convoy. Creeping in undetected, the U-Boat could have raised all sorts of hell and carnage.

Then, suddenly, their conclusions were shattered.

Through the voice tube from the radar room came the voice of George Ware. "Targets bearing dead ahead. Range, seven miles!"

The captain sprang to the voice tube. "How many? Can you tell?"

"They're kind of mixed up—hold it! . . . It looks like three. And, captain, they're closing awful fast."

Dead ahead, and coming toward them rapidly. Their speed plus the speed of the convoy added together on a collision course. How fast were they coming?

"Ben. Time their approach. Get the ranges from radar and find out their speed!" The captain slid down the ladder to the pilothouse, cursing that there was no TBS on the flying bridge. He was almost positive that the escort commander had picked up these bogeys on his own radar at the same time as *PC 1264* had, but he couldn't be positive, and he had to make sure.

In the pilothouse he grabbed the microphone and called a general alert. His message "rogered" he sprang back up the ladder.

Ensign Shanker straightened up from the voice tube. "Look like they're making fourteen knots, captain."

Fourteen knots. Fourteen nautical miles an hour plus about eight that the convoy was doing. That was twenty-two. Less than six miles away, they'd meet in fifteen minutes.

The captain was now sure he knew the reason for that surprising, momentary appearance of a surfacing enemy submarine. A courageous, but well-planned gambit. The German had surfaced deliberately, drawing attention to herself, knowing that the Allied antisubmarine doctrine required an endangered convoy to turn to a course 45° away from the peril.

For what could be fairer game for a so-called Wolf Pack—waiting on the surface for their victims to turn towards them, ready to come full-tilt at the vulnerable merchantmen, guarded only by three small subchasers, whose guns they outclassed now the frigate had been lured away?

A large, slowly moving mass of merchantmen takes time to form up on a new course. It can be a time, too, of self-inflicted hazard, wheeling the lumbering freighters and tankers together without running afoul of each other. The danger was heightened, also, by the preoccupation of these ships in avoiding collisions with their own kind; an immediate peril replacing their watchfulness for any the enemy might cause.

"Mr. Shanker, alert the gun crews for imminent surface action."

Even at this moment, when he felt his stomach tense, a strange constriction across his shoulderblades, and his muscles tighten in an arc around his belly, and he recognized that this was fear, the captain was intellectually struck by the formality of his semantics. Could it have been fear, or rather the wish to hide such human reactions that spawned Jones' "I have not yet begun to fight," or the host of phrases that have eagerly been preserved to build each nation's traditions.

"Ben," he said, "think up something deathless for the history books."

Ensign Shanker understood, as did Jarvis Guice by the signal lamp, Richard Bennett, the bridge talker with his phone; Louis Ellison at the 3"50 gun forward with his crew; Emmett Caul by the 40 mm gun aft and the men by the depth charges; Chief Charles Harvey and his engineroom gang; and none more so than George Ware, crouched before his radar scope, marking the pips as they came closer to the center of the screen.

No orders came from the escort commander. He had been alerted and was now undoubtedly girding for the battle that would come within minutes. To USS *PC 1264,* ahead of the convoy, would be given the honor and distinction of first interception.

USS *PC 1264* no longer was patroling but headed directly at the oncoming targets. Through the tube from the radar came a steady stream of ranges: "Eight thousand yards . . . seventy-five . . . seventy . . ."

"Guice," the captain ordered. "Challenge them! Dead ahead!"

Jarvis Guice bent swiftly and switched on the signal lamp, swung the lamp forward and clattered the Morse of

the single-letter challenge for this segment of the day. All
on the bridge peered through their binoculars for the answer they did not expect to see.

Ensign Shanker, the ship's gunnery officer said quietly,
"Forward gun loaded and ready, captain."

"Six thousand five hundred . . ." came from the radar
room. Three and a quarter miles. What were those shapes
ahead? . . . They couldn't be submarines or, if they are,
they're mighty big ones.

Then a light blinked. "Dah-dah-dit-dah." Q for "Queen."
The memory jingle rang in each officer's and signalman's
head: "No-balls-at-all—Queen."

"Correct reply," said Guice calmly. "Friendly."

The captain leaned back, letting his glasses held by the
leather strap around his neck, drop to his chest.

The leprechauns had taken pity. They'd taught the
captain his lesson. And he learned it. Never again would
he tempt fate—certainly never at sea.

They were friendlies . . . the friendliest ships that KN
382 could have met, especially now.

Task Group 02.10 was a Hunter-Killer Group on the
prowl for just such meat as USS *Natchez* had found. The
three destroyer escorts—USS *Thomas,* USS *Coffman* and
USS *Bostwick*—under the command of Captain G. A. Parkin-
son, USNR, aboard the *Thomas,* couldn't have arrived at a
more propitious time. Quickly they ran down the port side
of the convoy and joined *Natchez* in her hunt.

All night long they stalked the U-Boat, employing every
trick known to antisubmarine warfare. And below the surface, Kapitanleutnant Gunther Pfeffer manuevered his 750-
ton U-548, and tried every trick to avoid his pursuers. He
released *Pillenwerfers,* chemical air bubbles that remain
suspended at the depth, and reflect the sonar waves so the
tracking ships mistake them for the submarine. He, evaded
by quick turns, doubling back, sudden dives and releasing
oil and debris to make the Americans think they'd sunk him.

Gunther Pfeffer was an experienced submariner. In the past two weeks he had sunk three merchantmen, but now it was his turn. At 1:15 in the morning, an attack by USS *Bostwick* resulted in several underwater explosions, but it was not until 4:47 A.M., after an attack by *Coffman*, assisted by *Thomas*, that very heavy explosions, followed by breaking-up noises and the floating to the surface of large quantities of oil, that the death of U-548 could be established.

This was the last submarine action of the war in the Atlantic. But Alling Woodruff and his escorts couldn't know this, and the positive identification of this submarine stretched the nerves and reactions of everyone aboard escorts and merchant ships alike.

At 10:25 on Monday morning, the last day of April, USS *PC 1084* received an echo on her sonar, and promptly attacked with depth charges. Five minutes later, as she attempted to contain this suspected submarine, she sent a message to USS *PC 1264* to take charge of the screening of the convoy.

As the *1264* headed for her new station ahead of the convoy, signal flags fluttered from the masts of the merchantmen, showing an emergency turn to the right was underway.

Then a lookout on board a tanker saw something in the water he thought was a periscope feathering down the space between two columns of the convoy, and gave the alarm. For a while there was cofusion. Two of the merchantmen opened up with their guns and, with the order for another 45° emergency turn to the right putting the ships' columns in disarray, put the ships themselves in added danger from the shells being fired at the bobbing object.

Fortunately, no damage was done—not even to the wooden crate that had caused the excitement—but this wasn't the end.

At 11:30 A.M., with the convoy in order on its new course of 050° and the order about to be given to return to the original course toward New York instead of towards Greenland, another suspicious object was spotted—this time the jettisoned wing tank of an aircraft, glinting in the sun as it floated almost submerged between the ships.

Again, the armed guard crews aboard the merchantmen opened fire, and again the convoy was ordered to make another emergency turn.

At long last, with the identification of the wing tank and no damage done, calm came again to KN-382 and she was turned back to her northerly course and the end of her voyage a day later.

Ensign Ben Shanker had been OOD during this Donnybrook, too. When it was over, he asked the captain, "Can you hear that?"

"What?"

"Those chuckles coming over the water. Sounds Irish to me."

Decommissioning the PC 1264 at Tompkinsville, Staten Island, New York on February 7, 1946. The officers are (left to right) Ensigns H. E. Kohler, D. G. Maxwell, William L. Fanning, Jr., Samuel L. Gravely, Jr., and Lieut. (jg) Jack W. Sutherland

Seven

A Black Officer Reports

The evening of Wednesday, May 2, 1945, was softly warm. Supper was over. Everything was quiet. The liberty party had gone ashore.

Ensign Ben Shanker was alone in the wardroom. He was bored. It was too nice a night to be stuck aboard, but there wasn't anything he could do about it; he was the duty officer.

He switched on the radio and played with the dial for a few moments, but the music from the New York stations only added to his feeling of Fate's injustice. He wandered out on deck, and leaned on the rail. In the deepening twilight, the lights of Manhattan across the bay were beginning to glow; the Bowery with its ferry landing was hidden by the end of Pier 6 on the other side of the slip, but Ben could imagine those luckier than he leaving the sidewheelers and disappearing into the ground to the subway.

He heard footsteps on the steel deck. He turned, straightening. Emmett Caul, the gangway watch, preceded a tall, young Black in an ensign's uniform.

"Mr. Shanker." Caul was even more cheerful than usual. His voice and face reflected both enjoyment and pride at the announcement he was to make. "Ensign Gravely reporting aboard, sir."

The ensign came to attention and saluted. "Ensign Sam-

uel L. Gravely, Junior, United States Naval Reserve, reporting for duty, sir," he said formally.

Ben Shanker stuck out his hand. "Welcome aboard.
Have you had chow?" The other nodded, and Ben went on,
"Come on into the wardroom. I'll show you where you'll
bunk. . . . Am I glad to see you!"

How pleased Ben Shanker was to see Sam Gravely was
soon apparent to the latter. In later years, increasingly important assignments would be given him, but command responsibility was never given him as quickly as aboard the
first ship he served in.

"Okay," said Ensign Benjamin Shanker, ten minutes
after Ensign Gravely had first set foot aboard USS *PC 1264*.
"You sure arrived at the right time. I've got a date ashore.
So you have the duty."

Ensign Samuel L. Gravely's assignment to USS *PC 1264*
was a natural extension of this naval experiment. A black
crew had been assembled aboard a small ship to see if they
could operate it. They could, and without any of the dire
results so gloomily forecast. There had been no excessive
disciplinary problems; the black petty officers had shown
they could be leaders, fulfilling their responsibilities as well
as those of any other ship; the shibboleths of racial inferiority
were scientifically doubtful. As a demonstration, USS *PC
1264* had already provided an important example of human
similarity; certainly there were differences, but these differences were individual, of culture, of the environment in
which they had been raised, of past opportunity—or lack—
for adequate education, and obtaining a job commensurate
with their skill and training. But these differences were
present aboard other ships too, whose crews, except for the
stewards mates and cooks, were white.

When Ensign Gravely came aboard, he was twenty-two
years old. He had attended Virginia Union University in his
home town of Richmond, Virginia, but had enlisted in the
Navy before receiving his degree; he postponed this until

after the war. He had been among the first recruits at Camp Robert Smalls, Great Lakes, and then trained to be a machinist, attending the Navy's engineering school at Hampton Institute.

As a Fireman first class (F1/c) he was assigned to the Naval Section Base, San Diego. For three weeks after his arrival, his training as an engineer was used to ensure that the barracks were washed down every day, well swept and sanitary. In May 1943 he was promoted, and for five months he was put in charge of the pool hall of the Welfare and Recreation Department, maintaining the tables, collecting the five-cent charge for their use, racking the cues and balls, lucky in the responsibility that was his.

The program for commissioning Negroes had been approved, so in October, he was selected to be a V-12 student at the University of California at Los Angeles. This was a program for potential officers to complete at least three years of college—a requirement for a commission. Sam Gravely needed two semesters to fulfill this necessary prerequisite, so he was at UCLA from November until June, 1944. Then he was transferred to the Pre-Midshipman School, Asbury Park, New Jersey, to take a two-month course. Appointed a midshipman, USNR, in August 1944, he was sent to Columbia University to work for his commission as a Naval Reserve ensign.

He became an officer on November 14, 1944.

His first assignment as an officer was a two-month stint as a battalion commander, training Negro recruits at the Great Lakes Training Center, where he had taken his own "boot training."

He knew his life as an officer would be different from that of an enlisted man, but he never expected his new status would cause such difficulty as he now experienced. A seaman's life is circumscribed by the Establishment; he is assigned a bunk in a barracks; he is fed regularly in a mess hall. But an officer is on his own. This was no problem for

a white junior officer in 1944. He could check in at the Bachelor Officers' Quarters and eat at the Officers' Club.

But not Samuel L. Gravely, Jr., the first black reserve
ensign to be commissioned from an ROTC. And, if it was
impossible for him to find a room or a meal on the naval
base, it was nearly so in the surrounding civilian community.

His enforced loneliness, the long commute back and
forth to the drab, uncomfortable room which was the best
he could rent, were far from pleasant, but fortunately this
period was short-lived. The Special Programs Unit in BuPers
at last decided to give USS *PC 1264* her oft-requested Negro
officer. In February 1945, Ensign Gravely was transferred
to the Submarine Chaser Training Center, with orders to
report to the subchaser upon completion of his three-month's
training.

He had studied diesel engines at Hampton Institute at
the same time as Gibson, Turner, Means and Ike Davis. Gibson had left the ship when Ensign Gravely arrived, but the
other three were still aboard. At Hampton, they had known
him as "Sam." Now, he was "Mr. Gravely."

Last Convoy

The other expected officer, Ensign Donald G. Morman,
arrived an hour and a half before the ship put to sea for
convoy patrol on Monday, May 7. He had been drafted into
the Navy in April, 1944, five months after graduating from
the General Motors Institute in Flint, Michigan. After boot
camp, he had been sent to Midshipman's School at Notre
Dame University, and after commissioning, to the General
Line School in North Hollywood, Florida. Strangely, for a
subchaser officer, he had not attended SCTC. Moreover, he
had not been required to volunteer for *PC 1264* duty; he had
no inkling that she was a predominantly Negro ship until he
reported, two days after his twenty-fifth birthday.

Officers' Country was now decidedly crowded. Lieutenant Otto had been detached on May 3—there had been a farewell party for him and for Ensign Rhodes at the Harlem Defense Recreation Center that night—but Stan Rhodes' orders hadn't arrived by the morning of May 10, when the ship left with a convoy to Key West. With six officers, she was loaded.

But it was helpful, too. Every new officer coming to a ship, before he can stand a deck watch underway alone, has to be qualified by the captain to do so. The captain, obviously, must be confident that the officer of the deck can handle the responsibility of the ship, and the lives of those in her, under any sort of emergency. The method the *1264*'s skipper used was to stand each new officer's watches with him until he was satisfied, observing his reactions, his orders to the bridge, the way he maintained discipline; generally, how well he performed. It was on-the-job training. With two new officers aboard, the executive officer was relieved of watch-keeping duties, and with the captain helped with the training and qualification of Ensigns Gravely and Morman.

Sharing the watch with Ensign Gravely, the captain was impressed by the added smartness of his watch section. The crew was immensely proud that a man of their race had achieved commissioned rank, and it was obvious that, in their eyes, he could do no wrong. It was also apparent he had done his homework at midshipman's school and the Submarine Chaser Training Center; he seemed to have no trouble in putting the theory of the duties and responsibilities of an O.O.D., underway into practice; in fact, he was more "regulation"—more spit-and-polish Navy—than most officers on small ships.

His ability, the way he conducted himself as an officer, was appreciated by the crew . . . to a point. And that point was reached when the inevitable happened. A man was caught by Ensign Gravely doing something he shouldn't, and was promptly and properly placed on report. A Captain's Mast followed, and the miscreant received his just punishment.

It was nothing out of the ordinary, but a few of the men felt they had been betrayed. Their Man was part of the Establishment. Some bitter words were spoken in the privacy of the crew's mess and living compartments; thoughtless words that the more mature petty officers countered with unemotional reasoning and calm argument. It was a short-lived phase and part of the continuing learning process life aboard USS *PC 1264* for both whites and blacks.

The convoy was numbered NK-686 and started from New York with twenty-seven cargo ships and tankers. The war in Europe had officially ended the day before, and the day before that, on May 8, General Eisenhower's Naval Deputy, Admiral Harold R. Burrough, RN, had issued an order for all German submarines to surrender; they were to surface, fly a large black flag and await escort to an Allied port.

To escort a convoy now seemed rather pointless, but Commander Eastern Sea Frontier wasn't taking any chances with the possibility of a fanatic U-boat skipper deciding against surrender. It was a sensible decision, for two such submarines were in the Atlantic, *U-530* and *U-977*. Neither did any damage and eventually made their way to Argentina.

When USS *PC 1264* heard about the order for surrender, her captain vainly tried to get the ship assigned to accept a surrender and escort the submarine of the late Master Race to port. The idea smacks too much of a public relations stunt, he was told. "That's just the point," the skipper agreed.

This last coastal convoy headed south. At six in the evening of May 11, fifteen ships came out of Chesapeake Bay and joined up. Two days later, four ships left to go into Charleston, and on the 14th, two more went to Savannah and Jacksonville.

Then at eight o'clock in the morning of May 15, Eastern Sea Frontier was confident that danger from diehard Nazis was over, and the convoy was ordered dispersed.

The escort ships, USS *Fury* (*PG 96*), USS *PC 1085*, USS *PC 1219*, USS *PC 1264* and USS *PC 1265*, were told to continue on together to Key West for a week's training and then return to New York.

It was early afternoon when the escort ships of Task Unit 2.9.10 came singly through the entrance to Key West harbor. A signal lamp blinked from the roof of the Naval Base Administration building. It was addressed to USS *PC 1264* and requested that the commanding officer report to the base commander on arrival.

The ship secured from special sea detail at one minute before two o'clock. The captain climbed down from the flying bridge, changed into a clean uniform and started trudging up the hill.

The commanding officer of the Naval Base was a Regular Navy captain. He came right to the point.

"I understand," he said, "you have a Negro officer on board your ship."

"Yes, sir."

"Will he be using the Officers Club?"

"Yes sir, I presume so. In fact, sir, I expect that all my officers and I, except, of course, for the duty officer, will have dinner there tonight."

The captain was silent for a moment. Then he said, somewhat hesitantly, "Do you think that is wise?"

"Wise, sir? . . . I don't think I understand."

"I think you do, Captain. This is a southern town. We've got a lot of southern officers. Mind you, I don't condone this. But, what if one of them tonight has . . . er, perhaps a little too much to drink, and takes exception to a Negro eating—and even drinking—in the club? There might be trouble."

"Sir," the lieutenant answered, "whenever the *1264* reaches port, it's sort of S.O.P.—standard operating procedure—that at least for the first night in, all the officers usu-

ally have dinner together. We'll do this tonight. . . . As
for any officer who might make trouble—I'll be there, my
officers will be there, and so will the officers of our task
unit, with whom we've operated before, and are our friends.
I assure you, sir, that if anybody—or even two or three—
are stupid enough to start anything, it will be over in a couple of seconds."

The captain smiled. "Pretty sure of that?"

"Yes, sir. Definitely."

"Very well." He rose and held out his hand. "You take
the responsibility. I don't want to hear of any trouble. Good
luck!"

Goddam, the subchaser skipper thought, as he walked
down the steps of the building to the street, this Key West
sure is a festering boil on the ass of civilization. I guess,
though, I'd better take care of this little matter.

He turned from the way back to the ship, and walked
on to the Officers Club.

The club officer-in-charge was a young lieutenant. He
was found behind the bar, checking the number of bottles
decorating the glass shelves. "Hi," he said affably. "What
can I do for you?"

The skipper explained. "I'm C.O. of a *PC* that's just arrived. My officers and I want to have dinner here tonight.
One is a Negro."

"Fine! . . . Hope the food's okay. As a matter of fact,
we've got a new shipment of steaks. Recommend 'em; it's
my job to." He grinned.

The captain repeated. "One of the officers is a Negro."

"So? . . ." the lieutenant seemed genuinely unim-
pressed. "He's an officer, isn't he? . . . This is an officers'
club. We've got all sorts of officers—American, French, sometimes some Limeys, and even Italians now—former enemies.
We cater to them all. Matter of fact, the Frenchies have been
good for the club; they've scared the cooks into putting out
better chow. Which reminds me, we've got pompano on the

menu tonight. Try it—or the steak. Both good, I promise."

"Thanks."

Before liberty started that evening, the captain went into the wardroom for the opening gambit of the S.O.P. The eight-by-twelve foot room seemed small with all six officers in it at once.

"Who's got the duty tonight?" he asked.

Stan Rhodes answered, "Unfortunately, I have."

"Okay," said the captain. Sam Gravely and Ben Shanker were standing by the pantry service table. "Then let's the rest of us head up, in about half an hour, to the club and a drink that I trust is the first any of us has had in six days."

"Fine," agreed Ernie, Ben and Don. Sam Gravely said nothing, but continued pouring a cup of coffee from the urn.

The captain tried to be casual. "Sam, I hope you can come. The chow's pretty good."

"Thanks." Ensign Gravely looked and sounded thoroughly candid. "I'd like to, sir, really. But—" he went on hurriedly—"not tonight. You see, Captain, there's a young lady I met when I was at SCTC who lives here. I've been looking forward to seeing her again, and I've already made a date with her. So . . ."

Was this true? Or was Ensign Gravely trying to forestall possible unpleasantness at a white officers' club, and save himself and his brother officers the resulting embarrassment? . . . What can I say? the captain thought desperately. How can I get it across to him how much we want him to come with us? . . . But how can I doubt him? He probably has a girl here, and who's to blame him for preferring her company to ours? I sure as hell won't interfere. "I'm sorry, Sam," he said.

Sam smiled. "Thanks anyway, Captain." His smile widened "I'm not sorry, sir. I've been looking forward to tonight for a long time."

The captain believed him. It wasn't until much later that he discovered his first hunch was right.

Preparations for the Pacific

The war in Europe was won; there was still another war to finish. Half a world away, the Allies were crawling up the outer islands toward the home islands of Japan. For over a month, the bloody battle for Okinawa had raged; another month and a half would have to pass before it was captured, at the cost of 12,520 American and more than 111,000 Japanese dead. Thirty-six ships, none larger than a destroyer, were sunk by fanatical Kamikaze pilots guiding their planes to certain self-destruction.

In Washington, the Joint Chiefs of Staff were putting the final touches to the plan for an expected final assault against Japan. The target date for the invasion of southern Kyushu was set for November 1.

The fierceness of Japanese resistance was shown at every step along the island chain. None doubted that before the Japanese capitulated, casualties would be overwhelming. But similarly there was no doubt about the ultimate outcome. The Allies would win. The only question was, when?

During the calm and peaceful nights in Key West, after a day in the Florida Straits with the task unit, practicing more than antisubmarine exercises, but others they well might use far away—shore bombardment, antiaircraft defense, and fueling at sea—the men would sit and lie topside on the decks and talk.

In the darkness there was a certain anonymity, although by now, each knew the others' voices by intonation and speech pattern, from the Geechee dialect of one young Georgian to the clipped New England accent of the ship's lone Wampanoag Indian.

Now, they spoke of going home, or where they might live, and what they would do. There was talk of emigration; they had read that Brazil was a land of opportunity, with no racial prejudice. New York, from their experiences there, seemed more hospitable than some of the places they had lived and grown up in. And there was talk of everything else, too; usually of women, both serious and jocular talk, and at least at one time a combination of the two. In the darkness, under a cloudless sky, with the stars bright and filling the heavens, one voice spoke tenderly of his girl and how they had watched the stars one night like this in Central Park. "Perhaps," he said, ardently, "tonight she's watching these same stars." "I guess she is," another answered, "if she's flat on her back again."

They talked of the immediate future. What the ship would do, now the Atlantic War was over. "Pearl Harbor, here we come," said one. "Knock off that Harbor stuff," another answered. "It's 'Pearl, here I come,' back to Jersey City." They knew whom he meant.

Where the ship would now be deployed was of natural and consuming interest. There was no reason to keep her on the east coast of the United States, no justification not to let her go to an active war zone. The scuttlebutt was that the Naval Frontier Base had changed to a shipyard, that all the escort ships would be extensively overhauled, remodeled and outfitted; their armament changed to more modern weapons, that the *PCs* would be converted to *PGMs*—gunboats—with thicker steel covering the superstructure; that when this was done, they would be sent directly to the western Pacific, to act as radar picket ships to spot and hopefully stop the human bombs—the Kamikazis—or to act as decoys for the Japanese shore batteries during island invasions and, eventually, the coast of Japan, whose positions could then be revealed to the guns of the mightier ships offshore.

These rumors were partly true, as USS *PC 1264* and the other ships of Task Unit 02.9.10 saw, when they returned to Tompkinsville, the afternoon of Friday, May 25.

They had left Key West on Tuesday and steamed together at fifteen knots back to their home port. In the early afternoon of Friday, as they approached Staten Island, blinker messages told each ship where to moor. USS *PC 1264* was to go to the south side of Pier 7, between berths 6 and 7.

Assignment was necessary, as the ship could see long before she reached the pier. Thickly clustered tops of masts jutted above and between the roofs of buildings on the wharves. Every other Tompkinsville ship must have already returned.

Slowly, carefully, USS *PC 1264* turned into the slip between Piers 7 and 8. Subchasers were nested three and four abreast on each side; there was scarcely enough room for her to pass, and be the fourth *PC* at her allotted, numbered berth.

Yoeman Paul Davis was the mail clerk, too. Before the lines had been secured to USS *PC 1549*, he jumped across the narrowing distance, his leather pouch over his shoulder. His was always the first, most important errand on reaching port; his return always the most eagerly awaited—for personal mail, of course, but he also picked up official mail. Today, the captain wondered if he would bring the word of this ship's future.

He didn't. Then the weekend came, but there was little mail expected. Then Monday.

The first day of the week brought the usual slew of strangely useless notices—modifications to allowance lists of battleships and cruisers, safety precautions in operating aircraft catapaults, and changes in the channel buoys off Attu, Alaska; the only important official message was the orders for the transfer of Ensign Stanley W. Rhodes.

All the other submarine chasers knew what their future was, and their decks were busy with activity. Their K-guns, that could fire the 300-pound depth charges from the sides, were being removed, their 20-mm machine guns to be replaced by twin-barreled guns of the same caliber. Ships were leaving for, and returning from, drydock. And, in the middle of them all was USS *PC 1264*, untouched, forgotten.

"I've no idea what's planned for you," the base operations officer said. "We've had no word."

It was the same at Eastern Sea Frontier headquarters across the bay. But there, a chilling, insupportable possibility was raised. "I honestly don't know," the captain was told. "Maybe you'll be decommissioned."

Outraged, the captain called the special programs unit in Washington. "I'm coming down to see you. Something has got to be done. This is the biggest kick in the teeth we've ever had. It's pretty goddam obvious why we are the only ship doing nothing. . . . I'll see you tomorrow. Set me up with someone—anyone—who can get us out of here. . . . Ernie King, I'll see him. Dammit, the war's not over yet. . . ." He hung up.

He took the train that night and was one of the first to enter the Bureau of Naval Personnel building the next morning.

The special programs unit was sympathetic, as always. "We'll work on it," they told him, "but, frankly, the feeling among the Ops guys is that they don't want to saddle Nimitz with any racial problems—"

"Racial problems! What the hell are they talking about? . . . What 'racial problem' is the *1264*? . . . God—" He stopped. "Who told you that? I'll change his mind."

He wasn't told. He might have met him, for he saw a number of officers who worked for the Chief of Naval Operations; none of whom professed any power in detailing such an insignificant ship as a *PC*—nor, indeed, any interest. He was so dispirited by late afternoon that he was easily cowed by the Administrative Aide to Fleet Admiral Ernest J. King, USN, and left to catch the earliest train back; ashamed, angry at himself for his ineptness, his ignorance of how to achieve agreement to such a simple, understandable, necessary request.

As he walked down the dock the next morning, and climbed over the intervening ships to his own, he saw that his men were waiting for him, lined along the rail and packed by the gangway. Some of them, he knew, thought he was nuts to try and take them where danger was more certain, but he knew, too, that they honored his reasons. Their faces were impassive, grave, grimly concerned.

"How did you make out, Captain?" Someone asked.

He shook his head. "I didn't," he answered, and went into the wardroom.

He was asked the same question by Lieutenant Hardman for all the officers who were also waiting for him there. And the answer was the same.

Elmer Bradford, the tall, thin, Cook Third Class from Arkansas, who had run the officers' pantry since the day of commissioning, silently put a cup of coffee and a plate of cookies on the table at the captain's place.

"What do you think we'll do from now on?" Ensign Shanker asked.

"Who knows? . . ." was the answer. Slowly he began to tell them what he had tried and failed to do. "Perhaps," he added, "we'll have Tompkinsville all to ourselves."

There was a knock. Ensign Gravely, being next to the door, swung it open. A messenger from the base handed him an envelope. "A dispatch, sir, from Base Communications."

Sam passed it to the captain. He slit it open with his coffee spoon.

"I'll be goddamned . . ." he said softly. He looked up. "Listen to this. *'From Chief of Naval Operations. To USS PC 1264. When in all respects ready for sea, and when directed by Commander Eastern Sea Frontier, you will proceed to Norfolk, Virginia, and report to Commander-in-Chief, Atlantic Fleet, for training. Upon completion of refresher training, you will proceed via Canal Zone and report to Commander-in-Chief, Pacific Fleet.'"*

He looked at them, relishing the pleasure, the sense of vindication, they shared with him.

"Ernie," he told the executive officer, "call the men to quarters. They should hear this. We may be the last to get our orders. But, by God, we'll be the first ready to go."

The captain apparently enjoyed being dramatic. He could bravely promise USS *PC 1264* would be the first subchaser to leave Tompkinsville for the Pacific, but his ship had to overcome a two-week headstart by the other sub-chasers. Not that most of them expressed any great rush to leave the hospitality of New York for an uncertain future, but there were just so many workmen the Naval Frontier Base could assign to the overhaul and outfitting of so many ships. Some of the work could be done—and was expected to be—by the ships' companies themselves, but there were schedules to be followed for the removal of ammunition, engine overhaul and drydocking the vessels to refurbish their bottoms. With so many ships, all to be worked on at once, the short-handed base engineering and ordnance departments had a mammoth job to do.

Structural changes to the ship began June 12, with the removal of the K-guns from the afterdeck. Seven weeks later, on Tuesday, July 31, all work was completed and the ship left for Norfolk, ahead of most of her sister ships.

In the meantime, as much leave as possible was taken. All were sure that this was their last opportunity for some time, so a generous timetable was made up. The minimum number of men needed, remained, awaiting their turn to go or, after coming back from home, working on the ship's refitting and going to the ever-scheduled classes on the base and at the Navy Yard in damage control, firefighting, gunnery, antisubmarine warfare, and the rest. And they continued to savor the delights of liberty in the evening in New York and Jersey City.

Well past one midnight, two gunner's mates and a quartermaster—Ellison, Bennett and Cork—returned from liberty. They were not particularly quiet coming aboard, but the gangway watch didn't hear them, for, contrary to all rules and regulations and indeed—being wartime—committing one of the most serious offenses, he was slumped in his chair, gently snoring. To make himself more comfortable, he had loosened the belt holding the .45 pistol, so its holster sagged to the deck.

Technically, Ellison should have awakened him, put

him under arrest for sleeping on watch, assigned another
to this sentry duty, and reported his action to the duty officer. This would have started a series of events, beginning
with a Captain's Mast and ending with a general court martial; the possible punishment, death by firing squad, probably
would not have resulted, but it would have been a messy
business. Ellison had another idea; the punishment might
not have fitted the crime by regulations, but it had a con-
structive effect upon the offender.

Quietly and carefully, he withdrew the .45 from the
holster. Beckoning to Bennett and Cork to follow him, they
went behind the deckhouse. "Get off the ship," he told them,
"and come back aboard. Make enough noise to wake him
up. Give him a little jazz, if you like, about being asleep on
watch, if he isn't awake by the time you cross the gangway.
But don't—and I mean, *don't*—notice that he hasn't his
weapon. Okay?"

Ellison, as the leading gunner's mate, was responsible
for the small arms locker. Keeper of its key, he held each
petty officer of the watch strictly accountable for the .45
issued. Before the change of watch, the seagoing Rip van
Winkle woke Ellison.

He was apologetic. "I need a .45," he said, "to turn over
Wheeler, who's relieving me." He went on, "A few minutes
ago I had to fix one of the mooring lines, and the gun fell
into the drink."

Ellison got up and gave him a replacement. "See me
after quarters, this morning," he said.

Following the morning muster, Ellison handed him a
grappling hook and line. "Find that pistol by noon," he
ordered.

For three and a half hours he dragged the waters between his ship and the *PC* to which she was tied, in an effort of futility he thought he alone knew, his conscience be-
deviling him. Urged on by his shipmates, who were in on
the hoax, he was advised, criticized for his grappling tech-

nique, their imaginations limitless in what he could expect if he didn't find what he was supposedly looking for.

At last, Ellison led him away and told him the truth in a short but serious lecture. He was never found ever dozing again, on duty.

During these two months in port, Ensign Gravely's relationship with the white officers was friendly but formal. His quick wit and sense of humor were welcome additions to the wardroom; a good athlete himself, and because of his rapport with the crew, he was able to organize the ship's sports, and field teams to be reckoned with in the subchaser leagues. But there was hesitancy to discuss racial problems intellectually in conversation, unless some incident had occurred ashore—group therapy had not yet been invented. They were all still too sensitive of each other's feelings to confront them head on. On board, the problems didn't exist.

Away from the ship, the white officers were often the butts of remarks, such as "Here comes the colored section of the Navy," but they took them good-humoredly, for actually, rarely, were they said with real spite, but rather in a curiosity born of ignorance, phrased in mistaken humor. And their own color was protection.

But there was always this possibility of embarrassment, of a disagreeable occurrence in the white society of naval officers, and Ensign Gravely stayed away from it. As an officer, he was not supposed to associate socially with enlisted men, but in this time of history, he was much more at ease with a number of the intelligent, well-educated men in the crew. With them, his race didn't set him apart; he could relax without strain.

Liberty—the term for time off, away from the ship—is semantically exact. It is freedom—from the confinement of small compartments, from the constrictions of military discipline, from the absence of female companionship. How an individual spends his liberty is a personal matter, or should be.

In the anonymity of New York, an officer with an enlisted man was unnoticed.

It was different elsewhere.

On Tuesday, July 31, USS *PC 1264* set off to win the Pacific war. In the words of the CNO orders, she "was ready in all respects for sea," even to the initially mysterious enlargement of her peak tank hatch. The peak tank, a triangular hold, formed by the bow, and running from the main deck down to the keel, was originally designed to hold extra water for extended voyages. Its hatch had been a manhole, but now it was a large, square, hinged covering. Questioned about this, the base engineer had said, "It's for your supplies when you get beyond civilization. How the hell could you load cases of beer or whisky through that manhole?"

The ship tied up to a berth on the port side of Pier F of the Naval Operating Base, Norfolk, after a voyage of nineteen and a half hours, shortly after noon on August 1.

The sole purpose of her stop in Norfolk was to be inspected by Commander, Service Forces, Atlantic Fleet. He wasted no time. One hour after the ship's arrival, a Lieutenant Sarcone came aboard, and for an hour and ten minutes, he looked through the ship and observed a number of emergency drills. The following morning at 9:45, a group of officers, led by a Lieutenant Commander Scheveizer from ComServLant's flagship, USS *Nourmahal*, made a personnel inspection of the crew on the dock, and then went through the ship, checking each department's records and the condition of the compartments. It was a methodical, thorough, but swift inspection. They were finished by 11:00 A.M.

Officers and men were in their dress white uniforms for the inspection. They were scheduled to leave for Miami at around four o'clock in the afternoon, so, in the meantime, with the ship and her crew looking their best, the fleet photographer took a number of pictures; then it was back to khakis and dungarees, and to be off on the next leg of their journey.

The voyage to Miami took nearly two and a half days.

An hour and a half after midnight, on Sunday morning, August 5, 1945, USS *PC 1264* arrived at the Submarine Chaser Training Center's Pier 2.

The schedule called for ten days' training; a concentrated refresher in all subchaser operations. The ship was going to a different kind of war; one that could be expected to reach a crescendo of ferocity before it was over. Captain Mac was no longer at SCTC. He had managed to get himself back to the shooting war, and was now serving as executive officer of a cruiser, USS *Biloxi,* with a fast carrier task force in the Pacific. But his successors at SCTC carried on his traditions, and wanted to be sure USS *PC 1264* was prepared for that war, too.

She didn't stay ten days; she remained only five. The reason was an incident that occurred on the night of the day they arrived.

Sunday was quiet and hot. When the time for liberty came around, the captain, Ensign Shanker and Ensign Morman, left to go swimming.

"We'll be at the Tatum Hotel," the captain told Lieutenant Hardman, who had the duty. "If we go anywhere else for dinner, I'll leave word at the desk."

Ensign Gravely and Louis Ellison went ashore together. Having spent two months training at SCTC, which he had completed only three months before, Ensign Gravely was considered to be the most up-to-date authority on Miami and such pleasures as were available to Blacks. His advice had been sought by the crew, which he gladly provided, suggesting a small restaurant where they might meet.

It was early evening. The restaurant was doing a land-office business as the rendezvous for the men of USS *PC 1264;* they would come in, perhaps stay for a while, have a couple of drinks and move on. Nothing had been planned further; it was merely a place where they knew some of their shipmates would be. And conspicuous by his uniform as an officer was Ensign Gravely.

He, Ellison, and two others from the ship were seated

at a table. They had ordered dinner and were waiting for
it, when a fight started. Someone leaning back in his chair
was upended by another. The restaurant manager promptly
called for the shore patrol.

By the time the military police arrived, calm had returned. Two came in, a soldier and a sailor, their armbands
and truncheons their badges of office. Another, a Navy chief
petty officer, stayed in the patrol wagon outside. Caucasians,
they undoubtedly were ill at ease and nervous, surrounded
as they were by so many black faces; humanly, they covered
their insecurity with truculence.

By the door they paused, looked the room over and
saw a Black in an officer's uniform. Impersonating an officer
is a Federal offense. The MP walked over, leaving the SP
by the door.

Instead of asking for identification, or bringing in the
shore patrol chief petty officer, he said to Ensign Gravely,
"The chief wants to see you."

Ensign Gravely thought he meant Chief Charles Harvey. By protocol, his answer was correct in this case, too.
"If the chief wants to see me, tell him to come here," he
replied.

There are a number of possible explanations for why
the MP did what he did; none of them an excuse. He reached
down and pulled Ensign Gravely out of his chair. "Come
with me," he ordered.

The reaction of the subchaser's men who saw this was
immediate. If the MP had been nervous before, he had reason to be terrified now.

"Take it easy!" Ensign Gravely shouted. "This is only a
mistake." And to the MP, "Okay, let's go."

Outside, the word had gone out, up and down the
street, that Ensign Gravely had been arrested, and USS *PC
1264* men, in various stages of sobriety, had decided they
wouldn't let this happen. The shore patrol sailor, who had
entered the restaurant with the soldier, had ducked out as

soon as his companion had triggered the outburst, and the chief petty officer in the wagon had promptly radioed for reinforcements.

They arrived—two more paddy wagons. As they drove up, Ensign Gravely was desperately trying to calm his men. He explained it was a mistake, and that he was going down to the shore patrol headquarters and clear the matter up. He might have succeeded, if the shore patrol reinforcements had arrived as little as two minutes later. But they didn't, and with true riot control tactics, as soon as the trucks came to a halt, the doors were thrown open and the sailors herded into them.

It was fast and it was efficient. Every sailor but one was enclosed. Ensign Gravely, resigned, got into the chief's wagon, and the cortege with its prisoners sirened off to the shore patrol headquarters in the main police station downtown.

The one sailor who got away was Occonnar Young, the cook. As most cooks, he was not built for speed, but in an emergency he did very well. And this was an emergency. He must have covered the distance to Pier 2 in record time.

The *PC*'s men had been gathered up by the military police, but it didn't mean that all of them reached their expected destination. Halfway to the police station, one paddy wagon slowed for a turn. Jarvis Guice had managed to unhitch the bar holding the doors; the enclosed found freedom.

Whenever a liberty party of USS *PC 1264* got into trouble, Emmett Caul had the gangway watch. It had been so in Key West, six months before, when the Coast Guard had been difficult about its movie. So it was now. Emmett Caul saw Occonnar Young steaming down the pier toward the ship and he had a presentiment. He went quickly to the wardroom and stuck his head through the door.

"Mr. Hardman," he said, "I think something's wrong."

The captain had finished dinner when the telephone call came. It took him twenty minutes to reach the police station by taxicab. Six enlisted men and Ensign Gravely were being held, the only ones to reach the jail.

Ensign Gravely was sitting in the office of the senior shore patrol officer. He had established his identity as a commissioned officer in the United States Navy, he had even volunteered for and passed a sobriety test; the shore patrol officer was apologetic.

The men were a different matter. Their loyalty had brought charges of "Refusal to Obey Orders of Shore Patrol," and "Interference with Shore Patrol," two charges of "Drunk and Disorderly," and one, lone, peaceful, "Drunk."

The captain took a copy of the charges, and signed a release of the men to his custody. A co-operative shore patrol officer assigned a patrol wagon to take everyone back to the ship.

Actually, it was a minor incident, brought about by a tragedy of errors, and blown up out of all proportion by misunderstanding, some fear and careless emotion. The captain would hold a Mast and try to convince those charged that violence is never successful against a shore patrol. And there the matter would end.

It should have ended there, but it nearly expanded more seriously. The following morning, the base duty officer asked the commanding officer to see him right away.

In an office overlooking the slips and the buildings where so many young men had learned how to navigate, to pilot, to fire guns, to run engines, to fight ships, a lieutenant commander sat the captain down in an armchair next to his desk and asked,

"What happened last night? I understand one of your officers was involved with the shore patrol."

The captain explained, ending with, ". . . so it was all a misunderstanding, sir. The military policeman couldn't believe a Negro could be a naval officer."

"The first thing the Commandant of this Naval District looks at, each morning," the lieutenant commander said, "is the shore patrol report. This morning, he saw that an officer and a number of enlisted men from your ship were picked up, following a fight in a public place—a restaurant, I believe. He does not consider that the officer showed much propriety in being where he was—in a place catering to enlisted men. . . ." He paused, then dropped the blockbuster, "The admiral has directed me to tell you he expects you to institute general court martial proceedings against that ensign for 'conduct unbecoming an officer and a gentleman.' "

The captain was stunned. "But, sir . . . that wouldn't be right! . . . Ensign Gravely conducted himself exactly as he should have, under the circumstances. It certainly wasn't his fault—"

"Associating with enlisted men?"

"Sir . . . Ensign Gravely is a Negro. Where in Miami can he go on liberty? . . . None of the hotels will let him in . . . none of the places catering to officers. He can't even swim on Miami Beach. . . . Sir, I can't do it! I checked it out last night—that shore patrol report doesn't charge him with anything wrong. It was a matter of identity—as a naval officer. He couldn't help it if some of the men from the ship wanted to come to his rescue. No sir, I can't do it."

"The admiral wants you to bring court-martial proceedings. . . ."

The captain took a deep breath. "Sir," he said, "when I was a student here at SCTC, there was one thing emphasized over and over again. We were told that the commanding officer of a commissioned ship was The Captain, regardless of rank; that a junior grade lieutenant in command of an SC had the same responsibilities, the same powers under *Navy Regulations* as the four-striper captain of a battleship. Sir, I am the commanding officer of USS *PC 1264*. The Commandant of a Naval District cannot order me to bring charges against any officer under my command. . . . And, I won't do it."

The duty officer smiled. "And what do I tell the admiral?"

"I guess . . . just that, sir."

The officer got up from his desk and walked around to the lieutenant, who had risen at the same time and stood stiffly polite.

"Very well," he said. "Old Captain Mac sure got his lessons across, *Captain*. But I took his course here myself, and I learned that the commander of this base has certain powers, too. We don't want any repetition of last night's incident. So, I shall recommend he restrict your enlisted men to this base for the duration of your stay here. Is that understood?"

"Yes, sir," the lieutenant answered. "And, as captain of my ship, I can restrict myself and my officers for the same period."

"Very well. I'll pass the word to the admiral. I suggest you concentrate heavily on your training."

The ship did. For the next four days, the log shows entries of the times various men left to attend classes ashore and when they returned, of the ship leaving for training afloat, being refueled at sea by an oiler, *AOG 45*, and firing the guns at targets towed by aircraft. With no evening liberty, there was no temptation to return early.

On Friday, August 10, the word came from the base commander. Formally phrased, its meaning was clear: Get the hell out of here! Go on to Key West!

The restriction was over.

The War Ends

Key West was as far as USS *PC 1264* reached towards the Pacific.

The morning after the Miami "riot," the President of the United States made a terse announcement: "Sixteen hours ago, an American airplane dropped one bomb on Hiroshima, an important Japanese Army base, and destroyed its usefulness to the enemy. That bomb had more power than 20,000 tons of TNT. It had more than 2,000 times the power of the British Grand Slam, which was the largest bomb yet used in the history of warfare."

Three days later, a similar bomb was dropped on Naga-saki. The Miami *Herald* ran a front-page story, with pictures of a gigantic, strange, mushroom-shaped cloud resulting from a test explosion some time before, somewhere in New Mex-ico. It identified its power as atomic.

Such a new weapon was impressive, but few, if any, aboard USS *PC 1264* took much stock in the newspapers' optimism that it would make the Japanese surrender. And when, indeed, they did, five days later, on Tuesday, August 14, there was almost as much surprise as there was over-whelming elation.

The sky above Key West that night was filled with the light from star shells that could never now be used against an enemy. Excitement was so great on all the ships that there was positive danger that more lethal shells might be fired. Quickly, the order was given to stop. And it was, with the exuberance redirected, spilling into the town; Key West forgetting the past—and future—with one grand night of celebration.

The war was over. Now what, for USS *PC 1264?*

Her orders to the Pacific were countermanded. She would await further orders in Key West.

She waited in Key West, moored port side to South Quay Wall, Berth 3, U.S. Naval Operating Base. She waited for three weeks.

Inactivity is supposed to breed poor morale. Not im-mediately at the end of a war. There were better things to look forward to. All knew that their military obligation was running out—the phrase for their service was "the duration and six months." The limit, then, was February 14, 1946. But they knew, too, through the newspapers and radio, that there was a growing sentiment throughout the nation "to bring the boys back home." What was the need, now, for the largest military force the world had even seen? . . . History showed there couldn't be another war for at least twenty years. . . . So, what was the need for the usual training at Key West—to practice sinking submarines on the Attack Teacher, or go out into the Gulf Stream and do the same thing with a tame submarine?

Until the Chief of Naval Operations, or Commander-in-Chief, Atlantic Fleet, decided what to do with all the vessels in port along the Atlantic coast, and especially here in Key West, and until the Chief of the Bureau of Naval Personnel announced plans for demobilization, then what else was there to do, except relax and enjoy as much as possible these strange, empty days of peace?

The only work done was the routine upkeep of the ship—the constant battle against rust, by chipping and painting. Liberty started earlier in the day, stretching back to noon.

And they waited. . . .

The Bureau of Naval Personnel announced its plans for demobilization in a series of AlNavs—notices to "All the Navy"—starting at the end of August. A Reservist could request release if, or as soon as, he had accumulated a certain number of points; a point representing time in service and family responsibilities. Those who had more than the required number—and the captain was one—could be recognized by their smug, satisfied expression; those with fewer points showed correspondingly lesser pleasure.

The day the first AlNav was received aboard the ship, the captain wrote his letter to the Commander, Service Force, Atlantic Fleet, requesting release to inactive duty, and nominating the executive officer, Lieutenant Hardman, as his relief as commanding officer.

It may have triggered the fleet operations people, for on September 5, four messages were received. One an operations order, directing the ship to proceed to Norfolk, Virginia, and three changes of duty orders: one for the captain to relinquish command after arrival in Norfolk; one for the executive officer to assume command at that time; and one, a copy of BuPers orders for an Ensign H. E. Kohler, USNR, to report aboard.

The next evening, at 5:30, special sea detail was set, and the ship moved over to Craig's Dock to take on fuel oil for her trip north. Two hours later, her tanks were full, the red "Baker" flag lowered, and she was on her way.

For two and a half days she steamed, past the Florida, Georgia and both Carolina coasts, the Gulf Stream adding to her speed. Early in the morning of Friday, September 10, she rounded Cape Henry and entered the Chesapeake. Slowly she headed into the Naval Operating Base, and at 8:25 reached her berth at Pier G.

Four minutes later, the captain gave his last operational command to his ship: "Secure main engines!"

The captain wasn't the only member of USS *PC 1264*'s crew eligible to be released from active duty in the Navy. Chief Motor Machinist's Mate Charles S. Harvey was the first to leave, being transferred to the Receiving Station for separation on Tuesday, September 11. The captain was the second. And in the afternoon of the same day the captain would leave, he would be followed by Electrician first class James B. Brown, Motor Machinist's Mate first class Ike Davis, Motor Machinist's Mate second class Willie L. Gray, Motor Machinist's Mate third class Dallas A. Jones, Motor Machinist's Mate first class Walter W. Means, and Ship's Cook second class Occonnar Young.

Three days before they left, Ensign H. E. Kohler, of Ithaca, New York reported, bringing the wardroom up to six officers. G. W. Cook, a radioman second class, also arrived the same afternoon.

The change of command ceremony was set for Monday morning, September 17. During the week since the ship's arrival, the captain and his successor inventoried all the materials for which the commanding officer is responsible, such as codes and classified documents, and custody was transferred.

Monday morning was clear and bright, with a light breeze blowing, tempering the 73° warmth. The ceremony was to follow morning colors—the raising of the flag at 8:00 A.M.—and the muster of the crew at quarters.

Following breakfast, the captain was in his stateroom finishing his packing. Immediately after the ceremony, he would leave the ship for the Navy Separation Center in Shelton, Virginia. Elmer Bradford waited to take this last suitcase ashore.

The captain snapped the clasp and straightened up. "There we are," he said. "I hope I haven't forgotten anything." He held out his hand. "Bradford," he said, "I may not have a chance later to thank you for all you've done for us in the wardroom; me, especially. I appreciate it and . . . good luck!"

Bradford grinned. "Good luck to you, Captain." He picked up the bag and, pushing past the green curtain of the door, climbed up the ladder.

The captain took a last look around the cabin and started to follow. Feet clattered on the ladder steps, and Ensign Sam Gravely was at the door. "May I see you, Captain?" he asked.

"Sure, Sam. Come in. Sit down. I guess we've got a couple of minutes."

"It's very important. I don't know where to start." His face wrinkled in concern. "I just don't know . . ."

"Good lord, Sam, what's the trouble?"

Ensign Gravely sat there, letting his head sink to his chest. What in the world had happened? The captain became increasingly concerned. "What is it?" he pressed.

Sam gave no answer. He sat there, his big, lean, muscular body shaking. "What the hell is the trouble, Sam?" The captain leaned forward. "For Christ sake—"

Gravely moved his head and looked at his wristwatch, then he raised his head, and the perplexed skipper saw that he was trying to control his laughter.

"I'm all right," he said. "I just had to keep you down here for a few minutes longer. We can go up now."

Before the official ceremony, the crew had arranged their own ceremony, to present him with a desk lamp as a present from all of his shipmates. It bore a simple inscription: "USS PC 1264. We Will Never Fail."

Navy Day, 1945

The ship had waited for orders in Key West for nearly a month. She now waited in Norfolk for over six weeks.

The actual transfer of command had taken only a few minutes, and, after the ex-captain had left to become a civilian again, the ship was moved from Pier G in the Naval Operating Base to Pier 3 in the Portsmouth Naval Shipyard, a few miles up the Elizabeth River.

That afternoon, the departure of five old-timers of the crew, James Brown, Ike Davis, Willie Gray, Dallas Jones and Occonar Young, emphasized a difficulty every ship in the Navy was beginning to experience. It would get increasingly worse. With men eligible for discharge, the personnel offices of every Navy command had a serious predicament in trying to find qualified replacements. Two did arrive, before USS *PC 1264* left Norfolk. But with them came another grave administrative problem; their rates didn't correspond with those of the men who had left. This meant that the ship's organization, which called for a specific number of rates—for men trained in a certain specialty—had not enough of some, and too many of others. Chief Harvey and four of the five men who had left on September 17, were from the engineroom force. Engineers proved to be the hardest to find. Eleven days later, one motor machinist's mate, third class, Bernard Lavette Johnson, reported. And, two weeks later, Thomas Perdue, Boatswain's Mate, first class, arrived.

All the military forces were under tremendous pressure to release their personnel. Two million soldiers had left the Army between V-E Day and October 1; another 1,200,000 left in the month of October. The Navy was attempting to bring its strength down from 3,300,000 to 558,000 officers and men. With such a gigantic task, it is not surprising that the unique characteristic of one small subchaser and the arrangement for ensuring the assignment of Blacks to her should be forgotten; many orders of seamen and petty officers reporting to the ship had to be revoked in the next four months, as they were white. USS *PC 1264* may have been another ship to the Enlisted Detail Office, but her character remained the same. To the end, her enlisted complement was segregated. Only her wardroom was integrated.

No operations at sea were called for, so the ship's company tried to keep busy maintaining the ship's appearance—chipping and wire brushing the rust spots as soon as they appeared, and even anticipating where they might show, then painting and polishing. Norfolk's reputation as a liberty town was extraordinarily bad for a city that existed on Navy payrolls. But these were the days of the signs, "Dogs and sailors, keep out!" It was less hospitable to black servicemen, especially in providing any pleasurable, healthy recreation.

Ensign Gravely was now the third-ranking officer on the ship. The delay in Norfolk was no hardship for him; Richmond, his home, was less than a hundred miles away; his family was easily accessible, and he could have visited them nearly every weekend if he hadn't become involved in an activity that kept him busy every evening he had liberty and required his talents on weekends, too.

Sam Gravely, while a student at Virginia Union University, had been an excellent athlete and a mainstay of the football team, before leaving to join the Navy. One day, one of the shipyard workers told him a semi-professional team, named "The Brown Bombers," had been formed of sailors, soldiers and civilians with college football experience, and invited him to join. They played a game every weekend and practiced every weekday evening.

In inhospitable Norfolk, Sam Gravely's recreation was taken care of. One of the teams it played was Virginia Union. The Brown Bombers won 14–0. An interesting sequel came the following year, when Sam Gravely had returned to his alma mater to complete his college education. Playing for Virginia Union against the Norfolk Brown Bombers, he helped reverse the score—Virginia Union, 14; Brown Bombers, 0.

At the end of September, there were again six officers aboard when Ensign D. G. Maxwell, a Pennsylvanian from Lansdowne, arrived. As Ben Shanker had succeeded to executive officer, he became gunnery officer.

At last, in the first week of October, USS *PC 1264* was given an assignment. No more popular one could have been made, as far as the crew was concerned. It meant that the ship would go back to New York, but, more than that, it was an honor, a well-deserved recognition of the ship's operational efficiency. It was proof that the experiment of USS *PC 1264* was acknowledged a success.

USS *PC 1264* was selected to be one of forty-seven representative warships in a fleet review by the President of the United States on Navy Day, October 27. Among battleships, aircraft carriers, heavy and light cruisers, destroyers and submarines, she would be the smallest, but not any less important than any of the others as a type of ship that brought victory to the allied cause. By being chosen, she demonstrated a personal victory in a national, as well as a domestic cause.

Shortly after two o'clock in the afternoon of Wednesday, October 24, USS *PC 1264* left her dock, headed out into Hampton Roads, passed Old Point Comfort and left the

Chesapeake for the Atlantic. It was to be Ernie Hardman's last voyage with the ship; he was eligible for separation and had been told that his relief as captain would be waiting in New York.

The following morning, the ship sailed up the familiar channel into New York Bay. Through The Narrows, she didn't point her bow toward her usual destination, the piers of Tompkinsville, but kept on northward, passing between the Statue of Liberty and Governors Island and into the mouth of the Hudson River. Her berth for the rest of the day and night was to be Pier 80, at the foot of West 40th Street, Manhattan. Tomorrow, she would anchor at the end of the line of warships stretching from West 60th Street to Spuyten Duyvil, beyond the George Washington Bridge, at the tip of the city.

As the subchaser turned into the slip, it was apparent how interested the citizens of New York were in the fleet review. The pier was crowded with people, for there had been an announcement that the ships could be visited from 1:00 to 4:30 P.M. This gave the *1264* fifty-five minutes to get ready for them; to clean up after the voyage and have the men stationed, to answer any questions and to guard against any pilfering.

It turned out to be a pleasant three and a half hours. Many friends and members of families welcomed the ship back. Adolph Cork's girl friend had remembered that October 22 was his birthday; she and her family were on the wharf waiting with a large birthday cake they had brought from Stamford. Friendships thought irrevocably severed when the ship left for the distant Pacific were restored— some through the newspapers naming the ships participating in the review.

The Hudson River on Friday morning was a busy waterway, filled with ships taking their positions for the following day's celebration, and the myriad types of small boats, tugs and naval launches scurrying among them; the last, ferrying back and forth between the Navy landing slips at 72nd Street, 79th Street and 125th Street.

By the middle of the morning, USS *PC 1264* was at a point in the river marked on the chart as Anchorage 58. Thomas Perdue, BM 1/c, who had joined the ship in Norfolk, and Henry Perry, BM 2/c, let the anchor drop into twenty-six feet of water. Then all hands turned to polishing the brightwork, making sure that even the most infinitesimal rust spot would be hidden from a presidential eye. Ellison and the gunners prepared the 3″50 gun for its all-important job the next day of saluting the commander-in-chief.

In the afternoon, a lieutenant (junior grade) stepped into a launch at the 125th Street slip and waited to be taken out to the submarine chaser.

Two months before, Jack W. Sutherland had returned from fourteen months in the Pacific. He had served in a similar ship to the one to which he was going, on convoy and patrol duty in and around Hawaii, the Marshalls, the Marianas, the Caroline Islands, New Guinea and the Philippines. He had worked in every department of USS *PC 586* —communications, supply, gunnery, as first lieutenant and finally as executive officer. He had been qualified for command of a *PC,* so, after a home leave, he had been assigned to the Brooklyn Navy Yard to await orders.

He waited for about two weeks, occupying his time by taking courses at the Firefighter's School and also learning the intricacies of a new navigational system called Loran. Then he heard he was to take command of USS *PC 1264.*

While the war was on, it had always been a little difficult to find out exactly where a ship was on a particular day; this information was considered classified. But an officer, armed with his orders to report to one, could discover the general area where he should go to meet her. At least, he would be given a reliable clue.

Lieutenant (jg) Sutherland's misfortune was to receive his orders on October 18, from the Fleet Administrative Office in New York, directing him to "Proceed and report to Commandant Seventh Naval District for temporary duty awaiting transportation to USS *PC 1264.*"

It is inconceivable, considering the Navy's heavy involvement in the preparations for the Naval Review, his being told to go to Miami. He took his four-day's "proceed time" as vacation and caught the train for Florida the afternoon of the 23rd. If he could have waited one day, he could have seen a diagram in the New York *Times* of the positions of the ships that would be anchored in the Hudson, the topmost one marked *"PC 1264."*

The administrative officer in Miami was more knowledgable, and sent the errant skipper back to New York. By the time he arrived, perhaps the Navy at 90 Church Street had read the New York *Times,* for he was directed to the 125th Street landing.

There was a brisk October wind ruffling the Hudson into spume-topped waves as the Navy launch crossed from the landing slip to the subchaser's anchorage. As it approached, Lieutenant (jg) Sutherland saw that the *PC* was beginning to move; the anchor had been hoisted and dark smoke was pumping from her engine exhausts. He wondered if the ship was trying to avoid him. Not so, he was relieved to discover; the strong wind had made the anchor drag, so Lieutenant Hardman was getting her back to her proper place and, with a longer anchor rode, hopefully keep her there.

The launch approached from the stern and eased alongside. Dark arms helped him across and aboard. He asked to see the captain.

Jack Sutherland recorded in his diary, "I was amazed, but later pleased, to discover that the crew is all Negro! She is the only ship in the fleet with such personnel. . . ." His initial amazement made him remark to Ernie Hardman and

Ben Shanker, when he met the captain and executive officer on the flying bridge, "I've never seen so many steward's mates on one ship before . . ."

Ben Shanker asked, "Didn't anyone tell you about this ship?"

Sutherland shook his head. His diary records that he spent the rest of the afternoon "getting acquainted with the ship and crew." They impressed him. "This is a good ship," he wrote. "It's in fine shape and is clean. The exec tells me the crew is excellent—the gunners fine and the ship set a record for loading depth charges. He also said he enjoys the duty and that all of them do. It's obvious that they are proud of the ship and want to see it better than any other *PC*. I'm proud to be assigned to it."

Every prospective commanding officer is impatient to take over his new responsibilities; the present captain was anxious to return to the Northwest and the apple-growing country of Wenatchee, Washington. But the Navy Day celebration delayed the transfer of command.

None minded, for the fleet review by the President of the United States was a great and glorious climax to the career of USS *PC 1264*.

Navy Day, 1945, was planned to be a dramatic presentation of American naval power. The first event took place at 11:00 A.M., on the other side of Manhattan from the fleet, in the waters of the Brooklyn Navy Yard. A new, super-aircraft carrier, USS *Franklin Delano Roosevelt* was commissioned. President Harry S Truman had arrived in his special train from Washington at Pennsylvania Station half an hour earlier and was whisked by car through crowded streets of cheering, clapping New Yorkers, in time to make the principal address.

Following this, the president's motorcade returned to Manhattan, where Mayor Fiorello LaGuardia received him at City Hall and escorted him to Central Park. Before a crowd estimated at 100,000, the president made a speech, promising to safeguard for peace the secrets of the awesome weapon of atomic power.

Then it was lunch aboard the ship named for his native state. At 2:20 P.M., "Ruffles and Flourishes," sounded on the deck of USS *Missouri* and the president's flag was hoisted to the masthead.

At the other end of the line of ships, USS *PC 1264* rocked at the end of her anchor line in the strong wind that was rolling great thunderheads and banks of cumulus clouds across the sky. The review was scheduled to start at 3:30 in the afternoon, with the president boarding a destroyer, USS *Renshaw,* which would take him up the river, past the ships, each one rendering a 21-gun salute. A few minutes before, the subchaser's officers and men mustered topside, in dress blue uniforms. Ellison and his forward gun crew readied the 3″50.

It was a case of the usual "Hurry up and wait!" The schedule fell behind by half an hour. But an air of excitement, of anticipation, made the time pass rapidly. There was also one event that was on time.

Promptly at 3:30, far to the south, beyond the midtown Manhattan skyscrapers, dots appeared from the massive, white mountainous clouds. Twelve hundred Navy planes— fighters and torpedo bombers—in V-formation, and in wave after wave, roared over the fleet.

Then, when they had passed, the men on the subchaser saw puffs of smoke from the *Missouri,* seven miles away. She was saluting the president, so he must be on his way.

They could gauge his progress by the flashes and smoke creeping intermittently nearer. With the wind from the north they could hear no sound, and it was not until the *Renshaw* passed beneath the George Washington Bridge and was almost upon her, could the subchaser hear the salutes of the nearest ships.

It was almost dusk, at a quarter past four o'clock, when it was USS *PC 1264*'s turn to honor the commander-in-chief.

The sun had set behind the Palisades, but its rays tinted the sky and clouds with purple and rose. As the last ship in the line, she was the first to render honors on the downstream leg. All hands saluted and the gun fired the twenty-one blank charges without hitch.

The next day, the New York *Journal-American* reported: "Above the bridge nestled many small ships, destroyers, destroyer escorts and submarines, the ultimate tip was entrusted to the USS *PC 1264*, too small to be given a name.

"But she was not to be snubbed on this proud day. The *Renshaw* circled her and the President waved gaily to the crew."

After the review was over, and darkness had settled over the river, for half an hour—from 8:00 until 8:30—a searchlight show swept the sky with lines of light, crisscrossed in the "V for Victory" sign. USS *PC 1264* joined in with her small 12-inch signal lights; by comparison with the searchlights of the ships downstream, Lieutenant (jg) Sutherland thought, laconically, they weren't very impressive.

On Sunday morning the ship weighed anchor and returned to Pier 80 for an afternoon of "open house." There were even more visitors than the ship had had the previous Thursday, making it almost impossible for anyone to move anywhere on deck or below. But there was a carnival air, an atmosphere of happiness and thanksgiving that the war, at last, had been ended; of pride that this ship, small as she was, had contributed significantly something more than this most-important result.

The visitors' faces, almost all of them black, reflected their recognition of this, and no sailor aboard could feel less than a deep and proprietary pride that he was a member of this crew; that he had had a part in establishing his ship's reputation, and so proving that human ability could no longer be judged by outward appearance. It was now up to society to recognize this now irrefutable fact.

New London

Lieutenant (jg) Jack W. Sutherland took command of USS *PC 1264* after a short ceremony on Wednesday afternoon, October 31, alongside a pier at the newly named Navy Yard Annex in Tompkinsville. Both he and Lieutenant Hardman read their orders. "I relieve you, sir," said Sutherland. They saluted, shook hands, and the last of the original officers of the ship had completed his duty aboard her.

The ship was scheduled to remain in Tompkinsville until the following Sunday, November 4.

The new captain anticipated their assignment would be pleasant and not very arduous. They were to go to New London, Connecticut, and operate daily out of the Submarine Base in a sort of reverse training the subchaser had experienced in Key West. The submarines at the Fleet Sound School had been tame targets to teach her how to sink them. In New London, USS *PC 1264* would be a tame target to teach student submarine officers to sink ships. He expected the ship would put to sea, make a number of runs for six or seven hours each weekday in Block Island Sound, and have the weekends off. Hopefully, the wintry weather would not be too bad, protected as the Sound should be.

These hopes were dashed as soon as the ship reached New London on Sunday afternoon. Her schedule called for operations each day except Sunday; on Thursdays and Fridays she would work from 7:30 in the morning until midnight. The ship was to find the waters off the Connecticut and Long Island coasts as rough, if not rougher, as any she had ever experienced.

This was her life during the month of November and half of December. And to add to the misery of the storms, the cold, the never-ceasing pitching, rolling and tossing, and days of fog, it became increasingly difficult to maintain and run the ship, as men steadily became eligible for separation from the Navy.

Guice, Rhinehart, Miller, Wheeler, Wade, Perry, R. M. Smith, Cork and Cleo Black all left at the time Lieutenant (jg) Sutherland took command. The loss of so many at once was serious, but only the beginning of a continuing predicament for the new skipper and executive officer, Ben Shanker. As time went on, and the complement shrank, the captain was tempted many times to report officially that his ship couldn't operate without qualified replacements.

But he didn't. He knew the problem was Navy-wide, and it is a credit to him and to many of the men who voluntarily extended their service aboard, that the ship continued to operate without a noticeable lowering of morale.

Under the most adverse weather conditions, seamen did the work of petty officers. Being so short-handed, it would have been impossible for the ship to make any extended cruise without dangerous loss of efficiency. As it was, the system of section watches had to be curtailed from three cruising watches to two. Fortunately, they were rarely at sea for more than a day.

But November was a month of constant storms, and even a day's operations would tax the men's strength and stamina. To stay out longer, Richard Bennett remembers, "was hell. It was cold, frigid, but hell." Only one lookout could be kept topside at a time. Every half hour he would change places with another from the warm, relatively dry pilothouse.

Jack Sutherland recorded one such voyage on November 19 and 20:

"We were out Monday and Tuesday with two submamines containing student officers. The (first) day's runs went very well. About 2000 (8:00 P.M.), the weather began kicking up badly and got worse. It got so bad a number of men got sick and I wasn't feeling too well myself. We finally had to secure early. Hoping we would not operate in the morning and looking for sheltered water, we hit north for the Sound. We arrived there after midnight and took up a

north-south steaming plan for the night. I sacked out fully
clothed in the wardroom. But we were pitching so much,
and there was so much noise with gear scraping across the
deck, that I didn't get much sleep. I was up and down several times during the night and got up for good about 0500.
I called one of the subs to enquire about the day's operations, hoping they would be cancelled, but they weren't. I
thought we could rendezvous with them in an hour, but it
was so rough it took 2½ hours.

"I have never seen such rough weather and I hope I
shall never see any worse, but I'm afraid I will. Thirty-degree
rolls were common, and a couple of times we rolled 45°.
There was water on the deck in the radar passageway and
the radar shack. Everything that wasn't secured throughout
the ship had been thrown on the decks. Every time the ship
would roll, there'd be a clatter of china and pans, scraping
of gear sliding on the deck, clattering of locked doors. When
moving about, it was necessary to hold on all the time. I
was not only feeling lousy I was getting very angry, too.

"Finally, I got mad enough to suggest to the subs that
we secure from the exercises and they agreed. What a happy
moment that was! But we were still miles from the base
and, while going in, we were headed right into the sea. I
was on the bridge—the waves were coming over the bridge,
and the wind brought them over with such great force that
the particles of water stung. Even though I had on rain
pants and parka, I soon got awfully wet. It was cold and I
was miserable.

"Sam (Gravely) relieved me and I went below to dry
off. I gave him instructions how to get in, and I had intended
returning to the pilothouse as soon as I put on dry shoes,
but I was so tired I fell asleep. When I was awakened, we
had just passed Race Point, so I got fully prepared for the
weather and went to the bridge.

"The wind was still blowing awfully strong, and the
water was choppy, but not as bad as on the Atlantic. I was

worried about tieing up—the wind was stronger than it had been last Thursday, and I had a foul time with it then. Steering the normal course up the Thames River forced us into the east bank, so we had to steam crabwise.

"Fortunately we were able to tie up next to the dock and I made the best landing yet—I allowed plenty for the wind.

"Just before we left the subs (it was sometime before noon), one of them sent, 'Thank you for services. We realize your difficulties and admire your guts.' We were tempted to reply, 'What guts?'"

Thanksgiving Day, November 22, was a holiday and marked, traditionally, by a feast. Ensign Sam Gravely, as commissary officer, planned carefully for it, forming a committee consisting of the executive officer, Ensign Shanker; Orentell Buchanna, SC2/c, designated Chef de Cuisine; Alfred G. Green, Jr., RdM3/c, Assistant Chef; Emmett Caul, QM3/c, Junior Chef; Edward Walker, SC3/c, and Alfonso Brown, S1/c, were Mess Hall Supervisors. Marshall King, PhM1/c, typed and mimeographed the menus.

The menu covered everything expected of such a celebration—and more. The appetizer was a fruit cocktail, not too delicately flavored by a strictly non-regulation ingredient. Officers and men sat together in the mess hall. There was no formal grace; the captain asked for a moment of silence, so each could make his own personal prayer of thanksgiving.

There was a short respite over the weekend from the weather that lasted through Monday and Tuesday, making the ship's operations during those days unusually pleasant.

But it didn't last. Wednesday was so rough that the training areas closest to shore were closed off, and the submarines and their surface ships were sent farther offshore. By Thursday morning, the visibility was so bad and the thirty-knot winds, gusting to over fifty, were slamming the waves over the diminutive subchaser so badly, punished

her so, she could not possibly make any accurate runs. The
training had to be cancelled; gratefully, the ships headed
back to port, the submarines gliding down to deeper and
calmer water.

The subchaser's part in this training was not only to be
a target for the student submarines, but to carry out simulated attacks to give them experience in evasive maneuvers.
The ship, making contact by her sonar, carried out all the
antisubmarine procedures of the hunt and kill. Instead of
the ultimate firing of depth charges, ordinary hand grenades
were thrown from the stern and sides. So, the storms of
Block Island Sound did not make a gunner's mate's lot a
happy or comfortable one; it was downright hazardous.
Louis Ellison, John Atkins, Dick Bennett and the gunner's
mate strikers, earned their pay, and more, in these New
England waters.

During these weeks in New London, Allen Connor, the
electrician, started a newspaper. Entitled *The Sub-Chaser,*
the first issue announced its policy as "a new venture to
express the ideas and fancies of the officers and enlisted
personnel of our good ship the USS *PC 1264.* . . . Among
us are poets, artists, and just plain good sailors—but we
all have some creative ability, so let's pitch in and make this
a swell paper. . . ."

It became one, although the publication dates were
somewhat haphazard, following no set schedule. Its interests
were wide. It published poetry, articles on educational possibilities under the G.I. Bill of Rights, puzzles, letters to the
editor, liberty bus schedules, and a highly controversial gos-
sip column by a mysterious author with the pen name, "The
Gangway."

"Einstein" Conner, as co-publisher with George W.
Cook, RM2/c, anticipated that the identity of "The Gangway" might be angrily sought by the column's victims, so
he sagely enlisted Louis Ellison, GM1/c, to be editor. Not
only was Ellison the most respected petty officer, for his

personality and character, but he was an experienced Golden-Gloves boxer. The vitriolic gossiper's name remained only conjecture, its owner safe. "Some of the items were pretty bad," Ellison remembers, "but I was able to censor the worst ones." This was the only censorship exercised. "The Gangway" spared none—rank was no safeguard at all.

The paper was catholic in its tastes. It undoubtedly was the only periodical with a medical director listed in the masthead, but the reason could have been the ability of Marshall King, PhM1/c, in running the mimeograph.

One popular item the paper published after Thanksgiving was the Christmas holiday leave schedule. The ship was to return to New York on December 15 and stay until January 7. One half of the crew would have Christmas at home, the other half, New Year's.

To give the first group an early start, USS *PC 1264* cast off her lines from the New London pier a few minutes before 3:00 A.M., on Saturday, December 15. A little more than six hours later, she had arrived in Tompkinsville.

Everybody aboard managed to take leave. But on December 20, Ensign Ben Shanker began his leave which would not end with his return to this ship. He had received his orders for transfer. With his experience as a subchaser executive officer, and not being eligible for demobilization for another few months, he had been tapped for a *PC* in the Pacific—the *1173*—operating between the islands of the Marianas group.

"I can remember at the time," he says today, "it felt suddenly like leaving home. It had been a real privilege to have been a part of the *1264*, with its very special crew and very special officers that served her." Comparison was natural when he reached his new ship. "Without taking away any credit due for the performance and morale of the white crew, I think that everything we did and performed on the *1264* equaled, and, in many things, excelled the morale and performance of duty on the *1173*. . . ."

With Ben Shanker's departure, Ensign Samuel L. Gravely, Jr., became executive officer of USS *PC 1264*.

Everyone who took the New Year's leave was back aboard one hour before the ship got underway to return to her submarine operations in New London.

Heading across the harbor into the East River and on through Hell Gate to Long Island Sound, none knew that two days later his ship would be back in New York. This trip was as unnecessary as the one the captain had made to Miami, two and a half months before, in search of his new command. And for him a constant worry.

There was fog all the way through the Sound. Off City Island, south of New Rochelle, the ship anchored for two hours, waiting for it to lift. When there was a slight clearance, the anchor was raised and slowly, carefully, the ship continued on. Only a few miles farther, the fog settled again heavily around her. But the ship carried on.

At about six o'clock that evening, the ship was at the entrance to New London Harbor. "When we got near New London Ledge Light," the captain wrote in his diary, half an hour later, "I headed for it by radar, checking the bearing by the sound of its horn. We caught sight of the light when we were a couple of hundred yards away and then turned, on passing it about 10 yards off. Then I got cold feet. The visibility was almost zero and although we were on the proper course, which should take us up the channel okay, I was scared. So we anchored, and so here we are."

It was certainly the prudent thing to do. At 9:40 P.M., suddenly, as is the way with fog, they could see again, and twenty minutes later, the ship was securely tied to the State Pier.

The next morning, the captain was called to the Operations Office. A letter had arrived from Atlantic Fleet headquarters, canceling all previous orders for USS *PC 1264*, and directing her to report to the Commandant, Third Naval District, in New York, "for disposal."

The days of USS *PC 1264* were now numbered. In the harsh words of the official jargon, within a month her name would be "stricken" from the active list of the United States Navy. The duty now of the crew of this unique subchaser was to prepare her for decommissioning, for naval burial.

On Wednesday, January 9, 1946, at 7:45 in the morning, USS *PC 1264* began her last voyage home. And with her were three who had been on her first; three of the original crew—plankowners—Allen M. Conner, EM3/c, Robert M. Jackson, MoMM2/c, and William D. Williams, SoM3/c. There was another, who was almost a plankowner—a grizzled veteran of nearly fourteen years at sea (as a dog's life is reckoned)—Gismo, Ship's Mascot First Class.

Decommissioning

At one hour past noon, on Thursday, February 7, 1946, the remaining five officers and twenty-eight enlisted men stood at attention on the afterdeck of USS *PC 1264*. Wedged between two other *PC*s on the north side of Pier 7 in Tompkinsville, there was no band, no crowd of spectators, no press nor radio reporters; only a Navy public relations officer and an enlisted photographer to record the thirty-second ceremony.

The decks were strangely empty. During the previous three weeks all the armament had been removed, all the equipment, supplies and records turned in to the base. A week before, Ensign Gravely, as executive officer, had to find accommodations for the men ashore; the ship had become so stripped that there was no longer adequate heat in the compartments. He also had a pile of paperwork to complete for the transfer of each officer and man from the ship.

Everyone had been busy, accounting for every item, making sure that those responsible for their custody has signed receipts when they turned them in, and preparing for the final inspection by the Commandant's Decommissioning Team.

The night of the transition from living afloat to a barracks ashore was memorable for another reason: the Decommissioning Ball in the Witoka Club on 145th Street, between 7th and 8th Avenues, in Harlem. Invitations had been mailed to all former members of the crew, and from nine o'clock in the evening of February 1, until late in the night and early morning, the last, great ship's party organized by Mrs. Willie Parris and her Defense Recreation Center was held. Men came from as far as Detroit and Chicago, the first captain arrived from Washington, D.C., and messages were received from many who couldn't be present.

This was the actual, the real farewell to the ship, from the men who had served in her; these men, and those who had served before, who had demonstrated their ability naturally and normally by their performance; doing their duty without fanfare, and doing it a little bit better than most. So well, indeed, that even before the special programs unit in the Bureau of Naval Personnel was dissolved by demobilization, it had almost forgotten this ship it had so purposefully established two years before.

But the reason for this seeming neglect was USS *PC 1264* had fulfilled her purpose. In the early months of her active duty, there had been constant dialogue between the special programs unit and the ship. By telephone calls, personal letters and visits for discussion, the quality of performance of Negro enlisted men aboard ship, their reactions under the stress of service afloat, any comparison with a similar, but white, crew was studied and evaluated.

As a result, the Bureau of Naval Personnel had a basis for its subsequent actions: the assignment in the Fall of 1944 of Negro general rates, up to 10 per cent of complement, to 25 auxiliary vessels, which was extended to all fleet auxiliaries in April, 1945. In 1946, BuPers Circular

Letter 48–46 abolished all restrictions governing the types of assignment for which a Negro was eligible.

It would be naive, and certainly inaccurate, to believe that the experiences of USS *Mason,* which had a predominantly black enlisted complement, and USS *PC 1264,* which had a totally black one, were solely responsible for the Navy's change in policy. But in these two ships, the Bureau had actual examples. USS *PC 1264* was, perhaps, a more definitive one, as the quality of black enlisted leadership could be determined without any suspicion—if the performance was good—that it was due to the white petty officers aboard; moreover, it could assess the qualities of a Negro officer.

Early in her career, USS *PC 1264* was adjudged a successful experiment by the special programs unit and it therefore turned its attention to much more pressing problems. This judgment was not official—the ship received no scroll, no certificate, no diploma. It was summed up in a remark by Commander Charles Dillon, "You know the saying, 'The sq⋅.eaky wheel gets the oil.' "

Even at decommissioning, she showed her superiority. "This ship," said the officer-in-charge of the final inspection party, "has done a better job of decommissioning—is in better shape—than any other ship; at least, here in New York." Because of her condition, the *PC 1264* became the subchaser used as a showcase for prospective civilian purchasers.

For a few minutes after the short, official rite of lowering the commission pennant from the masthead, the men remained in formation to allow more pictures by the naval photographer. The commission pennant was handed to the captain as a keepsake, with the charge he was never to wash it. Then, Ensigns Gravely and Maxwell took the men ashore for transfer; all, except the yeoman and storekeeper, who remained with the captain and Ensigns Kohler and Fanning to lock up the ship.

It was done. The last door was closed and locked by Lieutenant (jg) Jack W. Sutherland, the last commanding officer of USS *PC 1264*.

He looked quickly around the deck of his first and last command, then walked quickly across the gangway and the intervening subchaser to the dock, where the others were waiting.

He shook hands with and bade good-bye to Guy P. Randolph, Y3/c, and Irving Houser, Jr., SK3/c, then, turning to the officers, he said, "We'll dump these keys with the duty officer, then get some chow. I've got to get moving. My train leaves at 4:30, but I've got to check out at 90 Church first."

Behind them, nestled between two naked submarine chasers, *PC 1264* lay; moving, rolling gently as she always did from the faintest ripple, her duty done, her purpose accomplished.

Appendix

Crew

Officers

LT. Eric S. PURDON	Commanding	Apr. 25, 1944— Sept. 17, 1945
LT. (jg) George R. POOR	Executive	Apr. 25, 1944— Dec. 18, 1944
LT. (jg) Will F. OTTO	Gunnery*	Apr. 25, 1944— May 3, 1945
LT. (jg) Ernest V. HARDMAN	Engineering*#	Apr. 25, 1944— Oct. 31, 1945
ENS. Frank W. GARDNER	Communications	Apr. 25, 1944— Sept. 6, 1944
ENS. Stanley W. RHODES	Communications	Sept. 3, 1944— May 28, 1945
ENS. Benjamin SHANKER	Gunnery*	Dec. 16, 1944— Dec. 20, 1945
ENS. Samuel L. GRAVELY, Jr.	Communications*	May 2, 1945— Feb. 7, 1946
ENS. Donald G. MORMAN	Engineering	May 7, 1945— Feb. 4, 1946
ENS. H. E. KOHLER	First Lieut.	Sept. 14, 1945— Feb. 7, 1946
ENS. D. G. MAXWELL	Gunnery	Sept. 26, 1945— Feb. 7, 1946
LT. (jg) Jack W. SUTHERLAND	Commanding	Oct. 31, 1945— Feb. 7, 1946
ENS. William L. FANNING, Jr.	Supply	Dec. 20, 1945— Feb. 7, 1946
ENS. W. J. ALTSCHWAGER	Communications	Jan. 21, 1946— Feb. 6, 1946

* Later Executive
# Later Commanding

Enlisted

ADAMS, Norman, S1/c
ALEXANDER, George, S1/c
ALKINS, Irving T., F1/c
ANDERSON, A. C., S2/c
ANDERSON, Charlie D., S1/c
ANDERSON, C. O., S1/c
ANDERSON, Earl, S2/c
ANDERSON, Edgar, Ck3/c
ARTIS, Robert, Jr., S1/c
ATKINS, John Edward, GM3/c
BAGLEY, J. A., S1/c
BAHAM, P. R., Jr., F1/c
BELTON, Cortlandt, Jr., RM3/c
BENNETT, Richard H., GM3/c
BLACK, Cleo J., RM2/c
BLAIR, Robert E., S1/c
BOGGESS, Jack T., SoM3/c
BOYER, William P., Cox.
BRADFORD, Elmer C., Ck3/c
BRANCH, George W., F1/c
BROWN, Alfonso, S1/c
BRIDGES, Zebedee J., SM3/c
BRIGGS, Donald, BM1/c
BROWN, Dudley C., F1/c
BROWN, James B., EM2/c
BUCHANNA, Orentell, SC2/c
BURNETTE, Spencer M., SC3/c
BURNS, Homer L., EM3/c
BUTLER, Nathaniel A., Cox.
CARTER, Howard R., F1/c
CAUL, Emmett C., QM2/c
CHADWICK, Samuel, SK1/c
CLARKE, W. L., RM3/c
COLEMAN, Marcus, S2/c

COLEMAN, Ronald S2/c
CONNER, Allen M., EM3/c
COOK, G. W., RM2/c
CORK, Adolph R., QM2/c
COULON, Hanley A., S1/c
CRAWFORD, William, Jr., StM1/c
CUNNINGHAM, Australia, SM1/c
CYRUS, Henry F., MoMM1/c
DAVIDSON, William, RM2/c
DAVIS, Isaac N., MoMM1/c
DAVIS, Paul G., Y1/c
DOZIER, James D., S1/c
ELLISON, Louis T., GM1/c
FASION, William, StM2/c
FRAZIER, Donald C., RM1/c
GIBBOND, James J., S1/c
GIBSON, Arnett E., MoMM2/c
GOODE, H. J., S1/c
GORDON, Richard E., PhM3/c
GRACE, C., S2/c
GRAY, Willie L., MoMM3/c
GREEN, Alfred G., Jr., RdM3/c
GRIFFIN, Benjamin F., S1/c
GUEST, Rosco, SM3/c
GUICE, Jarvis E., SM1/c
HARVEY, Charles S., CMoMM
HAVARD, Gentle, RM2/c
HAWK, W. W., Cox.
HENRY, Ollie, S2/c
HIBBITT, R. C., S2/c
HOUSER, Irving, Jr., SK3/c
HOWELL, C., S1/c
HUBBARD, Richard, EM3/c
HUNT, Harold H., EM1/c
JACKSON, Robert M., MoMM3/c
JAMES, Henry J., SoM3/c

JOHNSON, Bernard L., MoMM3/c
JOHNSON, James E., S1/c
JOHNSON, J. T., SC3/c
JONES, Dallas A., MoMM3/c
JONES, Herbert W., PhM2/c
JONES, R. F., RM3/c
KING, A. G., Cox.
KING, Herman E., S1/c
KING, Marshall, PhM2/c
LEGGETT, W., Y2/c
MAEROWITZ, Aaron, Rt2/c
MAJOR, J. E., Jr., F1/c
MASSEY, Donnie B., S1/c
MATHEWS, Melvin L., S2/c
MATTHEWS, William A., StM2/c
McBRIDE, James H., Cox.
MEANS, Walter W., MoMM1/c
MILLER, Lee V., S1/c
MITCHELL, James A., RM2/c
MOORE, F. A., S2/c
MOORE, Jacob H., MoMM2/c
MORRIS, Victor O., EM3/c
MYLES, J. M., EM2/c
NIMMO, J. B., Jr., F1/c
OWENS, Saint M., S2/c
PASLEY, J., S2/c
PERDUE, Thomas, BM1/c
PERRY, Henry J., BM2/c
PORTER, Irvin B., RM3/c
PHELPS, Charles E., QM1/c
POWELL, Gilbert, MM3/c
PRICE, Ferdinando, F1/c
RANDALL, Irvin, SM2/c
RANDOLPH, Charles E., MoMM3/c
RANDOLPH, Guy P., Y3/c
RHEINHART, Paul, GM2/c
RICHARDS, Andrew O., S2/c

RICHARDS, Robert A., MoMM3/c
ROGERS, Cliff, QM3/c
SANDERS, L., S2/c
SIMMONS, Anderson, Jr., S1/c
SIMMONS, Myron E., GM3/c
SIMON, Alcide, Jr., Cox.
SIMPSON, John, F1/c
SIMPSON, Joseph, MoMM3/c
SINGLETON, Marquis D., BM2/c
SMITH, Robert M., S1/c
SMITH, William S., SF1/c
STEPHENS, Theodore, S1/c
STREET, John Z., CMoMM
TAYLOR, H., S1/c
THOMPSON, Jackie, StM2/c
TINSLEY, Paul, SF3/c
TRUITT, Pink B., SF3/c
TURNER, Martyn R., MoMM2/c
UNDERWOOD, Eddie, S1/c
VANDERHOOP, Alfred A., MoMM2/c
WALKER, Edward, SC3/c
WARE, George E., RdM3/c
WASHINGTON, Leroy, RdM3/c
WEBER, Edward, PhM2/c
WHEELER, Luther, SoM1/c
WHITE, Laureen, RdM3/c
WILLIAMS, David, SoM3/c
WILLIAMS, H. K., RT3/c
WILLIAMS, William D., SoM3/c
WILSON, Parley Davis, GM3/c
WINSTON, E. G., S2/c
WOODLEY, Herbert O., S2/c
WRIGHT, Oliver C., F1/c
YOUNG, Clarence C., SC2/c
YOUNG, J. H., S2/c
YOUNG, Leland A., GM1/c
YOUNG, Occonnar, SC2/c

The **Naval Institute Press** is the book-publishing arm of the U.S. Naval Institute, a private, nonprofit, membership society for sea service professionals and others who share an interest in naval and maritime affairs. Established in 1873 at the U.S. Naval Academy in Annapolis, Maryland, where its offices remain today, the Naval Institute has members worldwide.

Members of the Naval Institute support the education programs of the society and receive the influential monthly magazine *Proceedings* and discounts on fine nautical prints and on ship and aircraft photos. They also have access to the transcripts of the Institute's Oral History Program and get discounted admission to any of the Institute-sponsored seminars offered around the country.

The Naval Institute also publishes *Naval History* magazine. This colorful bimonthly is filled with entertaining and thought-provoking articles, first-person reminiscences, and dramatic art and photography. Members receive a discount on *Naval History* subscriptions.

The Naval Institute's book-publishing program, begun in 1898 with basic guides to naval practices, has broadened its scope in recent years to include books of more general interest. Now the Naval Institute Press publishes about one hundred titles each year, ranging from how-to books on boating and navigation to battle histories, biographies, ship and aircraft guides, and novels. Institute members receive discounts of 20 to 50 percent on the Press's more than eight hundred books in print.

Full-time students are eligible for special half-price membership rates. Life memberships are also available.

For a free catalog describing Naval Institute Press books currently available, and for further information about subscribing to *Naval History* magazine or about joining the U.S. Naval Institute, please write to:

Membership Department
U.S. Naval Institute
291 Wood Road
Annapolis, MD 21402-5034
Telephone: (800) 233-8764
Fax: (410) 269-7940
Web address: www.usni.org